Zen
and
Hasidism

Zen
and
Hasidism

The similarities between two spiritual disciplines

Compiled by

Harold Heifetz

*This publication made possible
with the assistance of the Kern Foundation*

The Theosophical Publishing House
Wheaton, Ill. U.S.A.
Madras, India/London, England

A Quest original, published by the Theosophical
Publishing House, a department of The
Theosophical Society in America. Inquiries for
permission to reproduce all, or portions of this
book, should be addressed to Quest Books, 306
West Geneva Road, Wheaton, Illinois 60187.

Library of Congress Cataloging in Publication data

Zen and Hasidism.
   (Quest books)
   Bibliography: p.
      1.   Buddhism—Relations—Judaism—Addresses,
essays, lectures.   2.   Judaism—Relations—
Buddhism—Addresses, essays, lectures.
3.   Zen Buddhism—Addresses, essays, lectures.
4.   Hasidism—Addresses, essays, lectures.
I.   Heifetz, Harold.
BQ4610.J8Z46   291.1'72   78-9073
ISBN 0-8356-0514-0
ISBN 0-8356-0512-4 pbk.

Printed in the United States of America

DEDICATION

"What's the best way to get to Ventura and Laurel Canyon?" he asked.

Matsu told him in great detail.

"That's crazy," he snapped back. "That's not the best way to go."

"You're right," said Matsu. "There are faster ways. But one of the most beautiful of all women lives on Emelita Street. You might just see her as you go by."

But what courage to let go! To leap over the precipice with no guarantee you will survive; to fall into the darkness without any assurance that underneath are in fact the Everlasting Arms. Are you girded for this voyage? (Then), perhaps in a moment of supreme unawareness hear laughter in strange places, good fat belly laughter, and see the smile of God in all about you, and be for the first time happy, and careless, and made free.

Christmas Humphreys
"Zen Comes West"

CONTENTS

ACKNOWLEDGMENTS

This book attempts to present a comparative study of Zen and Hasidism and the parallels inherent in these two paths of mysticism. The cooperation and endeavors of many people were required to compile it. In this connection I wish to acknowledge the following publishers: David McKay Company, Inc., for use of Jiri Langer's article "Life In a Hasidic Yeshiva" from the book *Nine Gates*; the Hutchinson Publishing Group Ltd. for permission to reprint John Blofeld's "Life In a Zen Monastery" from his book, *The Wheel of Life*, pp. 159-174; the Jewish Publication Society of America for the selection by Louis Ginzberg from *Students, Scholars and Saints*; the Zen Mission Society for Rev. Jiyu Kennett's paper "On Meditation" and to Pantheon Books for quotations from their 1972 publication, *Selling Water by the River*; George Allen and Unwin Publishers, Ltd., who gave their permission for use of "Concentration and Meditation" from *Zen Comes West* by Christmas Humphreys.

The Magnes Press of the Hebrew University, Jerusalem granted permission for the use of "The State of Nothingness and Contemplation in Hasidism" by R. Schatz; the University Press of Hawaii for "The Nature of Ch'an (Zen) Buddhism" by Chen-chi Chang from *Philosophy East and West*. Vol. VI, no. 4, pp. 304-342, January 1975; the *Chicago Review* publication of the University of Chicago for permission to reprint "Zen Psychotherapy: The Virtue of Sitting," by Akihisa Kondo, Vol. 12, Number 2, (1958); Horizon Press for their permission to reprint the Martin Buber selection from *Hasidism and Modern Man*, 1958; the NCC Center for the Study of Japanese Religions for the permission to print the English translation of Abraham Kaplan's lecture, *Zen and Hasidism*, as it appeared in their English language journal, *Japanese Religions*; and to Pantheon Books, Division of Random House, Inc. for their permission to reprint the excerpt from pp. 290-291 of *Memories, Dreams, Reflections* by C. G. Jung, which was edited by Aniela Jaffe and translated by Clara and Richard Winston.

Our thanks are also extended to *SH'MA*, a Journal of Jewish Responsibility, for permission to reprint articles by Chaim T. Hollander and Zalman Schachter. Additional articles by Schachter and Hollander were written especially for this volume as a dialogue in Section III of ZEN AND HASIDISM. We also want to extend our most humble thanks to the other contributors whc wrote specific chapters for this book including Gary Snyder, Whalen Lai, Paul Wienpahl, Hidenori Tashiro, William Kramer, Benjamin Weininger, Jacob Y. Teshima and Steve Sanfield. Their efforts are most gratefully recognized.

The contribution by Hyman Enelow was taken from a very old, out-of-print (1913) book *Studies in Jewish Literature*, pp. 82-107, and in spite of great effort we were unable to locate Enelow or any heirs but acknowledgment should be made of his article "Kawwana: The Struggle for Inwardness in Judaism."

To all who seek understanding and vision in comparative studies of philosophy and religion, recognition should be made to these others whose words and thoughts we have used herein: Meister Eckhart, Naragarjuna, and the Gautama Buddha.

H.H.

INTRODUCTION

From the first moment I read about Zen, I wanted to go live under a bridge in Kyoto, wear a straw hat and meditate on the koan: what is the sound of one hand clapping. I hoped to escape from becoming one of the millions of lost, unnoticed and unidentified people scurrying back and forth through the gates of the cities. I needed to discover myself, my own worth.

I was intrigued with the ancient as well as new psychospiritual lingua franca of the reflective life, meditation, the language that never starts and never ends, and like energy, just *is*, always was and will always be. However, as so many others, I was at first afraid to be tamed by silence, to remain alone, and when alone, forced to listen to myself.

But I soon learned not to fear that "state of inner sensory, affective and cognitive quietude (in which the) mind is poised and open to receive insights from the higher level of consciousness."[1]

Meditation was a means by which both knowledge and the mystical experience could be achieved not only in my pilgrimage toward total freedom, but in preventing the final looting of what I felt was a sensitive spirit. It was an expedition and hunt for "the human ego-snake . . . (which) must be caught not from outside but from within."[2]

I did not go but waited. I did not think but inhibited, conquering the thieves of my mind while subduing the emotions in that inner search. It was not easy to discover those treasuries of silence and undergo the necessary combat found there, the listening and lighting of my own lamp, of recognizing the archetypes of the deep subconscious pit of my private history without fearing them.

When man said "I" for the very first time, he stepped out of the savage cage and knew historical memory. He realized he was not alone but had come from the past and was heading into the future, that his life was one which had continued, was continuing, and would somehow go on. There was no need for him to know how, but simply feel the truth of it as he groped along, flowing with his own nature. But what he had to learn initially was to not be frightened of himself, of his own curling thoughts, of those seemingly forbidding shadows moving about within his internal murk.

Deep meditation is like flying through the night air without a moon, or sinking in deep, black water. It was even dangerous to sit still in such extended calmness, in the awakening dawn state as described by Thomas Merton[3], of listening hard in the hara of the Japanese, the belly of everything, for "turning within leads to the discovery of deeper layers of the self."[4]

This exploration can determine your own nature; who you are and what you are and why you are, asking not only 'what am I, what am I really,' but 'who you are, what are you really?' Rabbi Zusya said, "In the world to come I shall not be asked: why were you not Moses? I shall be asked: why were you not Zusya?"

Meditation was the process of digging for the secret, inner self, the lurker and furtive peeker from shadows, unwilling to be recognized, but available to tell all. It was the taking off and unpeeling of my onion body in a painful defoliation until the unravelling suddenly encountered the bursting out of intuition. This was truly a becoming and an arrival, "closer and closer to . . . the inner core of . . . (my) real self, (my) center of being, (my) soul, whatever terminology is used. For example, behind a tiger may be soft fur, and behind the soft fur some steel pikes which eventually dissolve into a mighty river, with a diamond in its depth and a point of light at the center of the diamond."[5]

There is nothing holy about meditation. It is more reasonable than holy. Some have said it is another form of prayer, praying with the whole person, the entire body. But the theology of prayer, in the Western sense, is alien to Zen. Though meditation is part of the prayer instinct, it need not be a religious prayer or prayer at all. God is not mentioned and is not involved. Insight meditation is the seeking of the original face, an attempt to capture the riddle to the koan: what were you before your mother's egg and father's sperm came together? It pursues communication with the elusive, aboriginal shadow, even if one has never seen it.

It is a state "of being where the individual transcends all imagery and finds his ultimate identity with pure space, invisible and unconditioned, the void,"[6] a letting go so the mind is emptied and the psyche is permitted to respond, for "inside is the one who knows."[7]

Zen meditation is based on the doctrine of this void, in which one "annihilates all vagrant thoughts . . . belonging to the externality of things, and all ideas of individuality and generality, of suffering or impermanence, and cultivate(s) the noblest ideas of egolessness and emptiness and imagelessness."[8]

As it is not prayer, it is also not faith, though faith requires listening, as does knowledge. So when the Jew meditates, or prays, mystic or atheist, he begins with the vital word, *Shema*; listen. The emphatic Hebrew of Deuteronomy reads in translation: listen will you listen.[9]

There are different kinds of silences:[10], communing silence and listening silence, in which words are considered superfluous and even a hindrance to intimacy and communication. To be at *satori* is to be beyond speech and beyond interpretation. "Enlightenment is the moment of . . . knowing without knowing and seeing without seeing, in which being is born out of nothingness."[11]

There is nothing mysterious or obscure about meditation. It simply goes beyond language. Information and facts have a tendency to change. How far can words be trusted? A flower does not talk. We agree when we are silent. When we start talking we disagree. Misunderstandings arise from the endless competitive use of words. "All the so-called great questions are just words, intellectual self-abuse, a self-creating and wallowing in mind-created problems through whose indulgence we miss the real problems facing us daily; problems of compassion, the ending of violence, brutality, war, and all the little ways we humans destroy each other through word and deed."[12]

Words bring suffering. The satori experience emphasizes the use-lessness of reason. It has been said that the first fall of man began when he learned to speak, and involved himself in deceptive logic and language. Is not intuition, the sixth sense and lightning knowledge born of the silence, a surer and less frustrating means of solving the mysteries and leaping out of the darkness into enlightenment? Do we have to speak in order to prove we have truly grown beyond the cave? Is it not perhaps better to be quiet more and use language less, to not need words all the time in order to live? We work in our own darkness. Each of us lives alone, travels in the pilgrimage of his loneliness alone. Each of us dies alone, however much we continue to struggle not to be left behind.

Zen has a disrespect for rhetoric. ". . . The noblest words are but noises in the air. They die and in the end is silence . . ."[13] It is not what they mean but what one feels hearing them, and those feelings may have nothing whatsoever to do with their meanings. "All words are nets in which to ensnare the flow of life . . . (Words are) a necessary evil."[14]

The immensities of the Zen silence, the emptiness of it that roars, contrasts to but is characterized by the identical thunder found in the vital and eloquent volubility of Hasidism which appears to contradict it. But both have their genesis in the Naught, the Hebraic *ayin*, and its *kawannah*—the intention of it. The nothingness, *mu*, that is some-thingness, is both unique to Zen and Hasidism. Reb Nachman said that when you totally give all of yourself, you become empty, and when you become empty, you become a vessel for the higher lights that are in the world.

The cup is only a cup when it has nothing, when it is nothing, when its void awaits to be filled. I bring myself to the point of being nothing, only a space without sound, yet not to the state of murdering myself, though "it is in stillness that one experiences the loneliness and anguish of his own existence."[15] I accept the self-discovery of my own image, and am prepared to destroy it in order to build a better one. It is the turning of the ego in upon itself, uprooting it, and when it is totally consumed and the ego truly dies in the Great Death, *taishi*, it is then replaced by self. There is no longer any ego consciousness. Only the enlightenment of satori is left. The Great Death in Zen is equivalent to the concept of Self Extinction in Hasidism. Both deal with ego destruction. But they leave something, rather than take away everything. "The middle way is not sheer nothingness. It is something that remains after every possible negation."[16]

The meditative self-search brought me to the pain of reality and the acceptance of the often difficult realization of not being other than what I was. To be or not to be were not the questions. How to be and how not to be were the questions. I was forced to look at myself and accept the reality of the I and the me and the self-serving and embracing us, us, us. I shook hands with my real self. How do you say hello? What do you do in the first critical five minutes with this previously hidden stranger? I greeted it quietly, with caution at first, slowly becoming acquainted with my ego-centered self-consciousness, searching to know who I was, where I belonged and if I was a worthwhile being. There, in that deep water, I tried to be able to see without prejudice, to not only identify the direction I needed to take, but also learn my chances of safe arrival and whether or not death might possibly miss me.

I sought to extend out and away from myself, to allow the tranquil mind to leap across the void to the other shore and look back. I learned the questions of Rashoman thinking: is the flag waving, or is the wind waving, or is my mind waving? Is the water flowing under the bridge, or is it the bridge that is flowing by?

From all this emerged the ability that allowed me to see others better and so understand them, and myself as well, all from another level, another sky. We suffer from dualism because we differentiate things; good and bad, I am wrong, you are right, shall I go or shall I stay? The escape is to the egolessness and non-dualistic, compassionate, intuitive revelations free of the entrapment of words and language, released from a bondage of never listening to ourselves as well as to each other.

I discovered new realities, colors and a new sun. I used silence as a lathe, listening hard while standing at the edge of the unknown precipice where the ego dissolves and the beautiful, clean simplicity appears, where one "cleanses the horrible darknesses of the mind."[17]

Sigmund Hurwitz, in his study of the psychological phenomenon of Jewish mysticism, followed the Jungian concept that "beyond the areas of personal consciousness we find ourselves in an unknown dark region in which we meet the more ancient strata of the human soul. . . . Out of these deeper realms of the collective unconscious stems the strange images and symbols which are often incomprehensible to us."[18]

Many of us are natural, introspective mystics, yet afraid of venturing into the dark, to even allow the quiet moment to happen, frightened that the flooding onrush of silence has the sound and surge of death. Someone has said (it may have been Daisetz Teitaro Suzuki), "I cannot tell you what it is all about, but if you understand Zen, you will not be afraid to die." Perhaps there may someday be a different kind of Zen and another form of Hasidism so it will not only be unnecessary to be frightened of death, but not to have to die at all. It must be emphasized that the Great Death in Zen and the Self Extinction of Hasidism, in which perfect peace is achieved when the ego is finally annihilated, has no relationship to death, the terrible interrupter.

There is an incident of a great satori told of Sri Ramana Maharshi: "One morning the thought struck him that he would soon die. This thought came to him with great intensity and filled him with fear. Nothing around him had happened which could have caused this thought or explained his fear. Soon his entire mind was filled with the thought, 'I might die, and I will die. I am a being unto death.' Yet his reaction was not an attempt to free himself from the thought of death, as one might expect of a young, vivacious person. Rather he met the challenge, looking the possibility of death clearly in the eye and made the decision to measure himself with death. He lay down on the floor and imagined himself dying, life slowly leaving the parts of his body, one after another, death coming closer and closer to his center; vision, hearing and feeling gradually diminishing; thoughts becoming nebulous; the flow of thinking frozen and self-consciousness slowly disappearing up to the moment when one enters the state of sleep. But exactly at the moment his consciousness disappeared, abandoned him so to speak, an intensely clear and liberating awareness of his being broke through. All had disappeared as if it had been blown away before the overpowering thought: I am. Neither his body, nor his senses, nor even any ordinary thinking or consciousness which might have borne this experience remained. There was only this experience, erupting of itself and flashing forth with remarkable clarity, free of any inhibition and limitation: I am. It was a pure light as blinding as the noonday sun and allowed no distinguishing of individual things. Everything was filled with this light, appeared only through this light. There was nothing other than this light alone. Along with all else, death also disappeared."[19]

We must be "close to the night," as C. G. Jung has said about himself, but not frightened by it. Out of the deepness and darkness of meditation grows light and awareness, not finite interruption; sensitivity and intuition, not decay. It is "trying to seek something deeper than death . . . to go beyond death even in this life."[20] Time is defeated in this kind of eternity, which "is the absolute present and the absolute present is a *sono-mama* life, where life asserts itself in all its fullness."[21]

It is not the death that is bad luck to the Oriental, and a monster to the Jews. Jews have an unremitting hostility toward the cult of the dead. The land of the grave, *Sheol*, is a place of all corruption and evil. The world of death is filled with chaos. Death is not a part of life. It is a part of death. It is dark in the grave and remains so forever. For the Jews, to think of a life hereafter through which man had to first die, was an abomination of time in this world. Jewish hope has a special and particular character, and a prime purpose for religion is the need for man to have more time. This is its promise, a promise which has not yet been kept.

The Hasid's meditation, as well as that of Zen, is a study in how to transcend time, "to see things on the other shore as if it were something beyond . . . birth and death."[22]

The ego, even the small ego sense of the Japanese, desires many things. Every state is a state of suffering since it is an unsatisfied time. "The highest vow . . . is that in which there is no longer anything to be accomplished."[23] But this is not a cessation of force and energy in a seemingly passive meditation. It is not enough to just float in some silent, lazy suspension. It must be controlled. The suffering of desire can only be ended by halting desire, to strive for nothing, wanting nothing, for not only is the object of the desire a cause of suffering, but the desiring itself is pain. So one must seek Zen without seeking it. It must be allowed to happen. The ego, surely ambitious in its greed for many things, pushes and prods and compulsively drives on. But the ego is also afraid of achieving its goals, and it is this frustration from which man must also find release. It squeezes. It is like a *samurai* in discontent who seeks out a way to die, while, at the same time, professing a desire to live.

Nirvana is the condition of being without desire, the sublime emptiness stripped of prejudices, the permanent state of unassailable desirelessness, where one has finally finished in making the ego one's own enemy. But that pure stillness, like the capture of the space between two thoughts, is difficult to achieve and tough to hold. The partner of the leopard is silence. Silence is also the partner of Zen and Hasidism. The problem is to learn if one can live with that much silence.

Japanese Zen and Hasidic Judaism meet on the common ground of suffering and the need to find relief from it. While Buddhism professes that craving provokes pain, and that life and suffering are unavoidable and inseparable, Zen seeks escape from that great grief, *kokoro-kanashiku*, from the constant awareness that even in doing the very best, that best is never quite enough. Zen is the victor over that pessimism.

Hasidism, profoundly disillusioned in the Jewish passage through years of agonized history, found in the quiet of the Naught their own Jewish satori and special ecstasy. It matched the Zen intuitive and mystical insight of finding ways to push aside the absurd and unfair suffering that was. It favored the joy that not only should, but must be.

The Hasidic stubbornness insisted in the argument: if you do not get joy out of this life, how can you expect to get any happiness out of the next? If there is a cause for suffering, there must also be an end of suffering. As Zen has found release from the pessimism of Buddhism from which it arose, in which God had created a world of endless disappointments, so Hasidism also brought freedom from the astringent struggles and anguish, and proved that suffering was evil and an unnecessary ingredient in the search for the integrals of man's existence.

Martin Buber's attitude toward orthodox Judaism was that he found no joy in its severe, unbending dogmas. He objected to the mechanical rituals of the religious commandments in organized Judaism, for they had lost their original meanings based on love. It was the humanism of the ecstatic and mystical Hasidism that so excited him, with its emphasis on permanent joy as one of the most important ethical principles. It was a new mode, born in a time of darkness out of rebellion against a history that had surrounded itself with persecutions, ghetto restrictions, and a special Dark Age for Jews. It was and still is Hebraic revivalism, supported by a tremendous sense of sureness without having to indulge in obscure talmudic somersaults.

It originated in isolated Hasidic villages and hamlets in Central and Eastern Europe, such as the Galician Polish village of Belz, the Jewish Rome of Hasidism, where the Yiddish spoken was a kind of medieval German, and Jews lived devout lives "in an unbroken mystical trance, a state of unending ecstasy entirely beyond time, space and matter."[24]

Man, like God, still loved the stranger. Everyone had the opportunity to become a silken man; learned, godly and virtuous. The legend of the Lamed Vov was amplified. In every generation there was also one saint whom heaven had inspired to know certain secrets, and each generation had its messiah who led a solitary life without anyone knowing of his existence, but who was unable to reveal himself because of the weight of guilt in the world. But it was due to his very presence and merit that the world existed and was held together.

The authentic Jew, stubborn in his faith and in his will to perpetuate his essence, still believed in these messianic expectations, "to dream the dream of God."[25] The goal of his history was unswervingly bent on the establishment of a kingdom of heaven actually and practically on this earth, not just in heaven. It was to be, always to be, soon, in our time. In order to hasten it, self-afflictions were to be rejected and the alleged purpose and need to suffer was disavowed. Penance was false and misleading, an ugly cul-de-sac of a primitive, vestigial time. All suffering outraged the "soul" and contributed to morbidity, depression and a plethora of sadnesses.

There was no agreement between Hasidic Judaism and the belief of St. John of the Cross that the three enemies who travelled in the dark night of the soul were the world, the devil and the flesh. The world did not have to be evil, nor the flesh wicked or the devil the constant winner. After all, said the Hasid, the devil was not Jewish. And as for God, as the Hasid saw him (or her), God also hated suffering and sadness.

Hasidism was a different kind of prayer called Jewish joy, and a new way of praying that combined *kawannah*, intention, with meditation, all filled with love, instead of fear, ecstasy and not abasement. Prayers uttered in tears only sank. They could not soar. The Hasid proclaimed that there was a spiritual nature in all things. "All matter is full of supernatural 'sparks' of the holiness of God, and purely human functions such as eating and drinking, bathing and sleeping, dancing and the act of love are dematerialized and considered as the most sublime actions in the service of God."[26]

Joy caused a chain reaction of sparks, ". . . and where two sparks collided, an additional spark was born, compounding the happiness. It broke the separateness of man; the shouting to the world that I am here and you are there; I am in my space and you have your different space."[27] Ecstasy was the vehicle by which it was possible to rise up to the seven heavens of the Cabbalists. But a trade was involved and mandatory; receiving joy required a Jew to reciprocate, to contribute the enthusiasm and love back into the world, each day and each moment, not only toward man but toward all matter. The striking similarity between Judaism and the Buddhism of Zen's origin even extended to the transmigration of souls, in which ". . . the Lurian Cabbala teaches that the human soul can be incarnated not only in animals but also in plants, waters and minerals."[28]

The Hasidic notion of joy came out of the afflictions, and with it the belief in luck which was of a higher destiny. It was a Kosher kind of Zen in the exaltation of the Hasidic Naught and the separation from the ego enemy, all required before reaching the stage where there was no doubt and no compromise. The pessimism that had attached itself to Jews had been left behind. "My delight in Jewish history has never been more than a gloomy delight, the reminder of an endless succession of disasters, flights, pogroms, emigrations, humiliations, injustices ... I have only to open a book of Jewish history ... What is called Jewish history is but one long contemplation of Jewish misfortune, despite the extraordinary originality of Hebraic thought, (and) its astounding impact on the world."[29]

Hasidism was an ecstatic flight from the pain of living among strangers. It was compounded by each Jew's sensitivity and belief that every man's pain is also mine, that he or she over there, on the other side of the mountain, cries, but they cry with my Jewish tears. I am the brother, sister and keeper. That is Jewish involvement. All destinies are tied together. This was also part of the great unselfishness in Buddha's fundamental vow that unless others attained Buddhahood, Buddha himself could not attain it; if anyone suffered in this world, then Buddha himself could not become free and enlightened.

Hasidism helped break the back of alienation, of the sense of never belonging. It released the Jew from anxiety and the ideologies of frustration as seen in Job and Jeremiah. It was spiritual freedom from an almost perpetual sadness, in which the Hasid avoided egoism and pride, and cultivated generosity.

Zen and Hasidism, beginning from an identical genesis, both found in the void, the naught, the *mu* and the *ayin*, the nothingness that swelled with a potential filling up, the emptiness that was like the uterus awaiting life. They commenced with and dealt from the position of "the seamless robe of emptiness."[30]

The Jew found his place within Hasidism which helped him exist without accepting the belief that suffering was a precondition to joy, who denied that joy without suffering was only lust, and refused to condone that pain was necessary for redemption. He proved them all false. It gives him, as does Zen, the ability to live with the least possible anxiety, free of anomie, doubt and apprehension, and confirms that he is not simply spinning helplessly about in a meteor-strewn and unfriendly space.

Both Zen and Hasidism were and are in harmony with each other. The miraculous stories told of rabbis and roshis by saintly people did not necessarily have had to occur. They were truly holy if related by a devout and honest man. In any case, the miracles were those which the roshi or rabbi would have been able to accomplish anyway.

The question that reared its head at my crossroad had to be whether I, as a Jew, could practice Zen and still remain a Jew. I was unwilling and unable to forget the orthodoxy of my growing up, the sound of my mother's encouraging voice and my father's admonitions to be careful in a world where I could easily be blinded by events and, like an actor, find myself too often surrounded by strangers. I had a steadfast awareness of always being Jewish that had no connection with religion or any possible disenchantment or lack of enthusiasm for religion.

"We are endowed with a very rare, a very precious consciousness, the consciousness that we do not live in a void. We never suffer as so many others do from a fear of roaming about in the emptiness of time. We own the past and are, hence, not afraid of what is to be. We remember where we came from. We were summoned and cannot forget it, as we wind the clock of eternal history. We remember the beginning and believe in the end."[31]

It was tribal for me, rather than theology. My social sense was always colored whenever I was away from my own people by feeling I was a Jew first and a man second. This is the way I wanted it to be, despite the ease of feeling alien in many situations.

I had been wearied by the old testament of belief that in the end, the only truth was that pain must prevail. It was Hebraic Buddhism again. Abraham Joshua Heschel has been paraphrased: "In reverence, suffering and humility we discover our existence and find the bridge that leads from existence to God. And this is religion."[32] But if this was religion, I wanted none of it. I do not respond positively to the biblical image of the man of sorrows, acquainted with grief, his suffering a sign of holiness as he is tested day after day. Pain has no merit, except to signal the existence of some hidden disease. Otherwise it was like death: my implacable enemy. I was interested in what was Hasidic and the exultation of its mysticism, not in the weeping and wailing of the sack-cloth wearers, the lapel tearers and the pounders of chests.

I enjoyed my sense of continuity in being part of a humanist and sensitive people who saw God qualities in man, while others saw them only in nature. So I wanted to find some way to accept Zen without compromising Judaism, though "Jewishness is always uneasy," as Albert Memmi has told us. I could not and did not want to become a deserter, though "it is utterly inconvenient to be a Jew. The very survival of our people is a *Kiddush Hashem*. We live in spite of peril. Our very existence is a refusal to surrender to normalcy, to security and comfort. Experts in assimilation, Jews could have disappeared even before the names of modern nations were known."[33]

Being a Jew was umbilical for me, inextricably involved in what I am, my archetypal shadows, the sounds I hear, the motor that allows me to function. I needed to remain a Jew, in sentiment and spirit, and in what was indefinable. Knowing what I think I know now, and after having made all the necessary but cruel comparisons, I would only have chosen to become a Jew if I had not been lucky enough to be born one.

I came back to the determination: can a Jew practice Zen, study and enjoy it, make it a part of himself, intellectually if not by ritual and service, and still remain a Jew? Was Zen a religion, a system of mystical psychology, or was it a non-religious disciplinary technique? Was Buddhism, its source, truly one of the world's religions?

Zen "refuses to make any statement at all about the metaphysical structure of being and existence."[34]

I turned to Martin Buber who believed Buddhism had an unmistakable religious reality, but that it was "neither proclamation nor worship of deity."[35] It was not a religion in itself. My own study taught me that Buddhism was atheistic, teaching no God and repudiating the "soul," that if it was a religion, it was a religionless one. It was actually anti-religious in origin, and Zen itself, a clearly separate discipline, had long been severed from its Buddhist antecedents and was now without any practical historical continuity with it. "That's the trouble with Zen," said Gary Snyder. "They don't know anything about Buddhism."[36]

But Zen made everything fresh and new, having come so far that it had now no sermon of its own, nothing that had to be accepted, no sacred writings or sayings upon which to rely. The real experience did not come from books, but from the fact of the experience of the enlightenment itself.[37] It was a particular form of, but distinct from, orthodox Buddhism, and there was virtually no resemblance between them. Zen, because of its lack of religiosity, allowed an active participation for Jews in their search for non-religious means of improving their spirituality. It was knowledge, not religion. The word God made many Zen followers uneasy, I learned. Zen did not seek theologic truths. "In Zen, God is neither denied nor insisted upon. Zen wants absolute freedom, even from God."[38] Buddha had refused to make any direct statements about God. "God ... is very much in the nature of supposition (in Buddhism)."[39] Buddha, himself, did not deify a creator distinct or separate from the world. "Buddhism is not philosophy or religion in the Western sense,"[40] and neither is Zen, though either might be describable in religious terms.

Buddhism is self-redemptive, dealing with a human, corporeal I-Thou, its acknowledged man-to-man relationship as the highest presence, in which man is expected to work out his own salvation. It contrasted with the Judaic belief that God spoke to mankind as opposed to the Buddhist belief that man spoke to his fellow men. Each of us can not only become a Buddha, but, in fact, can surpass Buddha himself. "In Buddhism, Sakyamuni Buddha is respected and thanked as the first Buddha, but we can all be Buddhas, and greater Buddhas than Sakyamuni Buddha himself. There may be a greater Buddha at any moment. It is a kind of personal, not absolute worship."[41]

It was thusly atheistic, lacking an image since the possibility of also becoming a Buddha must inevitably lead, if one would presume it to be a religion, to the probability of only worshipping oneself. "We are all apt to forget that every one of us is Buddha himself."[42] Be your own lamp, Buddha said on his deathbed. He actually forbade his followers from treating him as a god. He had no use for the God concept. "You see, the Buddha ... the real trouble was that he kept silent on the ultimate metaphysical issues ... because they do not help you solve the problems of daily life."[43]

Buddhist satori is an experience which has no relationship to the Western concept of a personal God. "The Zen-man, too, (has) no God that corresponds to the analogical Christian God...."[44] A personal God finds no place in all of Buddhism, least of all in Zen, neither in statements nor assumptions. The silent void, the *sunyata*, the ultimate reality, occupies the space that in a true religion is filled with the God idea. "If religion is taken to mean the union of two things into one, such as God and man, then I don't think Buddhism is a religion."[45] It teaches no soul, nor anything supernatural. "Buddhist thought, particularly as represented by Zen, has no image of God in mind."[46]

Japanese Zen is no longer a child of anything. It has evolved a great and remote distance from the atheistic Buddhism of its roots. It has become a separate thing. It is it, by itself, standing alone. "Zen is not theology, and it makes no claim to deal with theological truth in any way whatever."[47] It is unholy and godless, a technique and system of disciplinary psychology and discovery. "There are in Zen no (sutras), no dogmatic tenets, nor are there any symbolic formulae through which an access might be gained into the signification of Zen. If I am asked, then, what Zen teaches, I would answer Zen teaches nothing. Whatever teachings there are in Zen, they come out of one's own mind. We teach ourselves. Zen merely points the way. Unless this pointing is teaching, there is certainly nothing in Zen purposely set up as its cardinal doctrines or as its fundamental philosophy."[48]

I found it was without piousness but involved with humanity rather than theology, serving existential man instead of any deity. It was full of "impudent paradox," as Thomas Merton stated, a doctrine without words and without a saviour to offer. "Zen places no reliance upon the authority of scriptures as do other Buddhist sects. . . . Zen discards the elaborate metaphysical speculations that came to China with Indian Buddhism. It can be said to have no doctrine at all."[49]

Zen is opposed to the almost Islamic fatalism and potential passivity that arose from the Buddhist secret for survival; to accept life just the way it was, to believe one could not escape the grip of an immutable destiny, who always expected the worse no matter what was done, and so, one must do nothing. This was and is not Zen. Zen, for me, teaches how to love without being loved back, like the Hasid who knows that love is not give and take, but give and give. What both expounded was that one could find happiness and peace in the giving to the point of emptiness, without any wish to possess, to ask nothing in return and still remain content.

Zen and Hasidism refuse to brood over sorrow, and do not believe that life and pain are indivisible. They are both life-hungry, practicing a joyous mysticism, one quietly and the other with exuberance. They reject without qualification what is alleged to be beautiful or redemptive in suffering. They reject as false any axiom that states or implies that the amount of happiness received is proportionate to the amount of suffering endured. They believe, without a scintilla of doubt, that life owes each of us discovery and joy, and they are opposed to the concept of essential sorrow as a feeling of contrition for allegedly essential sin.

Harold Heifetz

Notes

(1) Robert Gerard, *Psychotherapy and Psychosomatics*, 24: 475 (1974)

(2) Daisetz Teitaro Suzuki, *Mysticism: Christian and Buddhist*, (Harper and Company, 1957) p. 40

(3) Thomas Merton, *Conjectures of a Guilty Bystander*, (Doubleday and Company, 1966) p. 117

(4) Heinrich Dumoulin in *Studies in Japanese Culture*, J. Roggendorf (Sophia University, 1963) p. 20

(5) Robert Gerard, op. cit., p. 474

(6) Robert Gerard, op. cit., p. 480

(7) Thomas Merton, *Asian Journal*, (New Directions, 1973) p. 15

(8) Dwight Goddard, *A Buddhist Bible*, (Dutton and Co., 1938) p. 323

(9) *Deuteronomy* 11:13, in Hebrew: shemoa tishmeu.

(10) N. N. Jackson, *Meeting Silence*, Ph.D Thesis, (Washington University, 1974)

(11) Heinrich Dumoulin, *Christianity Meets Buddhism*, (Open Court Publishing Co., 1974) p. 49

(12) Ed Muzika, personal communication, 1975

(13) Christmas Humphreys, *Zen Buddhism*, (George Allen and Unwin Ltd., 1953) p. 23

(14) Christmas Humphreys, op. cit., p. 20

(15) Heinrich Dumoulin, op. cit., (1963) p. 20

(16) Daisetz Teitaro Suzuki, op. cit., p. 97

(17) attributed to Thomas Aquinas

(18) Sigmund Hurwitz, *Psychological Aspects of Early Hasidism*, (Northwestern University Press, 1970) p. 8

(19) H. M. Lassalle, *Zen Meditation for Christians*, (Open Court Publishing Co., 1968) p. 54

(20) Thomas Merton, op. cit., (1973) p. 306

(21) Daisetz Teitaro Suzuki, op. cit., p. 112

(22) Daisetz Teitaro Suzuki, op. cit., p. 98

(23) Thomas Merton, op. cit., (1973) p. 91

(24) Jiri Langer, *Nine Gates*, (David McKay Co., 1961) pp. vii-viii

(25) Abraham Joshua Heschel, *Zionist Quarterly*, 1:83 (1951)

(26) Jiri Langer, op. cit., p. 28

(27) Shlomo Carlebach, personal communication, 1975

(28) Jiri Langer, op. cit., p. 25

(29) Albert Memmi, Portrait of a Jew, (Viking Press, 1971)

(30) The Recorded Sayings of Layman P'ang, (John Weatherhill Inc., 1971) p. 24

(31) Abraham Joshua Heschel, op. cit., p. 83

(32) Jacob Yuroh Teshima, personal communication, 1975

(33) Abraham Joshua Heschel, op. cit., p. 83

(34) Thomas Merton, Mystics and Zen Masters, (Farrar, Straus and Giroux, 1967) p. 14

(35) Martin Buber, Eclipse of God,(Victor Gollancz, 1953) pp. 39-40

(36) Aelred Graham, Conversations: Christian and Buddhist, (Harcourt, Brace and World, 1968) p. 72, quoting Gary Snyder.

(37) Aelred Graham, op. cit., p. 96, quoting Fujimoto Roshi.

(38) Daisetz Teitaro Suzuki, Introduction to Zen Buddhism, (Rider and Company, 1970) p. 97

(39) Aelred Graham, op. cit., p. 170, quoting Shojun Bando.

(40) Aelred Graham, op. cit., p. 115, quoting Abbot Hashimoto.

(41) Aelred Graham, op. cit., p. 99, quoting Fujimoto Roshi.

(42) Daisetz Teitaro Suzuki, op. cit. (1957), p. 107

(43) Aelred Graham, The End of Religion, (Harcourt Brace Jovanovich, 1971) p. 144

(44) Thomas Merton, Zen and the Birds of Appetite, (New Directions, 1968) p. 103

(45) Aelred Graham, op. cit. (1968), p. 179, quoting Shojun Bando.

(46) Aelred Graham, op. cit., p. 35, quoting Kobori Sohoku.

(47) Thomas Merton, op. cit. (1967), p. ix

(48) Daisetz Teitaro Suzuki, op. cit. (1970) p. 94

(49) Thomas Merton, op. cit., p. 219

I

THE MONASTERY
AND
THE YESHIVOT

Back in the womb from which I came,
I had no God and merely was, myself.
I did not will or desire anything,
for I was pure being, a knower of myself
by divine truth. The I wanted myself and
nothing else. And what I wanted I was,
and what I was I wanted, and thus I existed
untrammelled by God or anything else.

Meister Eckhart

LIFE IN A HASIDIC YESHIVA

Jiri Langer

... On weekdays I spend most of my time at the *Bes Hamidrash*, or House of Study. It is open day and night for all who thirst after knowledge. The high shelves round the walls are stuffed full of books from the floor to the ceiling. The tables are littered with a jumbled mass of folios. Anyone may take out any book he likes and study in the *Bes Hamidrash* whenever he wishes. Here of course there are only holy, theological Hebrew books. A devout man would not touch any other. Even to know a single Latin or Russian letter is an indelible stain upon the soul. I sit and study the books from morning till evening, leaving them only for a short while to go to evening prayers or meals. Yet even the nights are not made for rest but—as the Talmud says— for the study of the Law of God. Spiteful insects remind me of this impressively enough as soon as I lie down. It is forbidden to kill insects. I already know that it would be a sin, so I prefer to go to the House of Study. I either study or listen to someone else, in another corner, reading aloud to himself in a drawling, plaintive chant. The *Shames*, or caretaker, hands us round candles. We hold the lighted candles in our hands so as not to fall asleep over our studies.

One afternoon I dive into the ritual bath in the same way as before prayer, for on this day I am going to the saint with my *kvitel*. A *kvitel* is a small piece of paper on which one of the saint's clerks writes the name of the suppliant and the name of his mother—not his father!—the suppliant's place of origin and, in a few concise words, the substance of what he is coming to ask of God. The Chassidim, it must be explained, do not bring their petitions to the saint by word of mouth but in writing. On my *kvitel* are written the words: "Mordecai ben Rikel mi-Prag, hasmodoh be-limud ve—yiras shomayim", which means that I am asking God "that I may persevere in my studies and in the fear of God". Not one word more.

That was how the Chassidim advised me to write it. The saint's
entrance hall and room are already crowded—in Belz it is always
crowded—with scores of suppliants, mostly women. Some come
to ask the saint to intercede with God for success in their business,
others for recovery from an illness, others for advice for or against
a marriage. The needs of the Chassidim are many and varied, and
only *he*, the saint, can satisfy them through his intercession with the
Most High. After reading some of the petitions, the saint asks for
details before beginning to pray or give advice. He reads some
petitions with obvious displeasure, especially those asking for
cures. He scolds the suppliant and tells him to go to a doctor. But
he wishes him a speedy recovery. Some bring a *matbeya*, that is, a
coin which the saint will endow with secret power and which can
then be used as a *kameo*, or amulet. The saint places the coin on
the table and draws three circles round it. He does so with obvious
reluctance. But once the coin has been consecrated by the saint's
hand, the suppliant receives it back with an expression of radiant
joy on his face. Besides the *kvitel*, we place a *pidyen* on the saint's
table; this is a small sum of money according to one's means. The
saint is *in duty bound* to accept gifts. This custom was instituted by
the holy Baal-Shem, and it has a metaphysical background. When
the saint intercedes with God on behalf of us unworthy people, the
Lord asks him: "Of what importance is this sinner to you? Have you
any obligation towards him, dearly beloved son?" And the saint can
reply to God: "Yes, I have an obligation towards him. He has
assisted me and my family." Our money offering is thus the only
link, mean as it is, between us and the saint; it is the necessary
prerequisite for our prayers to be heard. Hence the saint accepts
gifts. But he returns the gifts of poor people immediately. From
declared unbelievers he will not take any gifts at all. The devout
who live outside Belz send their petitions and contributions to the
saint's office by post, or if the matter is urgent, by telegram. The
suppliant obtains relief as soon as the clerk unsticks the telegram
even though the saint has not yet received the remittance. Those
who come to Belz from Hungary kiss the saint's hand. The Poles
do not. I am last in the queue. The saint reads my *kvitel* with undis-
guised delight. When I come out of his room, the Chassidim are
waiting for me outside, to wish me luck: "Git gepoilt!"—"Well
done!"

   When the moon is full, the saint cures mental maladies. The
people stand in a sad queue in his room while the saint pores over

the Talmud by the light of large candles. I once knew a girl who was completely cured of melancholia in this way.

The saint never looks on the face of a woman. If he must speak to women—as, when he receives a *kvitel*—he looks out of the window while he speaks. He does not even look at his own wife, a somewhat corpulent woman, but still beautiful. On a later occasion, when the holy man was alone with his wife, it was only natural that the lad from Prague should seize this rare opportunity of peeping through the keyhole when no one was watching. She had come to ask her husband's advice about their domestic worries, of which they had their full share. Even on this occasion the saint looked out of the window, with his face turned away from her, as though he were talking to a strange woman, not his wife. The Talmud tells of one devout man who did not notice that his wife had a wooden stump instead of a leg, until her funeral. . . . That man was a teacher. Thus far the Talmud.

We"who are really in earnest" do not board at the inn like those who "merely journey" to the saint of Belz. We belong to our own society, or *chevre*, the members of which are called *Yoshvim*, or *sitting ones*, because they live, or sit in Belz permanently. Our society lives on small contributions earned with difficulty from the more wealthy visitors to Belz. We cook for ourselves. The dining-room is small. Deep holes yawn in the unplaned boards of the dirty floor. We crowd together round the table on a narrow bench. There is a great shortage of crockery. We young people often eat two out of one dish, with our hands, of course. To use a fork would be an indecent innovation. The menu is not very varied. For lunch we get a slice of heavy rye bread, a plate of vermicelli or potato soup, which of course we eat with a spoon, and a tiny piece of beef to which a large portion of broad beans must always be added. The older men drink vodka, all from the same bottle (though the Talmud, or rather the Shulchan Aruch forbids two people to drink from the same vessel on hygienic grounds). We often have the famous Belz *purée*, made from sweet-smelling brown buck-wheat flour, called *grapel*, which is remarkably tasty. Sometimes we have fish, small white fish full of treacherous little bones. It is my duty to help to scrape the fish in the kitchen when it comes to my turn.

On the Sabbath the crowd is even greater. It is a real squeeze. We do not eat in our mess, but press round the rabbi at his table, quite regardless of each other's comfort in our anxiety to obtain straight from his hands some morsel of food which he has first touched and tasted. Each little titbit of his sweet *kugel* (a hot pudding), each piece of his greasy *chaulnt* (chaud lit), each drop of his home-made raisin wine contains a complete paradise with all its accompanying celestial delights. He who eats of food which the saint has blessed is sure to obtain both earthly and eternal bliss. At the table the Chassidim sing their Sabbath songs in praise of Belz, songs whose changing rhythms are a dance of gaiety and sorrow, chaos and desire. Before the grace after the meal the rabbi expounds the Word of God. Every new truth which the saint brings out from the depths of the Law is fashioned by God into a new heaven. The saint's exposition is at the same time a sermon. I hear his deep mystic voice, but I cannot distinguish the words.

On festivals there is dancing. A hundred men take hold of each other's hands, or put their arms round each other's necks and form a large circle that rotates with a rocking dance-step, slowly at first and then faster and faster. The dancing begins in the *Bes Hamidrash*, but after a while the whole crowd spreads out on to the square and dances under the rabbi's window. A dance lasts uninterrupted for an hour, or maybe more, till the dancers are exhausted, intoxicated by the endless repetition of the same, mystically colored, dance melody. In the same way the celestial spheres dance eternally round the glorious throne of the Lord. We young people are not allowed to take part in the sacred dance of the Chassidim. We look on and sing, clapping our hands in time to the rhythm. The rabbi dances only a short while during the morning service on the autumn festivals. He dances alone. In his hand he holds a palm branch or a parchment scroll of the Law. The sight of the saint's mystic dance fills us with godly fear.

We take very good care not to catch the saint's eye during a service. As he enters the House of Study we press together in one confused mass, to leave him as much free space as possible. No true Chassid comes within a distance of *four ells* (about eight feet) of him either during prayer or before it. If we are not sufficiently careful and agile he shouts at us—using words like "cattle!" or even "robbers!"—and sometimes he slips off his *gartel* (belt) and belabors the careless individual who has got in his way. But, surprisingly enough, his blows do not hurt in the least. Nor do his words. We laugh quietly to ourselves with joy, because we know that they are not insults but a high mark of honor, a secret blessing which he disguises with blows and rough words. For the Devil must not recognize them, or he may stop them from ascending to the throne of the Most High. Nevertheless we try to keep our distance from the saint; the farther we get away from him the better it is.

Why?—Why do we take such care not to come close to him? Why does he warn us so sternly to keep away? After all he is well aware that not even with a whisper would we interrupt him but would only pray in the most devout fashion. It is not because we might say anything we ought not to, or knowingly disturb him, but because our *thought*—all those silly thoughts we carry in our heads, even though not expressed, even the most devout—would upset his spiritual, mystic concentration. For our thoughts are so material that they would sully his pure, mystic concentration and detract from the splendour of his thoughts, each of which is a glorious, living angel. Some Chassidim hide modestly behind the backs of those who happen to stand in front of them. That is foolish, for the saint knows about everybody—even those who are hiding or are far away.

The weekdays slip by monotonously. I continue my study of the Talmud. I have long been fond of these interminable discourses of the ancient Palestinian and Babylonian rabbis on ritual and law, their legends, moral teachings, proverbs, anecdotes, paradoxes, that go to form the Talmud. The Hebrew and Aramaic languages, with their ancient elegance and terseness, have never lost their charm for me. Those picturesque signs in Hebrew writing which even to this day are half hieroglyphic, without vowels or punctuation, have been my favorite reading matter almost from childhood. Now for the first time I can give myself up to this pleasure completely. I sit and learn. When I do not understand one of the complex Talmudic problems, I ask an older person to explain it for me. But mostly I study alone. I repeat each page at least six times as I have been recommended to do. I memorize the actual Talmudic text; I learn the remarkably exact mediaeval commentaries which are printed round the text on each page like a wreath of tiny flowers, the diminutive letters of a mediaeval rabbi's handwriting. Sometimes I use other large volumes containing notes about these commentaries to help me along.

Books are greatly respected here, worshipped in fact. Nobody, for instance, sits on a bench if there is a book anywhere on it. That would be an affront to the book. We never leave a book face downwards or upside down, but always face upwards. If a book falls to the ground we pick it up and kiss it. When we have finished reading we kiss the book before we put it away. To throw it aside, or put other things on top of it is a sin. Yet the books are nearly all woefully dilapidated by constant use. When a book is so badly torn that it cannot be used, the caretaker takes it to the cemetery and buries it. Even the smallest scrap of paper

with Hebrew characters printed on it must not be left lying about on
the floor, or trodden on; it must be buried. For every Hebrew letter is a
name of God. We never leave books open except when we are actually
learning from them. If we are obliged to slip away for a moment, and
do not wish to close the book, we may leave it open so as not to lose
the place, but we must cover it with a cloth. If anyone notices another
person going away from a book without closing or covering it, he goes
over and shuts it himself; but first he will look at the open page and
read a few lines out of it. If he were to shut the book without reading it
at all, his act of closing it would weaken *the power of memorizing* in the
other person who left the book open. The parchment scroll of the
Law, which is hand-written, is held in even greater respect than printed
books.

I am gradually becoming acquainted with *Chassidic* literature.The
first book I read is called "The Beginning of Wisdom" (Reshit
Chochmah), a cabbalistic book of exercises for the ascetic. It incul-
cates humility and self-denial and is full of beautiful quotations from
the mystical Zohar and a book called "The Duties of the Heart" by
Bachya Ibn Pakuda. "Reshit Chochmah" is the work of a famous
cabbalist named Elijah de Vidas who lived in Palestine at the end of
the seventeenth century. Another book I read is "The Joys of
Elimelech" (Noam Elimelech) by the "Rebe Reb" Melech of Lizensk
(Elimelech). I shall be telling you something about this book and its
wonderful author later on. The first of these books was recommended
to me by the saint of Belz himself; the second was brought to my
notice by the Chassidim. They accompany me on all my journeys; I
had them with me even when I was a soldier. When I am alone and no
one can see me, I dip into cabbalistic writings which we young people
have been forbidden to study.

My health is affected and I am conscious that I am becoming
physically weaker every day. The daily bath before morning prayer,
the bad food, the all too frequent voluntary fasts, the loss of sleep, and
the lack of movement and air, considerably weaken the otherwise
strong constitution of a youth who is not yet physically mature. But I
force myself to face up to things. I will not give in.

Why in fact are we here at all? Why not serve God at home? Is it
perhaps because we want to become rabbis, or perfect saints like the
saint of Belz? No, not at all. Nothing like this ever occurs to us. We
have no desire to be rabbis and we shall never become saints. We are
quite convinced of that. All we want is to enjoy the glory of God's
majesty which the personality of the saint sheds around him. We want

to enjoy it throughout our lives, continuously and unceasingly. We know that when the day comes for him to bid us his last farewell, he will leave us his first-born son, no less a saint than himself and perhaps even greater.

... On weekdays, at Belz, we do not say morning prayers until noon when the rabbi comes into the House of Study with his sons. We pray at the synagogue only on the Sabbath. The weekday service, which in other places lasts nearly an hour, is completed in an almost miraculously fast time at Belz—fifteen or twenty minutes. This speed is very important for "no pig can penetrate a fence if the stakes are set close together"; in other words, no sinful thoughts can steal into prayers if the words are spoken quickly and without any pauses. "A person who cannot say a thousand words with one breath has no right to be called a saint."

But ... excessive religiosity is not welcomed. But now that my beard and side-whiskers are well grown ... I am able to speak some Yiddish and have begun wearing a long *shipits* (an overcoat similar to a caftan) instead of a short coat. ... I have started wearing a black velvet hat on weekdays, as all the other Chassidim do. ... But ... why am I not gay, all the time, as a true Chassid ought to be? ...

At last, when my face is pallid from undernourishment and illness, and my emaciated body has acquired a stoop, it is clear to nearly all of them that "I am really in earnest". No longer will the gates of Chassidism be closed in front of the youth from Prague.

The Chassidim are becoming kinder to me every day. My lot is being improved in every possible way. Better bread, and milk. But my weakened stomach resolutely refuses all these extra comforts. Moreover, the insects are becoming crueller all the time. They have absolutely no pity on me. The mice nibble at my clothes. I sleep on the ground on a heap of old straw. My whole outward appearance testifies that I am gradually turning into a complete *chnyok* and *katcherak*. These two words are untranslatable nicknames used by the Chassidim to mock any of their fellows who are totally indifferent to their outward appearance.

The saint of Belz has fallen ill. After a great deal of persuasion he has decided to visit ... Marienbad. We are carrying him there along the paths through the forest. At other times he is separated from us by his secretaries and servants, as God is separated from our souls by myriads of spheres and worlds. But here among the forest trees we can all approach him. Although he is seriously ill, he talks cheerfully to everybody. We are conscious that his are no ordinary words even when he is talking about things which appear to be everyday matters. All his words, however small, are to be understood metaphorically. The whole time his thoughts are concentrated exclusively on supernatural matters. . . . When he is not speaking to anyone, he repeats the Talmud to himself, which he naturally knows by heart in its entirety—all thirty-six tractates in their twelve mighty volumes! Once, as we were walking through the forest, he remarked: "If I didn't have you, I would pray with these trees here." He has never made a secret of his pacifist opinions. We have often admired his outspokenness. Once, when he noticed a public collecting box for war contributions on one of the forest roads, he called out with passion: "Is that what we've got to do with our money—so still more people can be murdered?" And on another occasion he said: "The German says: The whole world belongs to me! The Englishman says: The whole sea belongs to me! But my Yossele—that was the name of the Chassid who led the prayers in those days—my Yossele sings so sweetly: The sea belongs to God, for He made it; the dry land belongs to God, for His hand created it."

Our heroes . . . are the *Tsaddikim*, the rulers of the Chassidim. The word *tsaddik* means a perfect and just person, a saint. The word *chassid*, which becomes *chassidim* in the plural, means a deeply devout person who is wholeheartedly devoted to a particular *Tsaddik*. The founder of Chassidism was Rabbi Yisroel Baal-Shem-Tov who lived and worked in Poland in the middle of the eighteenth century. (He died about 1761.) To this day hundreds of thousands of Chassidic communities live almost totally isolated from the surrounding world, faithful to their unique traditions, and it would be true to say that in Eastern Europe they form states within states. Their *real* rulers are the grandsons and great-grandsons of the saints . . .

To relate stories from the lives of the saints is one of the most praiseworthy acts a Chassid can do. He will tell of them at every opportunity—during a meal, during his studies, on a train journey, but especially on the anniversary of a saint's death. He must never forget to add the word "holy", or the phrase, "May his merits protect us!" whenever he mentions the name of a saint. Woe to the listener who protests that he has already heard this or that episode before! Everybody is in duty bound to listen patiently to each story even if he has heard it a hundred times already. In this way, over the course of years, everything becomes imprinted on the memory—the heroes' names, their wives' names, the characters connected with them and the place where the various events took place.

Anyone can be a narrator. If you know a nice story about a saint, it will be gratefully accepted, and one of your listeners will immediately reward you with another story about the same saint, or a similar anecdote about another saint, or something a saint has said. If you make a mistake in any detail, you will immediately be corrected by your listeners, for of course they know it much better than you do! ...

The story-teller does not speak with words alone. If his vocabulary proves inadequate, he can help himself along with gestures, miming or modulations of the voice. When relating something gloomy, he will lower his voice to a whisper. If he has a mystery to unfold he will content himself with hinting, breaking off in the middle of a sentence with a meaningful wink or squint. If he has to describe some supernatural beauty he will close his eyes and roll his head about in genuine ectasy. In this way the listener can understand much more than if we were to paint everything in detail with the choicest and cleverest words. The narrator's style is absolutely simple, without any special pathos, and completely inconsequent. He often wanders from one saint to another—so do not be surprised if I sometimes do the same.

The Chassidim are aware that by no means everything they relate about their saints actually happened; but that does not matter. If a saint never really worked the miracle they describe, it must still have been one such as only he was capable of performing. Rabbi Nachman of Brazlav goes out of his way to point out that "not everything related about the holy Baal-Shem (for instance) is true, but even the things which are untrue are *holy* if told by devout people. The fact is (says Rabbi Nachman) that man is perpetually sunk in a magic sleep throughout his life and is unable to rouse himself except by narrating anecdotes about the saints."

From *Nine Gates* (David McKay Company, New York). 1960

Life in A Zen Monastery

John Blofeld

To many people, my decision to enter upon a life of self-communion within the tranquil halls of a monastery may seem a very eccentric outcome of my concern for the sufferings of others; yet my decision was perfectly logical if judged from the standpoint of the Mahayanist philosophy of living. I had already come to have implicit belief in the doctrine that all life is One and that the One is spirit or mind only, its seeming division into myriads of entities—walking, leaping, swimming, flying, wriggling, crawling—being quite illusory or, at best, real in a strictly transient sense. Moreover I had learnt that the relation of the individual to the totality of all existence is more intimate than that of the part to the whole. Could the veils be drawn aside, it would be seen that, in an important sense, the individual *is* the Whole, that the self-purification of one is in a measure the greater purification of all, just as a cup of clean water cast into a great vessel of murky liquid lightens the color of all.... A Christian, though believing himself damned for his sins, may still feel able to assist others by preaching Christ to them; a Buddhist, with no Saviour to offer, can only illuminate the Way for others from his own wisdom and experience. Though he may not hope to save his fellow beings in the mass, he may aspire to nourish the spiritual growth of a few chosen disciples; and even this aspiration must remain a dream unless he has so far pierced the veils of his innermost consciousness that he can anticipate every difficulty and understand those dark problems which are beyond the disciple's power to express in words. He must be so steeped in intuitive knowledge that his disciples' groping for words can be brushed aside.... To be of the smallest help to a single human being in matters of eternal moment, he must himself be far along the Path to Enlightenment. Such progress is best achieved in that secluded tranquillity where, free from anxiety and obligations, he can practice meditation night and day, preferably inspired by the calm beauty of mountain, lake and forest.

Lest some should regard contemplative monks as *selfishly* seeking their own individual escape from the Wheel, it should be remembered that Mahayana monks must offer a solemn pledge that, for the sake of all sentient beings, when all desire is transcended and freedom won, they will remain voluntarily in *Sangsara* ready to offer their spirit and their flesh again and again, to be *reborn endlessly into sorrow* as Bodhisattvas or in any other form, as pools of strength from which other Path-climbers may drink, there to remain until every other being has entered *Nirvana* before them or is prepared to enter in their company.

I had no intention as yet of taking a monk's vows, for in the Mahayana countries such vows are taken only by those who hope to remain monks for life. In Thailand or Burma, a man may enter and leave the monkhood as many as three times; in China, to withdraw even once is to admit defeat and to be an object of shame. Unsure of myself, I formed the more humble intention of living *as* a monk, sharing the Zen life down to the smallest detail, but retaining my freedom to return to lay life or to take vows as might at some future time seem best. In other words, I wished to be a novice.

Having made up my mind, I crossed over from the city to the Western Hills in a large rowing-boat. A canal connecting the West Gate with the mouth of the lake led past the pagoda-like drum-tower, in which is suspended a tremendous horizontal drum used for warning the city of approaching invaders. During the two-hour journey across the lake, . . . I suffered from the midday sun which, even in the gentle climate of Yunnan, can be cruel when the water reflects and magnifies its glare. . . . At the further shore, . . . a short-cut through the woods which would bring me to the main road close to the monastery grounds. In less than half an hour, I reached its outer gate.

Hua T'ing Ssu closely resembles other Zen monasteries of its size. The whole estate . . . is enclosed by a low wall and closely encircled by the forest. Passing through the outer gate, I entered an informal half-wild garden containing a bell-tower from the upper story of which a deep, solemn note shivered on the air at intervals of about two minutes, a note believed to bring to the sufferers in the transitory hells Ksitigarbha's . . . message of comfort and ultimate release. Next came a second wall pierced by a moongate and, beyond that, a small formal garden leading to the gateway of the monastery proper, which faced straight across the lake into the sunrise. The principal buildings strictly followed the formal design which for two milleniums or more has been employed by the builders of Chinese palaces and temples. The two Great Halls raised upon stone platforms formed two north-south oblongs in the huge east-west oblong courtyard enclosed by the remaining buildings standing in an unbroken rectangle. These other buildings included an elaborate gatehouse, a library, refectory, guest-rooms, living-rooms, the novices' schoolroom, a block printing press and the House of Spiritual Ancestors, where the spirit-tablets of deceased monks were venerated. Attached to the north side of the rectangle were a series of smaller courtyards containing the Hall of Meditation, the Abbot's private quarters and garden, the offices of the administrative staff, storerooms, kitchens, bathrooms and wash-rooms. Seen from a distance in its wild setting, the monastery was a place of ravishing beauty; its red walls made it a square-cut ruby in the green-blue setting of forest, lake and sky. From close at hand, the recently restored colors looked overwhelmingly bright—the walls almost crimson, the lacquered woodwork scarlet and green, the eaves and roof-beams covered with multicolored floral designs against a blue background, the main buildings tiled with imperial yellow, and the smoothly flagged courtyards gay with flowers and flowering shrubs. . . . As soon as I entered the monastery for the first time, I hastened to pay my respects in the Great Hall, during which time the Reverend Receiver of Guests was informed of my arrival. Presently he came forward to welcome me and provided me with temporary quarters near the guest-hall. The next day I sought an audience with the Abbot who readily agreed to allow me to undergo a period of training exactly like a monk's. The outward symbols of my transformation were to be a shaven head, a wide-sleeved robe for ceremonial occasions and a narrow-sleeved one for ordinary wear. I must not, however, wear the *Kasa* or sacred toga which is worn during the performance of rites. When all had been arranged, I was given a private cell in the compound of the Meditation Hall (Japanese—Zendo); and, after some probation, permitted to spread my sleeping mat in the Meditation Hall itself.

On ordinary days, the refectory food was almost always the same—old rice thick with the dead bodies of weavils, a soup of water in which pumpkins had been boiled with salt, a pumpkin mush (the vegetable scooped out of the 'soup') to all of which was added a relish of pickled chillies. Such a diet would have been insufficient to sustain health without the weekly feasts including such luxuries as *fried* vegetables and health-giving beancurd. . . .

The Meditation Hall became the center of my existence. It was a big square chamber about the size of a hotel private banqueting hall or of an exceptionally large university lecture room, to which light was admitted through barely translucent paper windows on one side only. In the center rose a small, octagonal shrine and round three sides of the room ran a low cushioned platform almost eight feet wide. At night the monks slept on it, heads towards the shrine, feet to the wall, forming a long line of shaven-headed figures humped beneath quilts of coarse grey cloth. During meditation periods, they sat on the edge of the platform facing the shrine. I suppose there was enough space for fifty or sixty to sleep there with a short space between each quilt, but our meditation group consisted of between thirty and forty only. Subdued conduct was necessary at all times, silence only during meditation periods and the hours set apart for sleep. The hall was much too dark for study, but we were able to do such jobs as mending our clothes there. Opportunities for exercise were rare, so we enjoyed occasional visits to the monastery's own fields to help bring back the crop of chillies or for some such purpose. For health's sake and to assist in calming our minds, each meditation session included one or two short periods of marching briskly round the central shrine at an ever-increasing pace, the rhythm of our steps being marked for us by the tapping of a so-called wooden fish.

Suting, a youth who had already spent six years as novice and full-fledged monk . . . took me in hand from the first, showing me how to order my gestures and movements in the formal, ritualistic manner proper to the inhabitants of a strict monastery. He instructed me in my ceremonial duties and, more important than all the rest, tried to interpret the Preceptor's instructions which preceded each period of meditation, turning them into simpler language and providing illustrations from his own head. He also helped me to memorize the words of the morning and evening rituals which must be recited in full without the aid of a book.

Our day would begin an hour or more before dawn. . . . The Meditation Hall is in pitch darkness relieved only by a circle of light glimmering from the flame before the octagonal shrine. We are lying side by side in a long row which follows the alignment of three consecutive walls, our heads pointing towards the shrine. Whoever has been on 'night watch' is still standing before the altar, slowly prostrating himself and rising again in an endless succession of beautifully controlled movements. Suddenly a few of the sleepers awaken, roused by the sound of a stick being knocked sharply against the courtyard flags—

dik dik dik. Presently the soft note of a sounding bronze joins in—*dik dong dik dong dik dong*. The tapping ceases and we hear only *dong dong dong*. Then the giant temple drum breaks in and we get *dong boom dong boom dong boom* until the notes of the sounding bronze cease and the rhythm of the great drum slowly increases its tempo. Over the space of twenty minutes, . . . the drummer rains down blows with all his strength . . . finishing on a terrific crescendo.

By this time, Suting has dragged the quilts off me, forcing me to face the cold, and accompanied me, first to answer nature's call, then to wash, clean our teeth and don our ceremonial gowns. All this we have done without supervision but at the speed of recruits anxious to please a bullying sergeant-major. Now we are filing from the outer darkness of the courtyard into the Great Hall ablaze with lights, administrators and menials to the left, contemplatives to the right. As each takes his place before the altar, he prostrates himself three times; then, at a given signal, the prostrations are repeated in unison. The *ting* of a silver bell brings us to our feet for the last time and at once the solemn incense chant begins.

Long invocations follow, addressed to names which may be taken as those of actual divinities, or as universal forces and aspects of the One Reality, according to the individual development of each and the measure of his understanding. Besides the invocations, there are all sorts of reflections, undertakings, precepts and so on, as well as *mantras* or mystical formulae recited in Sino-Sanskrit. The chanting and the throb and chime of percussion instruments and the glitter of scores of candles reflected as sharp points of light upon the golden statues never fail to elevate the heart to regions of tranquillity and beauty hard to penetrate by other means. At last comes the final prostration and we file out of the Hall. Dawn is just breaking. . . .

Now it is breakfast-time, an informal meal of rice-porridge taken wherever we happen to be standing when it arrives from the giant cauldrons in the kitchen. I smoke a cigarette and offer the packet round, but it is seldom that anyone accepts. Smoking, while not forbidden, is somehow unbecoming to monkish gravity, besides being evidence of a minor attachment.

Comes the *gok bok bok* of a 'wooden fish'. . . . This is the signal to enter the Meditation Hall. Silence. The session has begun. For about ten minutes we sit loosely erect in the lotus posture which I alone cannot manage properly. Suting watches with a smile my efforts to make the soles of my crossed feet point skywards. Nothing is required of us during those ten minutes except that we should sit quietly, letting our minds grow gradually tranquil and trying quite gently to empty them of wayward thoughts. At such moments each mind is like a pool into which a restless child has at last stopped throwing stones.

We get to our feet, fall in line and begin to circle round the shrine. Gradually the tempo increases until, towards the end, we are moving as fast as possible without actually breaking into a run, our heads held forwards and our shoulders hunched in the special ritual position for speedy circumambulation.

Everybody stops dead. We hasten to the part of the platform nearest to where we happen to be standing. We sit down, folding our legs as before, and I attempt quite vainly to hide my failure to achieve the position under the folds of my long gown. From the height of my knees everybody can see that I am cheating, but this is a small matter.

The silver bell is struck by the Preceptor who now begins his daily instructions, most of his words being too technical for my understanding. Suting will have to explain them later. The main point of yesterday's instruction was that we should reflect on the old conundrum "Who reverences the Buddha?' in the sense of 'Who am I?' Mere repetition of the words is not enough. Equally, any attempt to answer the question by logical deduction is Zen-wise, a waste of time. . . . I wish I could question Suting again, but the silence rule is strictly kept and my friend is already sitting with half-closed eyes lost in a world to which I have not yet found the way in.

A stick of incense has been lighted and none of us will move until it has crumbled to a little heap of grey ash. . . .

Two young monks, chosen as lictors for the day, are padding softly round the room with their lictors' boards. If either of them sees a head too far forward or saliva dribbling from a mouth, he will know that the owner of head or mouth has fallen asleep. Accordingly he will strike the offender's shoulder to awaken him. The flat of the board will produce much sound and little pain; the edge will make no sound but cause much pain; which is used will depend on whether or not the victim is an old offender.

A long, long silence. I try hard to deal with yesterday's conundrum. Once or twice I congratulate myself on having entered some supernormal state, only to find that it is merely a sensation of vagueness induced by staring too long at the same point—purely physical, a tiny obstacle to progress rather than an advance. I try to remember Suting's explanation of the Preceptor's words. 'Don't just repeat the conundrum like a magic formula.' 'Keep it in your mind continuously.' Good, I will. 'Do not waste time seeking its logical meaning or trying to explain it to yourself.' If I avoid vain repetition, what remains but to think out its meaning? If I avoid thinking out its meaning what remains but vain repetition? Let me start again. And so on, and so on. The incense-stick smoulders downwards to the ash in which it was planted and I am still far from hitting upon the right method.

We get up and circumambulate briskly, some with minds already inward turned and oblivious, except in a very perfunctory way, of their surroundings. At least the others move briskly. As for me, I can scarcely hobble so frightful is my leg cramp and the sensation of 'pins and needles'.

Halt. Back to the nearest seating place. Time for the second and last round of this session. During the remaining hour I make scarcely more progress than before.

At the end of the session, the novices hurry to the schoolroom, while the rest of us are free to employ our time in private meditation or in some sort of recreation. Lunch-time is announced by the striking of a much bigger 'wooden fish' which actually looks like a fish besides being made of wood. We file into the refectory and stand while a long, musical grace is chanted, during which a few morsels of cooked rice are ceremoniously carried to a pillar in the courtyard and left there—a symbolical offering to wandering spirits. Judging from what we had yesterday and the day before, the lunch will consist of rice, pumpkin soup and pumpkin mush, with salt as the only seasoning except for the chilli relish served separately.

The second half of the day passes very much like the first and by 9:30 p.m. we are all in bed, except for those who meditate or perform prostrations before the altar throughout part or all of the night.

Naturally my most absorbing interest lay in the satisfaction of my purpose in coming to live as a monk. I wished to understand Zen, to see if it was the best method of approach for me and, if so, to practice it day and night that I might gain a closer understanding of life and, ultimately, stand face to face with Reality.

It was months before I came to realize just what I was looking for and approximately how to reach it. Zen had attracted me in the first place because it offers a short cut with some possibility of gaining a full insight into Truth *in this Life*; and secondly on account of its *apparent* simplicity which makes the use of images and ritual not wrong but unnecessary. An added attraction was that this 'doctrine without words' requires a knowledge of very few scriptures.

In time I discovered that it had been a great error to suppose that Zen is a *simple* approach to Truth. Despite the absence of insuperable linguistic difficulties, it is in some ways the most difficult of all possible approaches, just as a short cut to the top of a steep mountain is the most arduous route for the climber.

Yet, though I may be Zen-wise obtuse, my months in the monastery were not wasted. I believe I may claim to have made some progress in converting from theoretical knowledge to partial realization two supremely important truths—that the real man is pure spirit (Mind) and that this pure spirit is One with the Universal Spirit (generally called the One Mind). I also came to understand certain profoundly meaningful paradoxes and even to attain a certain degree of intuitive realization of their validity. When a Zen Master declared that *Nirvana* is *here and now*, or that the Present is the only reality, I think I really did understand the truth at which those teachings point; or perhaps I should say rather that I came closer than before to understanding it. I did see that the injunction 'When hungry, eat' is no less spiritual than, for example, 'Nothing exists but the One Mind (Spirit)'. Before I left Hua T'ing Ssu, if I had not passed beyond the iron peaks of dualism which guard the Ultimate Mystery from our eyes, at least I could now and then see the light shining between their jagged crests. If I was still far from having realized *Nirvana*, at least I knew better than to seek for it anywhere outside my own mind. I knew that, since *Nirvana* is no other than *Sangsara* seen with a pure vision, it was wrong to think of going *from* the one *to* the other. I understood that if a lump of filthy mud *appears* less beautiful than the loveliest imaginable jade, the fault lies not in the mud but in my vision.

It is difficult to describe how I came to have a clearer perception of these truths. No moment of *Satori* cast its light upon me; never for one moment did I behold Reality face to face. Nor did I reach to any state of consciousness more than a little 'above' my normal one. Yet, slowly, during the long, tranquil hours in that dimly lighted Hall, never quite without the faint perfume of incense (and never without the disturbance of its whining, cruelly biting mosquitoes), some little trickle of the water of Truth splashed drop by drop into my mind. The trickle was never the result of striving after a specific object; and I soon abandoned the *Koan* method ('Who reverences the Buddha?' 'Who am I?'), finding it barren and fruitless for me, though others have discovered deep satisfaction in it. Perhaps an analogy will best express what I did do with my mind during the long hours of meditation.

If we are gazing out of the window and I say: 'Look at that tree,' both the command and the action are meaningless except in relation to the tree. But suppose we are sitting on a mountain peak surrounded by uniform, motionless white mist, floating above, around and below—a nothingness, in fact; if, at such a moment, I say: 'Look!' the command does, I think, have meaning. Now, in Zen we are told not to examine a conundrum logically; so, even when we employ a *Koan*, our striving is in a sense without a specific *object*; yet we do *strive*; we do not just sit with minds like lifeless lumps of wood or stone. Were I compelled to do that for which I am so little qualified, to teach the method of Zen meditation, I should say: 'Do not look at that tree; it won't help you at all; on the other hand, don't just sit, *look!*'

I know this analogy is very imperfect, but unfortunately Zen, like all other methods of striving to come face to face with Reality, is not easily expressed in words, except where speaker and hearer have entered upon a relationship so intimate that the latter *intuitively* realizes what lies behind his teacher's words. I have only ventured to say as much as this because a long description of my life in a Zen monastery seems to demand *some* account of the fruit I gathered. I am sorry the crop was so small, for there was plenty of fruit on the higher branches of the trees for those who knew how to harvest it. Fortunately, I still have a transcription of something Suting said to me at a time when I was feeling very discouraged. Perhaps his way of putting things is clearer than mine. It is certainly much deeper. Noticing my despondency, he said:

'Elder Brother, I don't know how many of us younger monks here really understand the Preceptor. I find his lectures far from clear. Still, I have discovered for myself that if I just sit perfectly still, so still that I am conscious of the blood drumming in my ears, and open up my mind to—no, not to anything—just open up my mind; though nothing happens the first time or the second, one day I begin to feel some response. My heart seems to be talking to me, revealing secrets of which I had never so much as dreamt. Afterwards, I am left in a state of marvellous happiness. A Light shines within me and about me, and they are One. My heart seems to have seven doors which open one by one, the Light getting brighter and brighter all the time. And when the meditation period is over, I feel as if everything that happens to me is good; as if all of it is directed by the Light; as if, without thinking much, I do just what is best for me to do; as if I am being carried by a great stream just where it is best for me to go. Then sooner or later, from habit I do something which brings me against the current of the stream; the Light fades and I am as before, but for a while I am lonely as when I was first separated from my mother. I think this is because I have a heavy load of *Karma* which drags me back and sets me against the stream again and again. What gives me hope is that, each time all this happens, the Light seems to stay with me a little longer.'

Suting had gone a long way past me on the road to Truth. I did not understand all of what he said at the time, entirely missing its deeper implications; but, since then, I have come to appreciate his words more fully. I am quite positive now that the whole secret of life lies within the innermost being of each one of us and that, if only we could open the 'seven doors of the heart' and keep them open, we should be able to live godlike lives, strictly in accordance with the *Dharma*, the universal laws of life and being, without any strain or effort. So long as the doors remain closed, our senses lead us against the current and whatever attempt we make to live in accordance with what seem to us to be the universal laws involves tremendous effort and renunciation.

From *The Wheel of Life* (Hutchinson Publishing Group, London) 1959

The Rabbinical Student

Louis Ginzberg

What is it that gave the Jewish scholar his peculiarly important place in the spiritual economy of his nation?

The first communal duty as well as the highest—since all others depended upon it—was to provide for the broadest possible dissemination of a knowledge of Jewish literature among the members of the community. It was the conscious purpose to train every Jew to go to his national literature for draughts of spiritual refreshment. The boy was led to it; through it the youth was to develop into maturity; from it the full-grown man was to derive enlightenment and strength and courage for his work and his activities; and with its light as a lamp for his feet, the venerable in years was to travel the path to the hereafter.

Besides elementary schools, every Jewish community of size and standing had an intermediate school for the advanced study of the Bible and the Talmud.

The principle underlying the study of the Talmud in Poland was "non multa sed multum," not quantity but quality. Whatever was studied was searched out in every detail. For the Polish Jew it was an intellectual occupation.

It is incorrect to think of the Yeshibah as a religious school, as it is generally assumed to be. It was more, it was the institution for general Jewish education.

Errors are transmitted like diseases. The inaccurate rendering of the Hebrew word "Torah" by "law," has all along been a barrier from understanding the system of Rabbinism as a whole, but especially from comprehending the specific ideal of Rabbinism which is summed up in the term *Talmud Torah*, the study of Torah.

Torah is not law. It is an expression for the aggregate of Jewish

From Students, Scholars and Saints, (The Jewish Publication Society of America, Philadelphia), 1928 teachings. It comprises every field and mark of culture—morality, justice, society, education, etc. The term aims to gather them all up as a unit because the Jewish view is that all the nobler manifestations of human conduct must be connected with religion. The education of the Jewish child, from the Soferim down to our own day, has been exclusively Jewish, though not exclusively religious, certainly not exclusively legalistic.

Because in Christian countries education of any kind was clerical and, of course, inaccessible to the Jew, ... Jewish studies offered the sole and only field for the manifestation of their mental activity. As a consequence, even their religious literature was cultivated for educational and intellectual purposes....

From the first the school was raised on a national basis, the only firm foundation for the education of the young, and as religion occupies the most prominent place in the national life of the Jews, the Jewish school was a religious institution as well. So long as the Jews lived in their own land, and could develop their national life without let or hindrance, there was no objection to introducing elements of alien origin into the school. It had no difficulty in transforming them Jewishly and assimilating them.

But when a national life was precluded, the Jewish school perforce had to narrow its compass. This was the only escape from the dangers of absorption by the surrounding cultures which menaced Jewish intellectual life. But even after its aims suffered such contraction, the Jewish school did not fail to reveal the intellectual impulse as the mainspring of the education it afforded. In spite of its one-sidedness in excluding everything non-Jewish, therefore, the Talmud Heder did not cease to be the great national institution for the development of the Jewish intellect.

Of entrance examinations and graduating exercises there were none. The schools made demands upon their pupils without conferring privileges, and therefore such formalities as examinations were entirely out of place. The student merely presented himself before the master whose course of lectures he wished to attend, and a brief conversation sufficed to reveal the extent of his rabbinical attainments. If the teacher was satisfied with the prospective disciple, he was enrolled a member of the Yeshibah, as the Talmud academy was called.

In one respect the Jewish student was the superior of his Christian colleague; as he exceeded him in years when he entered the school for higher learning, so he surpassed him in knowledge. On the

average, the candidate for university work ... was a lad of fourteen
who had read Aristotle instead of Cicero and disputed about soph-
isms instead of doing Latin prose composition. When the *Bahur*
presented himself in the Yeshibah, he had endured a very much
severer intellectual discipline. In the Heder he had gone through the
whole or at least the greater part of the Bible, the instruction in the
Scriptures being based upon the commentary of Rashi from almost
the time of its appearance. If little stress was laid upon Hebrew
grammar, the implied loss was more than compensated for in that the
pupil learned *Hebrew*, the language itself, in the Heder. The commentary of Rashi had peculiar qualities that made it an eminently fit
introduction to the study of the Holy Scriptures. A simple, natural
system of exegesis which, through the frequent use of the Midrash,
was presented with warm, deep feeling, made the Bible a living book
to the child student. It enabled him to penetrate to its very recesses. At
the same time the study of the Scripture with Rashi was the best
possible introduction to rabbinical literature—the Midrash and the
Talmud—from which Rashi gives frequent quotations in his Bible
commentary, making them intelligible in his unsurpassed way.
Instruction in the Talmud was begun at an early age. When the Bahur
entered the Yeshibah at the age of seventeen, he could look back
upon at least seven years of Talmud study.... The Jewish student ...
not only was master of the Hebrew language, but also was acquainted
with a considerable portion of the post-biblical literature.

Thus equipped with knowledge that enabled him to follow the
advanced lectures on the Talmud, the Bahur entered the Yeshibah.
The lectures in the Yeshibah were of a twofold character. The Perush
is the simple explanation of the text as it stands; it concerns itself
neither with parallel passages in other treatises of the Talmud nor with
critical analysis. The model for this method was the Talmud commentary of Rashi, and as long as the correct understanding of the text
offered many difficulties, the Perush was the only method of explanation employed. With the development of the study of the Talmud, the
Yeshibah began to lay great stress upon criticism, the analytical
method of study, Pilpul as it was later called. Here the student of
Jewish history must be cautioned against a pitfall. The acumen and
dialectics of the rabbis are not to be confounded, as they sometimes
are, with quibbling and pettifogging. The treatment of the Talmud by
the scholars of the Middle Ages remains the standard to this day, and
that too in spite of the admission that they shared the defect peculiar
to the whole mediaeval world of scholars: very few of them were
endowed with a sense of historical criticism.

The two methods of explaining the Talmud were applied successively. First the lecturer confined himself for a considerable time to the mere elucidation of the text, and later the whole of the raw material thus acquired by the pupil was worked over again critically. The lectures were delivered daily with the exception of Sabbaths, holidays, and Fridays. In later times the practice prevailed of reviewing the lessons of the week on Thursdays, and the review frequently required the whole day and the better part of the night. Naturally, a review of this searching presupposed intense application on the part of the student. In general, great importance was attached to private study, and every student was granted complete liberty in the matter of attendance upon lectures. The industry of the *Bahurim* was phenomenal. They knew too well that there are no short cuts to knowledge. Many of them did not sleep in a bed except during the night from Friday to the Sabbath. All other nights of the week they spent in the Yeshibah, permitting themselves only a short nap as they sat over their folios.

The needy student received his meals free of charge in the Students' Refectory, the "Bahurim Room," which was maintained by contributions from the local and outlying communities. Very frequently the rector of the academy, the *Rosh Yeshibah*, lodged with the students, permitting his wife and children to live elsewhere, so that he might establish the intimate relations with his disciples which are a characteristic feature of Jewish student life. On Friday evening, as a rule, all the students dined with the rector, each one being provided with a beaker of wine while the host recited the *Kiddush*. This Friday evening meal was graced by the presence of the married students as well as the others. Those who had already established households were in the habit of first consecrating the beginning of the Sabbath at home, in the circle of their families, and then they would repair to the Bahurim Room for the common meal. And as the Sabbath was welcomed by teachers and disciples assembled together, so it was ushered out in the same way. *Habdalah* was recited by the rector in the presence of the students, who all drank from the chalice of the master.

The holidays peculiar to student life were the days on which the study of a tractate of the Talmud was completed in the academy. Besides, unusual festivities were connected with the first day of Pentecost and the last day of Passover. On these holidays the rector of the academy gave a banquet, to which not only the whole student body was invited, but also prominent members of the community.

The Jewish student was a teetotaler. Rarely were complaints lodged against the Bahurim for unrestrained drinking or indecorous behavior. Of course, here and there a black sheep was bound to turn up in the flock, and it happened occasionally that a Bahur managed to gain entrance to the wine-cellar of the master and drink his fill.

That ill-regulated living was impossible in the Yeshibah, is due not alone to the frugality, sobriety and ascetic habits of the Jews, but also to the severe discipline which the rabbis imposed upon those guilty of excesses and frivolity. Once, when a Bahur flung a dish at the head of the beadle with whom he was quarrelling, the Rosh Yeshibah could hardly be restrained from excommunicating the student. The master desisted only at the intercession of all the other students and after the offender had again and again begged pardon of the beadle. The affection in which the teachers held their pupils, so far from making them indulgent toward the faults of the young men, only increased their severity of judgment.

Boundless veneration for the teacher and paternal love toward disciples, these are in very deed the distinctive marks of Jewish student life. When a dangerous illness threatened the life of a famous teacher of the fourteenth century, his pupils and the members of the community determined to fast two days of the week until his recovery was assured. A wish expressed by the master was a command to be fulfilled with alacrity by the disciple. On the other hand, the teacher knew no greater joy than to be of service to his pupils. If a student took unto himself a wife, the wedding feast was held in the house of the teacher. If a married student celebrated a joyous event in his family, again it was the house of the teacher at which the festivities were arranged.

In sorrow as well as in joy teacher and pupil were lovingly united. In the prayers commemorating the dead, teachers were named along with the next of kin who had departed this life.

By no means may the epithet "people of the book" applied to the Jews mislead us into imagining that the teachers of this people were bookish men. The authority exercised by our great teachers radiated from their personality, not merely from their learning. Their individuality was far richer than their word. This is the explanation of their perennial influence. Life can be enkindled only by life; deeds produce deeds. Herein resides the secret of the wondrous power of our old teachers—great in what they did, even greater in what they were. They towered above their writings, for with their word they introduced us into their lives. That personal intercourse with the scholar by far outweighs the effect of his teaching is a principle laid down in the Talmud and accepted at its full value by the later generations of

Talmud students. The disciple was admonished to observe the teacher as well as heed his instruction. Our teachers were not in the habit of delivering lectures on psychology to their disciples, abstract disquisitions upon the soul, full of superficial ratiocination and finical introspection. Their whole life itself was laid bare before their disciples—all its motives and emotions, its aims and errors. The pupil observed the master from morn until midnight, and his daily doings were no less potent an influence in shaping the character of the student than his formal instruction and precept. For the Jew divine service was not limited to the four walls of the synagogue or the brief hours of public worship. His whole life in its most material manifestations and in its most trivial activities was a divine service. His workshop, his staff, his table, his household utensils, all were instruments in the fulfillment of his destiny. How such a life was to be lived was a question of fundamental importance, and to fathom its true spirit it was necessary to observe minutely the conduct of the great. The well-nigh superhuman industry with which the master devoted himself to his studies could not fail to exercise an influence upon the pupils. The intellectual enthusiasm of the rabbis communicated itself to all who associated with them. The Bahur completely forgot himself, he pursued learning without thought of a practical purpose, his studies absorbed his being wholly and entirely. The only return he desired from his toil was the happiness which is experienced by the investigator who devotes himself with single-minded interest to the study of a scientific subject.

On the other hand, the rabbi was not a monk averse to life with its pleasures and responsibilities. The Talmud, whose study was his life-task, is not a work of abstract speculation; rather is it concerned with the concrete fashioning of practical conduct. The Rosh Yeshibah was not only a scholar, but also a judge who looked upon the administration of justice as the fulfillment of a religious duty. The impartiality of the master, his pitiless severity when the ends of justice were to be realized, taught a lesson which the student could not have derived from the dead letter of the book.

It is the specifically Jewish view that "Wisdom cannot become the portion of the evil-hearted." Character and learning according to this view are mutually dependent upon each other. Only he can be an original thinker of creative force whose character rises above the level of the commonplace for, to use the words of a philosopher of modern times, "Great thoughts spring not from the head but from the heart." This view grew to be so essential an element in the make-up of the

Jew that for him saint and scholar became almost identical concepts.

To be creative, mentality must rest upon a complete view of life that grants the worker a wide outlook upon all human concerns, that calls into requisition all its possessor knows and can do. Information may be useful, but knowledge is power, knowledge which permeates the whole man and which, transmitted into thinking and feeling, has become a live and active force. To impose limitations upon oneself does not necessarily lead to narrowness; on the contrary, the more the domain of knowledge to be cultivated is circumscribed, the more intense becomes the power of him who controls it. Here in part lies the explanation of the remarkable influence which our teachers exerted. Their knowledge was confined within the boundaries of the Talmud and the literature growing out of it; but over that field they ruled absolute. Their knowledge was an integral part of their ego. They mastered it and it mastered them, and therefore they were able to exercise mastery over others. If they were one-sided, it was with a superb one-sidedness. Knowledge and learning in them were moral forces because they were not extraneous possessions but constituted their real life. Their knowledge being a quick force by reason of its intensity, it was invested with creative, vitalizing power by virtue of which their views spread abroad until they became the common property of the people as a whole. Jewish learning it was that offered full compensation to a scorned, oppressed and baited people for all it suffered in the course of tens of centuries; it was Jewish learning that preserved the clearness and energy of intellects which all else conspired to brutalize and deaden.

The Bahur who went forth from the Yeshibah to take charge of a congregation sought to realize the ideals he had learned to revere in his teacher, the ideals which possessed the soul of the rabbi and were expressed not in well-sounding periods and well-turned phrases but in acts and deeds. Those ideals may be summed up as an identification of true knowledge with true faith, a faith not merely metaphysical and abstract but of concrete and effectual content. The Jew was convinced that his actions were to be estimated only according to their moral and religious worth, for he was animated by the belief that God does not view with indifference the doings of man be they good or evil. If the Jew of average standing and intelligence held this belief, it was the distinction of the scholar to verify and apply it in the walks of everyday life. He recognized but one judge, his own conscience, and therefore he valued his independence beyond all things.

II

THE VIRTUE
OF SITTING

Nagarajuna's Doctrine of the Eight No's:
there is no birth,
nor is there death;
there is no beginning,
nor is there any ending;
nothing is identical with itself,
nor is there any diversification;
nothing comes into existence,
nor does anything go out of existence.

Treatise on the Middle Way

On Meditation

Jiyu Kennett, Roshi

What is required is that you just sit. Now because your minds are not closed, thoughts will come through. Just let them pass and do not chase after them. Because your eyes are not closed you will see things on the carpet. Don't analyze them or discuss them in your mind. Because your ears are not closed you will hear birds singing. All of these will only disturb your meditation if you chase after them. What you have to do is sit, as if you were sitting beneath a bridge. Overhead the traffic is passing. It is no concern of yours. Although you know that it is there, just you sit peacefully. If you get caught up by different thoughts or sounds or smells or sights then don't feel that this has ruined your meditation. Just note that you have been, as it were, hijacked, and come back. You're just sitting.

Make sure that you are all sitting correctly. I will be in the process of coming around to check your back, because the thing that matters most is that the back is correct. It does not matter if you are sitting on a chair or on the floor, but the back must be correct and for each person that correct position is slightly different. Keep your eyes on the floor at a distance that is comfortable for you. Find what is a comfortable distance. Most of the books tell you that it is three feet. That would be true if everyone of us had exactly the same sight, but we don't. If you wear spectacles keep them on. You do not meditate in order to become different. You meditate in order to become completely you, completely normal, as you are for you. This is not an exercise in becoming a stranger to yourself. Find where your head is most comfortable, where it feels weightless for you as an individual and leave it in that position. Your hands should be, if you are right-handed, with the left over the right, and if you are left-handed, with the right over the left. Shake your shoulders a little so they become loose and unstrained in any way. When you first settle down to meditate it is normal to sway just slightly from side to side in order to position your body comfortably. When you wish to get up from sitting on the floor, since most people have difficulties with pain in the legs, you will find it very advantageous to again sway just a little, starting with tiny ones and getting bigger. It is amazing how much easier that makes it when you stand up.

You must have all discovered that if you would do it properly you have to maintain a very high degree of alertness while at the same time not being concerned by what is going on in your own head and what is going on in the world outside you. A lot of people have been very intrigued by the experiments that have been done with fastening electrodes to Zen masters' heads and discovering that however often or however regularly sounds are heard by a Zen master, he registers exactly the same amount of alertness each time. Whereas a person who does not meditate tends to register the first one alertly and then on a steadily declining scale notes the others. Now the reason for this is because a Zen master has gotten over the problem of being shanghaied by his own thoughts. The fact that something is the same makes him react no differently than as if his mind were constantly being stimulated by new and interesting sights and sounds. In other words, he has been able to zero in on the center of himself and hold still upon that center. He cannot be swayed from it, he cannot be pulled off of it. Interesting sights, interesting sounds, thoughts, discussions in his own mind: none of these affect him because he can sit still beneath them. They are all going on, but there is no disturbance. There is no question, "Oh, what a nuisance, outside a dog is barking; I wish it would stop because it is messing up my meditation." Just, "Outside a dog is barking." It is just that simple. That thought has gone through the mind and straight out the other side. There is no question, of, "Well, I better . . . what am I going to do in here, what am I sitting here for?"—and then discussing it in your own mind. Because there again you have not learned to zero in upon the center of yourself and find that center which is completely peaceful.

Now I don't have to tell you the value of being able to do this in everyday life because most people are pulled off center during the entire day at some time or other. And some are pulled off of it more or less every hour of the day, simply because they have not learned to be at peace within the center of themselves; and you're not going to learn that until you stop the racket inside your own head and stop being annoyed by external things.

So the whole purpose in the beginning of this type of meditation is to be able to sit still within your own center and let everything else go on. If you like, you are an oak sitting in the middle of a quagmire. Everything else is quaking but you are just sitting still, unaffected by anything.

But alert to everything that happens.... Now one of the ways in which you can tell if someone is doing this correctly is by the degree of efficiency he has at his everyday work. We find in Shasta that when new members of the community come, they go around in what we call a fog, and they're always asking us how to get rid of the fog. The answer is we can't get rid of it for you. You'll have to do it for yourselves. Nobody can get inside them and make them sit still. They have to learn the degree of alertness that it takes to really not be hijacked by one's own emotions and one's own ideas, because once you've gotten over being caught off guard by your thoughts, then you can get over being caught off guard by your emotions and then you can really and truly act.

So if you find someone's doing this sort of meditation and seems to be wandering around in a dream, you know quite well that he's doing it incorrectly. There is a danger because it can be very pleasant and you can tend to drift off—if you're not very careful—up into the seventh heaven or up onto cloud nine, and then you are worse off than if you had never meditated at all. The purpose of this meditation is to stop being pulled off center and to make you a hundred percent more efficient, more still, more capable than you've ever been before. If you find that it is making you less efficient, then go and see a Zen master very, very quickly because you've done something wrong and you need it checked. You'll do no harm to yourself except that you will wander around looking as though you're not very much here which will worry your employers and worry a lot of other people as well. I've often seen people who have been hijacked in this way, if you like, by their own meditation methods, and the second state of them is worse than the first. Meditation should make you a hundred percent more alert, more alive.

Audience: Boredom is really a thing that plagues me a lot and I wonder if you have any suggestions about getting through that.

Roshi: The only method I know is a slightly cruel one. It's the one that was employed in the monasteries in the East where they made the thing so infuriatingly boring that you either got over it or you got out of the temple. That was done deliberately. It's quite fascinating what you can do with that to see how well somebody's doing getting rid of it. There's nothing like taking a bunch of trainees for a holiday by the sea with absolutely nothing organized to see how well they're learning to handle boredom. You can handle it in the monastery where it's beautifully structured and you know exactly what's coming next and exactly what each bell means. All right, the days get a bit boring because they're all the same but you're still structured by the bell. It's like having a corset on the spiritual body, but when the corset is removed, I'm afraid the only answer to your question is sheer downright hard work. You have to learn to live with the boredom. I remember asking about this when I was in the East and they told me you've got to learn to live with it—which is cold blooded but honest.

Student: It should be clearly understood when dealing with something like this that boredom is something you do to yourself. There is no such thing as a boring situation. There are only people bored by situations.

Roshi: There is something they feel they are missing. Now that involves an inadequacy thing within oneself. Maybe there's something more. If you zeroed in on the center of yourself, boredom just can't enter into it. There's no way that it can. But that's taking it a step further, quite a long way further.

The characteristic of people who have done a tremendous amount of meditation and who've done it properly is their quite incredible alertness, their enjoyment of life. Every day is the best day they've ever lived no matter what is going on, and never under any circumstances are they bored. However bad the TV program they happen to be watching or however annoying the company they are forced to keep, they are just zeroed in on the center of themselves and it doesn't matter—nothing pulls them off, nothing fazes them, nothing throws them. I remember asking my teacher what he did when things pulled him off center, when thoughts were grabbing hold of him in meditation and things like this. His answer was, "Well, this morning under my robe a flea was walking; just I noticed it had strong legs." It marched straight through and out the other side. That's the only way you can really do it. We do have to make a very considerable effort. The real problem with boredom and other things of this sort is that a lot of people are not willing to put in the amount of effort necessary to get over that, and that happens also in meditation—they are not willing to put in the amount of effort necessary to really zero in upon themselves. Because of that the Rinzai system invented the koans which gave them something to chew on while they were trying to zero in. Soto says, "No, we're not going to do that for you, you're adults, we're not going to give you baby comforters. You're going to do it right from the start, right from the very beginning." Which means that it's rather harder but the end results are much deeper and much freer and the mind is less manipulated by external circumstances.

Audience: Is there any role-playing in meditation by the relationship between the master and the student?

Roshi: The only role that is played for certain in the very best monastery is the fact that the master is always telling the student, "Remember thou must go alone, the Buddhas only point the way." All I am doing is pointing. I'll not attempt to take over your mind. You will do everything for yourself. I'll show you how but I will not in any way take hold of you or manipulate you or tell you what to do with your life. You must want to know. You must want to come to me to know what I did but I am only telling you what I did. You must find it true for yourself." And that goes right back to the very heart of Buddhism in which Shakyamuni Buddha said, "Don't believe anything because I've told it to you. You must prove it true for yourself." I would say this: if you find a Zen master who is trying to manipulate your mind or who is trying to possess your mind in any way whatsoever, instead of making it quite clear that you must do all the work, get away from him very quickly. Because he's doing it completely wrong. There must be absolutely no manipulation. There is a beautiful relationship once the person has learned how to do this because it is as if you are all one family, but there is no possession. If the disciple says "I'm going off tomorrow," the master says "good," and if the disciple says he's coming back the day after, the master says "good." There's no holding on, no pushing away. They are at one with each other, but completely different. It is another meaning of the Buddhist belief that all is one and all is different. All is one in the Buddha-nature but each one of us is totally different externally, and totally individual in that sense.

Audience: What's the role of surrender?

Roshi: Surrender to what? There's no surrendering to anything except in the sense of transcending the ego-centric ego into what it really is, which is your own Buddha-nature. The ego as we know it has had all this selfish muck put on top of it: we are beautiful within when the Buddha-nature has gotten rid of its ego-centric ideas and wants and wishes. But if you like to call it surrender you can, but it is surrendering to your true self, it is not surrendering to anything else. There is no surrendering to something external. There is no giving up to anyone or anything. There is only the perfection of you as an individual and, in so doing, finding that you always were and always will be, perfect within. Only you have made an awful mess of yourself and have got to clean it up. In other words, you clean up your own house.

Audience: What role does work play in meditation practice?

Roshi: What role does work play in meditation, or in everyday life?

Audience: I don't know if either of them aren't the same.

Roshi: Well, some people make a difference between the two, and I wanted to make sure that you didn't. The whole purpose of this meditation as I said, is not to be pulled off center, not to get hijacked by your emotions—to be able to function in everyday life without being pulled off of your center. Now if you think that this is only something that can be done in meditation, then the meditation is useless. Religion was invented by man to help man; it was not invented to help religion. At least the Shin Buddhist church got that straight and openly admits it, although nobody believes them. They say, "First man invented God, then he worshipped Him." Now the whole purpose of this is so that in your everyday life, what you are doing, you will not be pulled off center by the worries of the world outside. You'll be able to handle the situations that come up. As such, the work is incredibly valuable because it gives you a chance to see how you can be pulled off center and thus be able to work harder on your actual meditation.

You'll need to be able to keep yourself still within your own center much more when you are out in the ordinary world, especially if you are not actually in the meditation hall. It's very easy in a monastery in that respect and because of that the curriculum is made deliberately difficult. It's made more uncomfortable than the world would be. It has to be made that way. Because if it's not, what you're going to get is a bunch of people who are escaping into a beautiful Shangri-la and who are afraid of the world outside. We make work of some quite revolting varieties up in Shasta for people who want to escape. The septic tanks are always needing re-digging—this sort of thing, you know. You get people who really want to live in the holy monastery and do nothing else except worship and the second day they're there they find themselves digging about up to the ankles or a little over. And if you can't zero in on your center then, just as much as when you are sitting in the meditation hall, then you'll need to be trained much more strictly because what are you going to do when you get back out into the world and the boss is grumbling and grouching, and the traffic is in a snarl and you can't get your car going—you have got to be able to handle all these situations from the center of yourself without being pulled off that center. Therefore the work is extremely valuable because if you cannot understand the center of yourself from the position of the work, you are never going to understand it completely. You're going to be, as it were, a person with one eye. In Soto Zen we have work and meditation and both are equal, absolutely equal and both absolutely necessary. If you like, they are the two pillars that hold up the temple.

Audience: You talked about the center. Can you say something about where that is located?

Roshi: The center is located everywhere, at every moment. Sometimes you'd find it one place, sometimes you'd find it another. For convenience, so that the head shall not take over, we tend to think of it somewhere in here, in the *hara* (the heart and belly area). But that is only a matter of real convenience....

Audience: Can you say more about the heart?

Roshi: The heart comes out as an awful lot of different things. For some people the heart is everywhere. For some, it is just something that they feel within themselves. When you first start meditating you are usually told to put your mind in here, in the *hara*. Now the mind they are talking about is not the mind as you know it. It is the *kokoro* in Japanese which translates as heart, mind, soul, deep knowledge. It is not a thinking thing.... If you've got something therefore that partakes of all three, the heart, the mind, and the soul, you cannot think of it as being located here, or here, or here. You'll have something that is in all three which shows the facets of all three in different places at all times, and also shows the facets of everything in everything else around you at all times. For example, when we come to sit down we bow to the floor; we recognize, if you like, the godheadness of the floor. It doesn't owe us the right to sit on it; we take that right, so we say thank you for allowing us to sit. Thank you to the carpet for making it comfortable. Thank you to the cushion for allowing us to sit on it. The attitude of gratitude is the first one that has to be cultivated if you would really understand Zen—the attitude that you do not have the right to take everything over that you happen to feel like taking over simply because you have the power to do so, because that is actually getting into a power complex. People don't seem to realize that when they sit down on a chair without thinking, they are showing their power over the chair, instead of looking at the chair and saying thank you. After all, why should the trees be sacrificed to my personal wishes? Just for my own personal comfort? In other words, you have to start thinking of other than self, so we bow to the cushion.

We then turn and we bow to the other side which we are going to be looking at. If I were a floor, would I want to be stared at all the time? No, just think about it. It sounds strange, but it is true. We do it because it doesn't grumble back at us, the same way that we eat vegetables because they don't yell. You should know that being a vegetarian is a purely selfish act. Like it or not, you are maiming a cabbage when you pull its leaves off to cook. But you think, oh well, the cabbage doesn't kick up a racket, so why worry; I mean, I'm not doing harm. Well how do you know? So when you come to breakfast—for lack of a better word I'll use the term "grace" that is used by a Buddhist—we must think deeply of the ways and means by which this food has come. We must consider our merit when accepting it. We must, we will, eat, lest we become lean and die, not because we just feel like eating anything or something specific. We are doing this for a purpose. What we are actually saying is, "Have I done enough today to have the right to sacrifice these things?" What have I been up to that makes me so special that I can sacrifice something else to my personal wants? That doesn't alter the fact that I still don't eat meat unless it is offered, which sometimes happens when I'm out for dinner, and then I will be wrong to refuse it. Because then an animal would have died in vain and I would have insulted it. You cannot say no unless you are pretending to be holy and I quite genuinely mean pretending. But you don't go out and buy the meat for fun just because you feel like having meat. And if you've got a lot of stale food you don't think, "Well I'd like something different so I'm going to go out to a restaurant or a coffee shop rather than eat that." You eat because you do not wish to become lean and die and thus a nuisance to other people, because then they've got to bury you. That is part of the morning grace. This is the reason you eat. But you must think sincerely about the ways and means by which the food has come to you. You must consider your merit when accepting it. All this comes out of the heart and the recognition that the trees and the leaves and the ceiling and the roof and the stones and everything around you is part of that heart. And so when you sit down on the ground you bow to the ground: "Thank you for allowing me to sit." When you walk into a room: "Thank you for just being here, for keeping out the cold." After all, these things don't have to stand up like this for us. It's very nice of them to do so, very kind of them, but they don't owe us anything. We imagine that everything does. That again comes out of the selfish self, the ego-centric self. But when you get that out of the way you can really start enjoying everything and everyone around you in a totally different way.

Audience: When you were talking about not eating the meat that was offered to you I was wondering how you would fit that attitude with people who are giving and giving and giving.

Roshi: Well, you're invited out for dinner and somebody doesn't know you're a vegetarian, so you eat. When you finish the meal you quietly let it be known that in the future if they are inviting you would they be good enough not to serve meat. But you don't embarrass your host by refusing his dinner. . . .

Audience: One more thing about food. When you said that you would be considering someone else's comfort in not becoming lean and dying, could you also say that you don't want to inconvenience your own self by becoming lean and dying without that being an ego-centric wish?

Roshi: One would like to do that but the hairline between it being an ego-centric wish and a completely pure one is an awfully thin line. You could do it, I suppose, but I don't know that I'm good enough yet that I could.

Audience: I have some confusion about this attitude of being non-judgmental about what goes on as opposed to responding to what's going on in terms of being joyful about something or sad about something. There's one school that says it is healthy to respond with your emotions and if you don't then it's being repressive, so how do you reconcile this?

Roshi: It's not a matter of repressing emotion, it's a matter of not being hijacked by it. A Zen master can grieve and he can cry and he can feel sad. . . . It's a matter of not being hijacked by the emotionalism. There's nothing wrong with emotions so long as they don't hijack you. Most people get pulled off center by them. You are going to feel sad, you are going to feel happy, you are going to feel joy. But you don't have to be pulled over by them.

Audience: You mentioned both the words "soul" and "transcendence."

Roshi: These are only abstractions for something you can't put a name to.

Audience: I'm a little uncomfortable about using them.

Roshi: I'm uncomfortable about them too, but what terms can you use? You see, they've used mind, they've used Buddha-nature, they've used heart-mind, they've used soul—all these things are like the moth going round and round the flame of a candle. The only way you're going to know what that flame of the candle's like is if you stay in the middle of it—and you're not going to be able to come back and tell anybody. I find that I know what the thing is, each one of you knows what it is, but could you put a name to it? They're terms of reference. The only thing I can say is, please don't be pulled off center by their connotations.

Audience: Do you have any comments about meditation with children?

Roshi: With children? Children meditate marvelously. I'm always telling young mothers to meditate holding their babies in their arms when they're very small. In the East as soon as a child can crawl, the parent will either bring it to the temple or will sit with it in front of the family altar—so it sits for a couple of seconds and then it starts crawling, that's fine. If you do that as soon as it can actually begin to move, it will eventually sit beside you and it will look at you and it will wonder in the same way as your cat does when it catches you watching a wall. But it will look at you and then it will sit down and look at the wall. They learn incredibly fast. . . . Cats, kittens, dogs, everything will do it. They give you a very strange look, they wonder why, but they'll do it, and I have seen a whole bunch of two-year-olds in Sojiji sitting in the meditation hall doing the most marvelous meditation, far better than any of the monks got up to—completely by instinct, because they weren't being pulled off center by an awful lot of bright ideas as to what this would do to them and what it would not do to them. They were just sitting, which is exactly what they were required to do. They were automatically in that zendo. Bringing them up like that from the very beginning, without putting any doctrine or anything of the sort into their heads, just letting them sit still, in their rightful center—by the time they are eight or nine they can tell you why they are doing it far better than you will be able to tell them; because they will know by instinct, having done it right from the beginning at the correct age.

I'm sure all of you know the story of Shakyamuni Buddha, who discovered how to meditate properly when he was seven. And he goes through all this other lot of stuff later on and he hangs himself upside down over fires and he sits under waterfalls and he does all these beautiful ascetic things, including sitting underneath the Bodhi tree, and in the end he says, "But wait a minute, when I was seven, I discovered how to find peace, and all I did was just sit." . . . He's made it, all the way up. Because he knew the right way of doing it in the very beginning. Just to be still within his own center and listen to what was going on outside.

Now I can guarantee you, if you take your children to sit with you don't worry if they can't sit more than two or three minutes, just let them crawl away; they'll come back again. Don't be bothered by them, don't let them pull you off center because instinctively they'll wonder what you are doing. Just don't you be pulled off center and they won't be pulled off center. Children know the second their mother or father is off their center, and start crying, but they don't do anything so long as the parents are still within. Everything and anything can go on during the day and the children just do not create problems, but you let the parents be swayed in the least bit from the center, and those children know. I strongly recommend you to let your children sit with you; don't worry if they don't sit exactly right or if they crawl about; just you continue to sit and you'll see what'll happen.

You've got the perfect pattern for this right from the very beginning in Shakyamuni Buddha, who did it the same way himself. I don't think you can have a better example. It's fascinating that he had to give up all his bright ideas and his studies and all this sort of stuff and go straight back to doing what he had done in the very beginning before he could find what he was really looking for. This is the reason why you frequently hear the Zen stories of the monk rolling about on the floor when he's found out—laughing his head off. He's thinking, "What a downright idiot I've been. I knew it all along and here I've been worrying my brain with all these bright ideas which were just bright ideas and they weren't all that bright."

On Meditation in
The Jewish Mystical Tradition

William M. Kramer

Over a century ago Austin Phelps, a professor in Andover Theological Seminary, offered some thoughts which are helpful in understanding the mystery and meaning of meditation. After William Cowper, he wrote of what it means to feel the non-nearness of God, what it was like to experience "remoteness from God's presence, in comparison with which the distance from East to West is vicinity, is cohesion."[1]

Phelps beautifully presented the cause which elicits from sensitive souls the adventure of meditation and the hunger for the *unio mystica*:

> One of the most impressive mysteries of the condition of man on this earth, is his deprivation of all visible and audible representations of God. We seem to be living in a state of seclusion from the rest of the universe, and from that peculiar presence of God in which angels dwell, and in which departed saints serve Him day and night. We do not see Him in the fire; we do not hear Him in the wind; we do not feel Him in the darkness.[2]

The Jewish mystic did not feel deprived because he was not in possession of or possessed by "visible and audible representations of God." Judaism has long walked the *via negativa*.[3] The mystic was, as the phrase has it, God-intoxicated. Schechter said, when writing about Hasidism in his day, "Their faith is still real enough to satisfy the demands of a Luther."[4]

Among the Hasidim, particularly those of Lübavitch, there were spiritual exercises and physical counterparts which would help the devotee to attain an ecstasy in the Divine Presence. An 1859 account, reflecting an earlier decade, gave the usual picture of Hasidic dance and song, but it also included elements too often unaccounted.

The Khasidim in their worship are very noisy, and fond of singing, clapping hands, and jumping, in order to banish worldly thoughts. The more pious of them continue their prayers from six in the morning to three in the afternoon, when they take both breakfast and dinner at once, for no Jew will take anything before his morning prayers, except, when delicate in health, a single cup of tea or coffee. They return to afternoon and evening prayers, in which they are engaged till midnight. Before morning prayer they all go to the Mikvah, or well of purification, both in winter and summer; and some also attend to their ablutions before their afternoon prayers.

Previous to prayer they employ half an hour or an hour in meditation; some walk about in silent thought; some are singing in an undertone; others are smoking their pipes while thus engaged. When the Reader feels prepared in his mind he begins prayer, and is joined by that part of the congregation that may be in readiness to enter upon their devotions. Some, for the sake of greater privacy, retire to a private room, called "the Meditation room," (in Hebrew, *Baith hithbon-nanuth*), for they say they would rather not pray at all than come hastily before the Lord, not perceiving clearly in their minds whom they are about to address, and for what they are about to ask. They say, prayer without the mind is like the body without the soul.[5]

Lazarus described the righteous Hasid as one who should always "be occupied in meditating upon the goodness, holiness and majesty of God." He recalled the face of a *rebbe*, whom he had evidently known in his youth:

His countenance is still fresh in my memory, in which I am persuaded there was something heavenly; and this indeed is not wonderful when we consider that such a man, even from childhood, knows nothing of the world, and is occupied day and night in fasting and prayer, and in studying how he may serve God.[6]

There was, of course, meditation in Judaism since first there was wonderment and methods of achieving it have been quite fully delineated in the spendorous tradition of Zohar. The Jewish *locus classi-*

cus for kabbalistic meditation, one which is thought to have influenced the work of Sigmund Freud,[7] is to be found in the writings of Abraham Abulafia (1240-circa 1291-1300).[8] He taught that one who seeks to channel the heart to God alone should prepare by cleansing the body and dressing it, preferably in white, and then selecting for the experience a meditory, an isolated place, where one's voice would be unheard by man.

He suggested that meditation begins best by day and is best completed in the night. The night was not for its darkness, but rather that one could light many lights creating a brightness of fact and symbol. The isolated silence should be gifted with the mediator's voice speaking out to God the thoughts of a mind unencumbered by worldliness. The conditions are set so that a revelation of God's might could come as a dialogal response to the human cry.

This is not a Sabbath of the soul but the spirit at work. The Sabbath comes when the meditator returns. And so the head should be covered with the shawl of daily prayer and the prayer thongs be affixed to forehead, arm, and hand as visible signs of the beauty of the invisible Deity, adorning the adorer who becomes a worthy receptacle for the flow of holy wonderment streaming from the nearness of the Presence.

Then, according to Abulafia, the time has come to sit at a table with an ink-dipped pen in hand and a mind concentrated on the thought that what will be is a service to God from a heart of joy and gladness. Letters come. On a tablet the meditator should write them, grouping, regrouping, arranging, rearranging, permuting in a kind of free association, until there is a meaning that warms the heart, a meaning from words if not of them.

Then the letters will sound, their combinations chord, and there will be a music that travels from ear to heart to spleen. And the music is a feeling and the heart hears and understands and in the spleen the hearing feeling evokes emotive response. The inked letters tell secrets which are lyrics of a joyous hymn.

Whosoever meditates with letters must be mindful of what can come from their movings. When the heart is truly warm and the letters have given what would otherwise be unknowable, the meditator, Abulafia instructed, has opened the channels for Divine Power and the envisionment, as it were, of the Holy One and His messengers as close as intimate companions, investing the meditator as an emissary to take the forthcoming word as mandate for a mission.

In the vividness of this achieved reality, the mind must be directed to comprehend the multiplying thoughts which letter combinations stimulate. All this to be done as one would analyze a dream or profoundly examine a work of science. Reason is not to be set aside but to be charged with interpreting.

As reasoning mind takes over, the consciousness of its strength contrasts sharply with a sense of the inner and outer weakness of the body. Pen, ink, and tablet are forgotten; the meditative state has climaxed. The body quakes with the lushness of its emotion. Life is precious as it is at death's brink; the soul seems so expanded that it must shatter the body. Fully prepared to accept death, the meditator is ready for the Divine Emanation, filled with an enthusiasm to serve and honor the Holy One with all the vitality of body and soul committed to the Sacred Glory.

The time arrives for the face to be veiled with the *tallit* before the awesomeness of looking Godward. This is the beginning of the returning. It is the time for the thoughts to return to the body and the meditator to arise and eat a bite and drink a bit and perhaps know the enjoyment of a goodly scent. This helps to return the spirit to its sheath unresistingly, for there is an awareness that there can be another time, and there is a rejoicing in the good fortune of knowing that a loving God loves you, Abulafia stated.

NOTES

[1] Austin Phelps, *The Still Hour; or, Communion with God* (Philadelphia: Presbyterian Publication Committee, 1866), pp. 13-14.

[2] Ibid., pp. 17-18.

[3] See Louis Jacobs, *The Via Negativa in Jewish Religious Thought*, Third Allan Bronfman Lecture (New York: Judaica Press, 1967).

[4] Solomon Schechter, "The Chassidim," *Studies in Judaism* (Cleveland: World Publishing Co., and Philadelphia: The Jewish Publication Society of America, 1962), p. 189. He was aware of what he considered abuses in that it was sometimes the worship of man, a specific Hasidic leader, and he felt that if it were to be reformed and viable "it must be brought back again to the source of all "Beauty, all Wisdom, and all Goodness; it must be restored to God" (p. 189).

[5] J. G. Lazarus, "The Sect of the Khasidim in the North of Europe," *The Israelite*, Cincinnati, 27 May 1859, p. 375, and 3 June 1859, p. 382.

[6] Ibid.

[7] A. A. Roback, "Freud, Chassid or Humanist," *B'nai B'rith Magazine*, January, 1926, pp. 118-30. See also David Bakan, *Sigmund Freud and the Jewish Mystical Tradition* (New York: Schocken Books, 1965).

[8] On mystical meditation in Abulafia, see Gershom G. Scholem, *Major Trends in Jewish Mysticism* (New York: Schocken Books, 1946), pp. 119-55; Gershom Scholem, *Kabbalah* (New York: Quadrangle, The New York Times Book Co., 1974), pp. 53-59 and passim.

Concentration and Meditation
in Zen

Christmas Humphreys

1. Meditation is necessary

The more the Western mind is subject daily to physical, emotional and mental stress in the very task of keeping alive, the more is it necessary to spend some time, daily if possible, in drawing on the deeps of our innate wisdom, strength and serenity, in aligning the part with the Whole, in returning 'home' for comfort, strength and peace. From moving at the edge of the circle we need the 'still center of the turning world'; from peripheral fog, the dust of the market place or the darkness of unlit illusion, we need to lift our heads into the Light; from the exhausting heat of the 'three fires' of hatred, lust and illusion, we need periods of self-mastery and that peace which lies at the other end of desire.

But the occasional 'return home' is insufficient. Even flashes of what we are pleased to call direct experience are only indications of a movement in the right direction. The total development of that complex entity, man, is a task of many lives, and though learning and morality have their place in that process, sooner or later the enormous task of the mind's development must be planned, and begun, and unceasingly continued. In this great enterprise I have formulated two good rules, Begin, and Walk On!

In the ideal, and it is a very far ideal, it will be enough to 'meditate,' whatever that may mean, at every moment of the daily round. I do not say that this is impossible. I do say that I have never met a man who could do it. True, we can and shall increasingly infuse the deed of the moment with the spirit of Zen, but that, well done, is the product of long mental training, produced in the 'soul's gymnasium' of the meditation hour.

Meditation, in brief, must pass from the phase of an interesting hobby to that of a valued amenity, and thence to a necessity. When the art and craft is mastered there will be time for it to be applied.

2. Why meditate?

Before taking on any new enterprise it is well to ask oneself, Why? The answers can be many, and all are selfish or unselfish, with results accordingly. To develop the mind in order to develop 'powers' is at all time folly, and generally what is popularly called 'black magic', that is, the abuse of spiritual powers to selfish ends. That way lies suffering untold, madness and spiritual death. The only right answer is to fit oneself the better for the service of mankind, whether immediately, as in the Bodhisattva ideal, or in due course, when one's own development is well-progressed, as in the Arhat ideal. But the dedication must be thorough, irrevocable and frequently confirmed. On the Path to Nirvana 'the first step is to live to benefit mankind', and the sooner the would-be pilgrim on that Road is steeped in that great truth, the better for his salvation. . . .

3. Are you fit?

Are you physically fit enough to breathe deeply and regularly, to sit still for a quarter of an hour or longer at a time? Do you sleep well, to recuperate from the extra effort on the brain? As for 'pure' living, bear in mind what you are trying to do. Towards the end of the journey you will have to give up all meat, all alcohol, all drugs, whether tobacco, tea or coffee, all sexual indulgence of any kind and even contact with other humans. But to do this at once will make you very sensitive, and psychically sensitive, so that life in the crowded, filthy psychic atmosphere of our cities will be repulsive and almost impossible. Of these indulgences of the self meat-eating produces the greatest problem. On the one hand, it is cruel at our stage of evolution to be party to the killing of other mammals for our food; on the other hand, it is not easy in City life to get enough to eat of other forms of protein without producing the fat and pasty appearance which was at one time almost synonymous with vegetarianism. In these conditions one can only work out

From *Zen Comes West* (Geo. Allen and Unwin Ltd., London), 1960 one's own 'right' way at the time. For myself I confess to the view that there are more important ways of spending time and mental energy than in troubling about what one eats, and I am certain that the ancient teaching is right that a false belief is a far greater obstacle on the road to enlightenment than a host of misbehavior on the physical plane. For the rest, the rule is moderation and common sense.

Are you emotionally fit? The man in love, the man pursuing a vendetta, the man full of troubles, worries, hates, and fears, is not yet in a condition to concentrate, much less to meditate with any hope of success. Are you mentally balanced? If beset with complexes, projections, violent views; if aggressive to all differing opinion, fixed in your conclusions; or the reverse, too timid to hold any views at all lest someone of a stronger mind cry "Boo' to you, then wait. The development of the mind must rise from sure foundations, and as the building rises any latent faults and cracks may bring it tottering to the ground. Cracks in the mind should be found and healed before meditation is undertaken; later, the crack may widen and split the mind.

4. *Only methods can be taught*

Work out your own salvation, said the All-Enlightened One, and this is the heart of 'Buddhism'. No books, no lectures, not the greatest master in the world can do one hour of the work for you. All these are fingers pointing to the moon. *You* must do the work, and would that all of you had already learnt this lesson, which is probably the most difficult of all to learn. The amount of ingenuity exercised by the human mind in getting someone else to do its spiritual labor is staggering, and we are all still trying! Methods are endless in their variety, and more are being invented day by day. But all have this in common, that one must begin, and one must continue. The effort will produce its stress and strain; there will be difficulties innumerable, and adventures grave and gay upon the Road. But whatever the method chosen, the pupil and the pupil alone must produce an inexhaustible supply of 'guts' to keep him moving on the Way.

5. *Commonsense is needed all the time*

There is nothing mysterious about meditation, nothing holy, or occult. But in the early stages new habits are being created, new channels in the stubborn mind deliberately dug and widened. As in the development of new muscles there must be patience and persistence, regular practice but never too much. It is useless to begin with three hours a day, as it is foolish to attempt to develop biceps with three hours' work on the first day with the dumb-bells. At first there will be a struggle with the mind; then the new habits will be formed, and the practice will become a habit as much as shaving or doing the hair; then the habit will become a necessity, and the most longed-for hour of the day. There will be no quick results worth having, nor should the eyes be looking for them. But there *will* be results, pleasant and unpleasant, and in time the joys of hard-won achievement, in which the teacher, if any, will take some pride but claim no share.

6. *The whole man is involved*

The self, the Self, and the SELF, all these are one, and aspects of one unity. The whole man climbs, and takes his muddy boots to the summit of his spiritual Everest. The self is called the 'shadow' in modern psychology, but a shadow needs an object to cast it and a light. The object is the Self, the growing, evolving something which moves to Enlightenment. The light that throws the shadow is the SELF, the Light which is not yours or mine but the one Light born of the Darkness of the unborn Universe. The shadow must die, fade, become no more; so must the Self in time, leaving but the Essence of Mind which is All-Mind, which is No-Mind. Meanwhile, take your boots with you, cleaning them at times.

7. *The immediate purpose should be clear*

Fix the immediate goal and reach it; there is time then to reach further. There is too much vague and hindering talk of the nature of Satori, or the comparative value of this and that 'experience'. There will be time enough to discuss the view from the mountain top when you get there. For most of us the Goal can be the One; there will be time enough to discuss what lies beyond when we have achieved so far. While none of us has yet achieved the One does it matter *what* is neither One nor two? Let us be modest in immediate purpose, enormous only in our 'spirit of enquiry' and our insatiable will to achieve.

8. Concentration versus Meditation

I use this word versus to emphasize the profound distinction between these two uses of the mind. By Concentration I mean the deliberate creation or development of the mental faculty of focusing consciousness at will on a chosen object. It is the forging of the instrument, the cutting of the tool, the development of the special muscles needed for a special job. It is the building of the car which a driver will drive where he will, the creation of a searchlight which, under the technician's hand, will focus as directed, for as long as directed, and can then be switched elsewhere or switched off. By Meditation I mean the deliberate use of this instrument to a chosen end. There can be no meditation of value until the mind used is under the control of the will. . . . I am pressing this point because too many would-be meditators are quite incapable of Concentration of the type needed, and far too lazy to learn.

So to Concentration. First, it is a faculty used every day by every human being who is not an idiot. . . . All the usual examples of concentration have this in common, that the object is holding the subject's attention, emotionally or mentally; the pull is from the object end of the piece of elastic; hence such phrases as 'My attention was held by . . .', 'I was spell-bound, fascinated . . . I could not tear my eyes away.' Now the process must be reversed. In cold blood the subject, which is you, must decide the object, even against desire for something else, active dislike of the object, or at least boredom and resentment at the exercise. The object now may be the doorknob, or abstract, such as the relation between devotion and pity, or with no meaning at all, like a koan. Now comes the rub, indeed the enormous problem, how to exclude from this chosen field the host of thoughts, emotions and desires which will fight, as though with a life of their own, to enter the roped-off field. This problem is so large that famous scriptures give it their whole attention. The opening sentence of Patanjali's famous *Yoga Aphorisms* may be translated, 'Yoga is the hindrance of the modifications of the thinking principle', or in simpler English, is the power to stop the mind from running about. . . . Some fight the intruders; others welcome them, examine them and let them go; others just ignore them. But sooner or later, by one means or another, control is gained. Then, and only then, is the pupil ready to begin to meditate, to use his trained and obedient instrument to do what he wants to do. . . . Given this new power of selectivity of wavelength, of focusing the whole power of the mind as you will, for as long as you will, until you decide to switch it off—you may usefully and successfully meditate.

9. *And so to Meditation*

Again consider the purpose of meditation and see that the motive is at all times pure. For now the meditator enters the field of 'spiritual' forces. The term is of course comparative, for there is nothing completely spiritual or material that we know. But these 'higher' forces, as yet unknown to science and to all but a few psychologists, are immensely powerful, and have their own laws. Never should a claim be made to their possession, nor should they be unnecessarily displayed or money taken for their use. To abuse the possession of greater wisdom, strength or power of mind is utterly evil, and even to keep it for oneself alone is, according to tradition, that which distinguishes the Pratyeka Buddha from the Buddhas of Infinite Compassion, of whom Gautama was in history the one we know.

It is now more necessary for a regular time to be observed when the meditator can keep himself apart. This is to make it easier to protect the mind from interference, but also the body, for in deep meditation a sudden shock to the body can produce headaches, palpitation and the like. If such a place cannot be found in the home, the nearest Church will do nicely. As to time, let it be early or late, but the earlier in the day the better, for the whole being is fresher and the earth current is a rising rather than a falling tide. But it is more important for the time to be regular than to aim at any particular time....

As to posture ... I do not doubt that the full 'lotus' posture is the ideal, and next to that the ordinary cross-legged position known to all small boys. But I am equally convinced that for a long way on the Way there is no need for such a posture, so long as the head and spine be kept erect and the circuit closed. Let those who can sit comfortably on the floor in the traditional Buddhist posture do so, with the seat itself a few inches higher than the ankles. Let others sit as they will, erect and yet relaxed, and with the muscles balanced so that breathing is easy and regular and the body can so sit for half an hour without any movement at all. The 'circuit' should be closed by folding the hands and in some way closing the feet together. The whole 'Self' is, on several planes, a powerful generator of the force which in one of its forms we call electricity. Let the induced pressure be conserved and not dissipated from carelessly 'earthed' hands and feet. I do not myself approve the eyes half-open, as I believe that it tends to induce a fixed stare which is bad for the eyes. Even if the eyes being closed induces sleep, does that matter? When you wake you begin again.

The theme for meditation is for a long while immaterial. The breath itself can be used, and is perhaps the oldest of all. But use the breath just as you breathe, and without the Indian Yogic exercise of fancy breathing which can, when not supervised by a very skillful teacher, lead to the most serious results. I repeat, you are now developing and hoping to control the most powerful machine in the whole world, the human mind. Don't play the fool with it.

But whatever the theme, breathing, a phrase, a concept, it is better at first to begin with a few minutes 'warming up' exercises. Some watch the breathing, some take Pansil, some 'pass through the bodies' as I have shown you, discarding the body, the emotions, the thoughts, till nought is left but the silence or the white Light or whatever device you choose. For all these methods are devices; all are right for some at some time; none is right for all, or for anyone all the time.

But now you are going deeper, or higher, however you think of these things. You are withdrawing from the edge of existence to its center, moving higher above the world of men into that of the Enlightened Ones. You are raising consciousness above its habitual level to one less immersed in the unreal self or 'you', more free of the stains of hatred, lust and illusion, more that of the Self, the higher Self in the sense that we have agreed to use that term. The Goal, remember, is non-duality and nothing less, and the last thought of feeling of self must die before that moment of awareness can be attained.

At the end of the period, long or short, come gently back to 'reality', trying to preserve the link with Reality as long as possible. Then share your treasure with all mankind. Use the four Brahma Viharas to send your love and compassion and joy and equanimity to all that lives, above, below and everywhere. This helps to reduce the risk of an inflated ego, empties the unreal self, thus making room for the Life and Joy of the universe to enter in, and ensures that your period of time thus spent has been of some use to mankind. . . .

But this we must watch, that we do not leave the road. This Middle Way is infinitely narrow, and the blind alleys and worse to either side are infinite in number. Beware of trance conditions, from naked self-hypnosis to the subtlest and 'most enjoyable' condition of lotus-eating peace. The difference is that of a flash of lightning to the warm glow of an electric stove. He who touches the fringe of the Absolute *knows* and does not talk of it. The faculty by which this true experience will be gained is Buddhi, the intuition, and this is far beyond the most pleasant condition of high-thought repose—as of any trance of any kind. The right attitude for meditation is perfectly balanced between the opposites, positive/negative, alert/relaxed, receiving/giving, one with all. Beware of revolving like the proverbial squirrel in the thought-machine. You are still going round on the Wheel of Becoming, and Satori lies at right-angles, it has been said, to the plane of that Wheel.

10. Zen Meditation

The foregoing applies, I believe, to all meditation. What is there special about Zen? Only the precise definition of its object—Satori, and nothing less. But the Rinzai and the Soto schools use very different methods to this end. Rinzai, which we know in the West through the writings of Dr. Suzuki, Professor Ogata and those who have learnt their Zen from them, is short, and fierce, and sudden. It is also boisterous and joyous and enormous fun. It is ferociously subtle, nebulous yet certain in attack, indifferent in defeat, and laughing all the time. I will not have it that the school of gentle loving-kindness only is compatible with Rinzai Zen. Rinzai stabs at the balloon of self, tears down every concept and the stillness of serene delight. It hacks at thought as a desperate man cuts down the jungle to escape from it; it lives intensely in the Here and Now and This.

Soto Zen, I understand, though it is not easy to get information beyond the merest platitude, eschews the *koan* and *mondo* beloved of Rinzai Zen, is far more gentle, feminine, introvert and contempla-tive—as many of you, who have but doubtful place in a Rinzai circle. For the latter ignores the Bhakti element of mystical devotion, and some of you miss it. It is desperately direct, and therefore impatient of any moment spent in anything less than the direct assault on Reality. Zen . . . aims at such a goal. You appreciate the value of an agreed self-discipline, for the paradox stands that only he who is self-controlled is free. But gentle browsing in the mind will not produce those 'moments' which are out of time. The effort must be continuous and considerable. The 'Great Spirit of Enquiry' must be backed by a trained and indomitable will. Even as those who fight with naked swords, even as a man whose head is held under water fights for air, so must the man of Zen be fighting all the time for Enlightenment.

True, there are those who seem serene and simple, gentle and at peace—*now*, but this is the reward of achievement, the sign that the battle is over, and largely won. For us there is the need of immediate urgency. The form of that fighting is for each to decide; meanwhile we are trying to fight together, in the sense of side by side.

11. Group Meditation

Members of a meditation group should be, in the old phrase, 'as the fingers of one hand'. Any gossip or ill-will at personality level makes smooth and efficient work at higher levels of consciousness impossible, and the damage done by one person indulging in such can be remarkable. The teacher or leader must be respected, but in Western lands no more than respected. The devotion accorded a true teacher in the more devotional East is too apt in the West to degenerate into a psychological transference. . . . The pupils . . . must learn to stand on their own two feet, and not on the teacher's, and he serves them ill if he does not assist them to do so. When for any reason the leader considers a particular member can benefit no more from membership of the group, he must be allowed to say so. In the same way a pupil can leave when he will. But in either case the parting should be serene and dignified.

12. And so to Results

It is cold truth that results should not be sought, at least too strenuously. . . . The team, be it group or some greater Brotherhood, must be ever served, and the team that needs all our help all the time is mankind. Results for the individual are only of value to the extent that they serve that end. But they will come. The wise man is concerned with causes, seldom with effects. If the work is right, and carried out without pause, results, and the right results, *must* come. The inner effects are what matters to true spiritual development, and these may not appear for a long while to one's friends. The felt effects will come in time, serenity, certainty, and greater ability to 'cope'. Meanwhile, it is wise to forget results in the playing of the game for the sake of the game. . . . The Bodhisattva vows, never to take the reward that is earned until the last blade of grass has entered Buddhahood, will save the ego from its pride, and these vows are daily recited in Zen monasteries. . . . for the journey that I have found of value is this—right Motive, right Modesty, and unlimitied Guts!

13. *'Every Minute' Meditation*

. . . In the famous ten Oxherding Pictures (see Dr. Suzuki's *Manual of Zen Buddhism*), at the 8th stage both Ox and Man have gone out of sight, and the picture is a blank circle. But Picture 9 is 'Back to the Source', a state of habitual consciousness which is neither in Satori nor out of it; then comes the last Picture, 'Entering the City with Bliss-bestowing Hands'. In other words, back to the grindstone, in the office or the home or the market-place. Thereafter the all-but Sage is 'in the world but not of it'. He wears the Yellow Robe internally, he is, whatever else he is doing, meditating all the time. In the end this is the only form of meditation needful, but it is a high stage of development and must, like all else, be patiently attained. No sudden flash of intuitive understanding will produce this faculty, for the whole man is harnessed by it, and the wholeness is an integration of many lives.

How do we best approach this ultimate faculty, of living the spiritual life in the material, of achieving a devotion to minute, holy things from the saving of a pin to a healing meditation? How to infuse an active life with Zen, to do it all the time—and not to reserve one's Zen (as brandy) only for crises and best occasions? There seem to be two main ways, and they are not alternative. One is to leave the infusion to the unconscious, so to deepen and prolong one's periods of inturned meditation that the mind can be left to produce the flower of that practice in daily life. The other is to work consciously towards this spiritual infusion, allowing for periods of reaction, and avoiding the danger of becoming a spiritual snob.

There is nowhere for you but Here. In an hour's time you may be somewhere else; you will still be Here (though it may be a new 'here'). It is always Now, and will be Now tomorrow as it was Now yesterday. And you can only be concerned with This, what you are concerned with Now and Here. All else is memory or imagination, memory of the non-existent Past or imagination of the non-existent Future. And Now? How long is Now? In one sense no length at all, for a millionth of a second ago is Past, and a millionth ahead is not yet come. So only the Now exists, the timeless cosmic, everlasting Now, of Eckhart and a score of Western mystics, and of Suzuki and all those of the East. Thus there is nothing else which can occupy your mind than This, but you can decide very often what This shall be. It is always the product of your karmic past, and is not less holy for being manure to be put on the compost heap, or more so for being incense for the Shrine.

It will come! The practice of 'every minute' Zen will come, but it will take time as we use that term, and call for much patience. Difficulties will dissolve, distinctions blend and blur. You will be the more able to cope with all that life may bring to you, and see the terms good and bad, and pleasant and unpleasant, and other pairs of the opposites, as labels you attach to circumstance. Your friends will be less your friends in that you have less need of them; your enemies have less power to wound as that which alone they can injure, self, begins to fade away. Past and future will less tangle you with memories or hope. You will stand the more firmly on your own two feet, and walk on them happily to the (non-existent) Goal.

The State of Nothingness And Contemplative Prayer In Hasidism

R. Schatz

Contemplative prayer became the spiritual message *par excellence* of Hasidism. A Hasid who did not pray with the aim of divesting himself of corporeality, detaching himself from this world, and rising above nature and time in order to attain complete union with the divine "Nothing", had really not achieved anything of spiritual value. The intensity with which these doctrines were taught point to the nature of the longing which they express: prayer is a guide for breaking out of nature towards the spirit. From this point of view prayer is essentially spiritual; its means are meditation and intellectual concentration on the spiritual element which is embedded in the natural world. The breakthrough to the spiritual is possible according to both the transcendent and the immanentist view of God. According to the former it is the transcendent "nothing" which is the ultimate aim; according to the latter it is the "Nothing" immanent in man which is the goal of this breakthrough. Both formulas are used concurrently in Hasidic doctrine, and both share the basic assumption that prayer is essentially a supernatural act in which man seeks to break down the limitations of his natural existence in order to reach the divine. Man's natural existence, subject as it is to pride and to the desire for personal advantage and honor blocks the path to unification. The life of individuality is in fact a life of plurality, for it derives from nature, whereas the life of the spirit springs from the encounter with the one and only reality, which is the unity of all contradictions and the effacement of all individuality, and as such included, paradoxically, in the divine "Nothing".

Granted these premises, it is obvious that prayer should occupy pride of place in the religious life, since prayer is the "ladder set on the earth and its top reaches to heaven". Prayer is the embodiment of both the letters and the spirit of God. It is the symbol of the natural order and of differentiation, for it is fixed in the contours and shapes of the Hebrew alphabet, but is, at the same time, supernatural owing to the divine life which may become active in it when man is engaged in contemplation.

It is true, of course, that Hasidism has enlarged this conception and applied it to the whole of existence by distinguishing between the outer "shell" and the inner reality, and teaching that by meditation man can penetrate the shell and pierce to the mystical significance of existence. This subject requires discussion in the wider context of the Hasidic doctrine of serving God through material and even profane acts. For our present purpose it is sufficient to note that in spite of this wider aspect of the problem Hasidism has assigned an exclusive role to prayer, giving it—in keeping with Jewish tradition—pride of place in the religious life.

The initial stage of prayer is in its most concrete aspect, i.e. the letter, by means of which the Hasid elevates himself to its inner spiritual reality. This reality is devoid of distinct contents. It is a chaos of infinite light, but a living chaos which exists within an orderly and stable framework of divine manifestation. Each definite, outward manifestation of the divine contains the Infinite Divine. By breaking through the outer shell the mystic can, in a state of supreme spiritual concentration, bring about a meeting between the spiritual element that exists *within* him and that which exists outside him. Contemplative thought is therefore the sole means of achieving that true prayer which reveals the divinity behind the cover of matter. Hence prayer without spiritual purpose is worthless. Devoid of strength and essence, it remains enmeshed in the external; it neither penetrates nor breaks the chains of nature, nor does it liberate the spirit.

The Hasidic traditions regarding contemplative prayer go back to the founder of the movement, the Ba'al Shem Tov or Besht.

Meditation thus begins with what is here called "entering into the letters of the prayers". Man may be unable to enter this state and incapable (in our text: "unworthy") of contemplating the object of his meditation, because the external world (in our text: "alien thoughts") blocks his path and does not allow him to concentrate his thoughts and progress from one spiritual degree ("heavenly hall") to the next. He is thus exiled from the supernatural to the natural world. The

From Studies in Mysticism and Religion (The Magnes Press, Jerusalem.) 1967

spiritual vision of the object of meditation is described in Hasidic sources as seeing through a transparent object: as the mystic concentrates upon the letters, their concrete shape dissolves and the divine attributes that are concealed in the letters become spiritually visible. The Besht compared this (somewhat inappropriately) to looking at the stars through a telescope, which enables man to observe things which cannot be seen by the naked eye. According to the Besht, this kind of vision is possible only after the annihilation of the faculties of the soul. When man has annihilated himself and become "nothing", then the emptiness of this nothing is filled with a new kind of supernal being. But in this state man is no longer active and no longer does he speak; he encounters face to face the divine existence which acts and speaks through him.

The Besht is reported to have said:

> There are two kinds of fear [of the Lord], an external fear and an inner fear. The external fear simply means that owing to fear all the faculties and qualities and attributes vanish and become nothing. But the inner fear comes after the state of "nothing", when the higher faculties and qualities rest upon him. Then he becomes filled with shame, for the essence of life is the state in which the higher qualities rest upon man. But how do the higher qualities come to rest upon man? Like the astronomers who can see the stars during daytime with the aid of their looking instrument, so there are instruments with which it is possible to see the higher qualities and degrees, and these instruments are the letters. For instance, when man wants to see the greatness of the Creator he says *hagadol* ("the great") and contemplates in his mind the letters, *gimmel, daleth, waw, lammed*. In the course of this contemplation all his qualities and faculties become annihilated and God's greatness becomes revealed in these letters. In the same manner the might of the Creator is revealed through the letters of *hagibbor* ("the mighty")....
>
> For *the letters have the power* of condensing the higher degrees and drawing them down and containing them within themselves, and through these letters the higher degrees rest upon the man who utters them.

Man cannot grasp the Divine in its unlimited fullness. In the act of meditation he can encounter the Divine as limited. The extent of

God's manifestation to (or in) us depends upon the pupil's creative potentiality and receptive capacity.... The path to the Infinite Divine is opened up again by man's growing capcity for "thought". According to the Besht the teacher at first shows the pupil his great mind so that the pupil should stand in awe of him, but then goes on to show him his gradually more and more limited mind, until the pupil is capable again of grasping the great mind....

The spiritual possibilities which are thus opened up presuppose, nevertheless, the breaking of the chains of the material world. As man himself spares no efforts in concentrating his mind and directing it solely to the one thought about God, God himself comes to his aid and releases him completely from these chains.

> The desired goal is that before prayer he should divest himself of corporeality, which is finite and limited, and enter into the state of nothingness which is infinite. Man should therefore set himself entirely toward the Creator and to nothing whatever of his own self. And this is impossible unless man puts himself into the state of nothingness, viz. that he is not at all; then he will take no interest in things of the world, since he no longer is, and he will pay heed only to his Maker.... We pray to God...that He open the chains and fetters of corporeality so that we shall divest ourselves from it and cleave to the Nothing.

Prayer begins as a human activity speech, spiritual efforts to concentrate on God alone and the mortification of the external world. But before long it undergoes a transformation and becomes passive. Instead of man sending up his words, they are sent down into his mouth and infused from above in a kind of supernatural constraint. The mouth continues to utter automatic speech, although the spirit has already passed from the realm of "speech" to that of "thought". Another source quotes the Besht as saying:

> ....And through this power [which strengthens the attribute of mercy against that of law] he [scil. the tsaddik] arrives at the gate of Nothingness, where he forgets his existence altogether while his thought and his love and all his faculties cleave in the fear and in the attributes of God. Hence every Word of his is a vessel for the supernal Word...that is to say for the combinations of supernal letters.* Thus it also happens that words which emanate

*These spiritual combinations have their own laws and meaning and cannot be compared to the combinations of letters in concrete words.

from the higher worlds are infused into his mouth. This kind of speech can certainly arouse the higher lights and then one attribute can overcome the other in accordance with the combinations of the letters and according to need.

In fact, the *tsaddikim*, the men possessed of great souls, ... are capable of rising to the highest level and achieve the state, described above, in which their movement of speech derives from Him, Blessed be He. It is evident that their [apparently] simple utterances cannot properly be called "speech" at all and they do not function as ordinary speech. . . .

Here we have an explicit statement, to the effect that the words uttered in prayer do not exercise a magic influence on the sphere of the Divine, but that ordinary human speech is paralysed and its place invaded by divine speech, according to the transformations provided for the doctrine of the permutations of letters. The concrete combination of letters constituting the word ceases to exist as a result of the new power of the spirit, which is concentrated in it and which transforms it into the living word of God.

The moment of this transformation is beyond human comprehension because it comes about when man has annihilated himself and becomes "nothing". This psychological nothing represents a rupture in the continuity of time, and it is from there that man leaps into the sphere of the supernatural. At the same time, this moment of nothingness is also the link between material and spiritual existence. The neutralization of all specific contents and facts at the moment of nothingness actually guarantees their existence beyond their appearance in time. This notion of nothingness is applied to all spheres of existence, since they all, including the material world, are subject to the law of the spirit whose incidence cannot, however, be fixed, since it is a case of the supra-temporal working within time. This law equally applies to the transition from logical discursive thinking to contemplative thought; and the same applies even to the divine thought which, although timeless also in its attributes, yet possesses that quality of nothingness in which everything is annihilated only to be reborn in a new dimension. This analogy in the laws governing the relations of transcendent and immanent worlds renders an encounter between these worlds possible and provides the basis for the significance of spiritual prayer. Man's transformation into "nothing" is his bridge to the world of the spirit, for it is at this point only that the true spiritual processes begin. On the other hand, man's inability to abolish his temporal existence prevents the spiritual from breaking through and halts the progress of the causality of the spirit.

For instance when a person utters a word of wisdom or performs an act of wisdom, then the active force [of his wisdom] pervades everything that he has done or said, yet the wise man can still utter and perform more words and acts of wisdom. The Torah is the wisdom coming from God, and hence His power is contained in the Torah because the power of the active principle is present in that which has been acted upon. This power is truly infinite. There are many degrees ... and they all influence one another. Speech is in time, and [even] thought is affected by time, since a man's thought may change from one day to another. There is, however, an attribute which connects them all, but it is beyond human understanding, for it is the attribute of Nothingness ... as in the case of the egg that becomes a chick, when there is a moment when there is neither chick nor egg, and no man is able to fix this moment because that particular moment is a state of nothingness.

This law of transformation enables man to meet God, for the law of the spirit applies also to the human soul which is part of the Godhead.

When a man studies or prays, the word should be uttered with full strength, like the ejaculation of a drop of semen from his whole body, when his [whole] strength is present in that drop.

So long as the human mind is capable of dealing with itself, i.e. of self-reflection, it cannot reach Nothingness. Only the annihilation of the intellect, the complete extinction of the reflective consciousness enables man to liberate himself from "being" and to obtain a "new intellect", i.e. a purely spiritual mode of thinking that is beyond time.

Every day ... we have to detach our life force from material thoughts and from the being of ourselves, in order to enter the gate of Nothingness. Then we shall easily cleave with our roots unto the Cause of all causes. ... For as long as our intellect is concerned with our selves it remains in the realm of being and the activity of our mind is limited and finite, but when we come to the root then it enlarges [to infinity].

After its withdrawal to Nothingness the "limited mind" acquires a capacity for the divine; it becomes enlarged, capable of receiving the voices of the spirit which it was incapable of receiving prior to its annihilation. This "enlarged mind" with which the contemplative is clothed flows from the divine Nothing. . . .

The Besht's definition of man's existence in a state of Nothingness: "How can man attain the state of Nothingness? If he abstains from everything but that which pertains to his soul, then he is in the state of Nothingness, because the soul is a thing that no one can comprehend". By suspending all activites other than thinking, man can enter upon a new dimension of spiritual life. . . . The "life of the soul", or the intellect (in its second stage, after the annihilation of the original intellect) is regarded as a call that God addresses to man, for it is only in this life that God can thus reveal Himself to man. Without it there would be no meaning to man's existence in this world. . . . One should listen to the continuous call to rise above corporeality and eventually to attain the exaltation of the encounter with the *mysterium tremendum* and with the divine grace which becomes manifest in man.

> . . . When man elevates all the worlds by his [contemplative] thought, then a great awe and trembling seizes the angels because of their fear of God, and they behold a great and resplendent light. All this becomes manifest through lowly man who dwells in the world, and [through him] a great splendour is born. . . . through the body (i.e. matter) great beauty comes into being. . . . The person who performs a divine commandment brings new life to this world, for he brings prosperity to this world [if he intended so] or the world to come [if his intention was directed thither]. But man thinks: who am I, despised and lowly, that I should cause great pleasure to God in all the worlds? Let him not think that owing to his lowliness God cannot derive pleasure from him. On the contrary, God dwells with the downtrodden and humble.
>
> When God's presence rests on [man's] words, then a great fear seizes him and he does not know where he is and he neither sees nor hears, because all corporeality has been annihilated. . . . Man ought to pray with all his strength until he is divested from corporeality and forgets his own self, so that only the life that is in God remains, and all his thoughts are directed to Him. [In this state of orison] man must not be aware of the intensity of his prayer, for every awareness is awareness of his own self.

And all this occurs in one moment and in a flash, which shows that it derives from the supratemporal.

The suspension of individual existence and the union with the Divine lasts for a moment only and have no duration. The attainment of the "supratemporal" state is a supreme delight and a sudden illumination which has no comparison.*

All this refers to the power of the mystical experience. Further analysis, however, is required for an elucidation of the concept of metaphysical and psychological Nothingness, and of the manner in which human thought can bridge the gap between these two realities, if indeed they are two.

Man's activity is God's activity. Man speaks and thinks because the "world of speech" and the "world of thought" speak and think in him; he attains intellectual or mystical "illuminations" because rays from the world of the divine intellect reach his mind and illuminate it by virtue of the identity of the transcendent and the immanent worlds. . . . Human speech and thought are two stages in the process by which the spirit is "clothed", for even within the divine realm the spirit cannot exist in a pure, "naked" state. Even the Divine reaches itself and becomes conscious of itself in a kind of momentary flash, when the elements of its "thought" and "speech" become annihilated. Of course, within the Divine this annihilation into nothingness and creation out of nothingness is an eternal continuous process, whereas man is engaged in an unending and active struggle to shed the "garments" of speech and thought in order to attain illumination from that world of divine nothingness which is immanent in him, but to which, nonetheless, he has to travel a long and arduous road.

The stages of divine being referred to as divine "Thought" and Speech are completely annihilated, they rise towards the sphere of Divine Nothingness. On reverting again to "being" in a form that may be compared to spiritual vessels or "letters" the divine "Thought" and "Speech" can be infused to, and become manifest in, the man who is prepared to receive them. By "purifying" the instruments of his speech and thought, the contemplative may attain of the infusion of the divine vessels of speech and thought into his own, as the latter have become transparent to the divine influx. This, is the meaning of

---

*The emphasis on the ecstatic "delight" and in the encounter between the divine element in man and the Godhead outside him, raises a difficult problem for they have to be balanced against other texts which warn against the desire for "mystical intoxication".

true prayer: its words are vessels, capable of becoming (in the words of the Besht) "luminous and shining".

....The problem of the annihilation of human speech in human "thought" (i.e. contemplation) emphasizes the process by which man passes from the one to the other. Speech ceases to be possible when the particular is swallowed up in the "general" i.e., in the psychological process of thinking. Our spiritual efforts should be directed to the suspension of the faculties of the soul and our concentration upon the "one thought" that the whole of the earth is full of His glory. The unity of being—which is none other than the Godhead—can be gained by means of the intellectual stage of thinking, providing man has first eliminated all other faculties of the soul. From this point of view speech is only the starting-point for meditative concentration, and should be eliminated on the higher levels of contemplation. Mental prayer is, therefore, a necessary stage in the spiritualization of prayer, whilst vocal prayer plays a secondary role in the psychological process of man's passage from plurality to unity.

Speech prevents spiritual concentration and does not permit true understanding—the latter term signifying elevation of the spirit beyond time and that intuitive regard, which is the ultimate goal of the *homo spiritualis*. Speech still belongs to the sphere of the "distraction of the mind" whilst thought is directed to the supratemporal world of unity.

It would seem that the same spiritual motivation was also responsible for the relegation of the study of the law, a supreme value of traditional Judaism, to the periphery of the religious life. Discursive and intuitive thought cannot be reconciled as easily with regard to study as they can with regard to prayer.

There is not one action in the world that is not sustained by a spiritual principle immanent in it, though man is not necessarily conscious of it. It is precisely for this reason that the presence of such a spiritual principle does not disrupt the continuity of conscious thought. Only thought "with letters" is conscious, but there also exists a "hidden" thinking which feeds automatic speech. Silence and speech are equally legitimate: silence, because it befits this state of orison, speech because it can be automatic and hence does not interfere with contemplation.

The Besht repeatedly emphasized the value of the "prayer of quiet":

In prayer a person can offer to God the service of orison, in such manner that his service is not at all apparent to others. He will not make any movement with his body, but inwardly in

his soul his heart will be aflame and he will shout in silence,
owing to his enthusiasm. In this way his internal service will
be greater than when it would appear outwardly.

Serving God with thought only and without the body, clearly implies
utter silence. . . . Because the annihilation of the senses is a necessary
condition of the attainment of "supratemporal" contemplation, shut
the eyes and not look at the prayer book in order to rise above vocal
prayer.*

Two conditions obtain during contemplative prayer. There is the
utter silence which accompanies ecstasy at its height, when he "cries
out in silence owing to his enthusiasm", and there is the state in which
prayer is "uttered" in a manner that appears to the observer as
automatic speech wholly distinct from the person who utters it. Both
cases show that the identity of speech and thought is not necessarily
an ideal desideratum. On the contrary, a sufficiently advanced
spiritual state requires that speech and thought be not identical—in
the one case because there is no speech at all, and in the other
because the mouth utters automatic speech.

Sometimes one should serve God, with the soul only, viz. with
his thought, whilst the body should remain immobile so as
not to be overtaxed. At other times a person may *utter* his
prayer with love and fear and much enthusiasm but without
any outward movement, so that it will appear to others that he
prays without devotion. This is possible when one is in close
contemplative union to God, and then one can serve Him
with the soul only, with very great love. This kind of service is
better and proceeds more quickly and assists the union to
God more than prayer which is outwardly apparent on the
body, for the powers of evil have no hold on prayer that is
wholly internal.

This phase of transition from uttered prayer to mental prayer is
"forgetting of speech", a kind of suspension of the memory of particulars in the process of contemplation. Thus, the sound of the ram's
horn, the *Shofar*, blown on New Year's day is a more spiritual prayer
than words uttered with the lips, because it contains within itself all the
significances and contents of the discrete words and yet is devoid of
particular meaning.

---

*"When a person finds himself on a low level it is better for him to pray from the
prayer-book, because the sight of the letters of the prayer causes him to pray with
more intention. But when he is cleaving to the higher world, it is better for him to
shut his eyes so that the sight will not disturb him in his devotion."

Only spiritual prayer has any kind of meaning. Man cannot pass from his concrete personality to God except by way of the spirit, for only there does God reveal Himself. And God's "answer to prayer" can have no meaning except a spiritual one.

It would be wrong to infer that the abolition of vocal and verbal prayer is advocated. The Hasidic revolution should be measured by ... the strength of the pneumatic elements with which it informed the existing values and patterns. This is not to subscribe to a superficial and conservative interpretation of Hasidism, for the pneumatic energy is so restless that—blowing wither it listeth—it may at any moment destroy again the very objects which it had just fashioned. Hasidism was carried by its spiritual impetus to the crossroads but it stopped there. Its visible eruptions, albeit determined by its own inner logic, were restrained by Hasidism itself, no less than by the hue and cry raised by its opponents.

The Besht recommended a pneumatic way of life, detached from this world. Prayer with the lips becomes mere lip service. The pneumatic impetus imparted to traditional Jewish concepts a new, pneumatic charge; thus e.g. the idea of martyrdom no longer signified the readiness to sacrifice one's (physical) life under external pressure, but rather to annihilate one's awareness of physical existence under the pressure of the spirit.

The spiritual significance of Hasidic prayer is certainly not to be found in a (non existent) abolition of its concrete elements. The same applies to the attitude of Hasidism to other concrete elements in the cosmos. Its real contribution lies in the breaking of the concrete framework of prayer in an effort to illuminate thereby the "dark letters". The same applies to the Hasidic doctrine of the annihilation of all concrete things in order to raise the divine sparks imprisoned in them. The real revolution took place in the change of meaning of the concept of *kawwanah* (originally "concentrated attention and devotion", later "mystical intention"): the intention is now intended "upwards" in the sense of divesting the spiritual of the material and attaining the "pure", divine thought. It is this change which characterizes the role of the spirit in Hasidic doctrine.

Meditation of T'ieh-Shan

Chen-Chi Chang

We know that Zen enlightenment, *wu*, varies greatly from the shallow glimpse of the mind-essence of the beginners to full Buddahood as realized by the Buddha and a few advanced Zen masters. However, these experiences are different only in degree of profundity, not in essence or in basic principle. . . .

In order to give the Western reader a more genuine picture of how Zen enlightenment actually takes place, I have translated a short autobiography of T'ieh-shan, in which he recounts his personal experience of *wu* during his long striving for enlightenment. This story is first-hand information, which is better than any explanation or description given by eloquent and learned but inexperienced scholars.

According to T'ieh-shan's account:

I knew Buddhism from the time I was thirteen. At the age of eighteen I joined the priesthood . . . then one day I read a thesis brought by a monk from Hsüeh-yen, called "Advice on Meditation". After reading it, I became aware that I had not yet reached the stage mentioned in this book. Therefore, I went to Hsüeh-yen and followed his instruction in meditating on the sole word *wu*. On the fourth night sweat exuded all over my body, I felt very comfortable and light. I remained in the meditation hall concentrating on my meditation without talking to anyone. After that, I saw Miao-kao-fêng, and was instructed to meditate on the word *wu* without a moment of interruption, day or night. When I got up before dawn the gist of the sentence immediately presented itself before me. As soon as I felt a little sleepy, I left the seat and descended to the ground. The Koan never departed from me at any time, even while walking, preparing my bed and food, picking up my spoon or laying down the chopsticks.

It was with me all the time in all my activities, day and night. If one can fuse his mind into one whole, continuous piece, he cannot help but attain enlightenment. Following this advice, I was fully convinced of my actual arrival at such a state. On the 20th of March, Master Yen addressed the congregation:

"My dear brothers, it is of no use to feel sleepy while sitting for a long time on your meditation seat. If you are sleepy, you should leave the seat and walk on the ground, use cold water to wash your face and mouth and freshen your eyes. Then you may go back to your seat again, sitting with your spine erect, freshening your mind as if you were standing on a precipice of ten thousand measures, and take up solely your koan. If you keep on working like this for seven days, you will certainly come to the realization. It was such an effort as this that I made forty years ago."

I practiced according to this instruction for some time and soon I felt unusual improvement. By practicing in this way the next day I felt that I could not close my eyes even if I wanted to. The third day I felt as if my body were floating in the air. The fourth day I became completely unconscious of anything going on in this world. That same night I leaned upon a baluster and stood there for some time. My mind was so serene that it was as if it were in a state of unconsciousness. I collected my koan and lost it not, and then I proceeded back to my seat. When I was just about to sit down, I suddenly experienced a sensation that my whole body, from the top of my head to the bottom of my feet, was split. The feeling was something like having one's skull crushed by somebody; it was also like the sensation of being lifted up from the bottom of a ten-thousand-foot well to the high sky. I then told Master Yen about this [indescribably ecstasy] and the non-attaching joy that I had just experienced.

But Master Yen said to me: "No, this is not it. You should keep working on your meditation."

Upon my request, Master Yen gave me the words of *Dharma*, the last two lines of which read like this:

"To propagate and glorify the 'upgoing' affair of Buddhas and
    Patriarchs

From *Philosophy East and West* (The University Press of Hawaii), 1957.

You still need a good hammer-strike
On the back of your head."
I kept on saying to myself: "Why do I need a hammering on the back
of my head?"
I was not at all convinced of this. However, it seemed that there was
still some slight doubt in my mind, something of which I was not sure.
I meditated thus a long time every day for almost half a year. One day
when I was boiling some herbs for a headache I recalled a *koan* about
Naja, in which a question was put to him: "If you return the bones of
your body to your father and its flesh to your mother, where would
'you' be then?"
I remember that once I couldn't answer this question when I was
asked by the host monk, but now, suddenly my doubt was broken.
Later, the Master asked me: "When and where can one consider his
Zen work is completed?"
I could not answer this question. The Master urged me to stress my
effort on meditation to wash away worldly habitual thoughts. Each
time I entered his room and gave my answer to his interrogation, he
always said that I still had not got to it. One day I meditated from
afternoon to the next morning, . . . until I directly reached [the stage of]
profound subtlety. Arising, I went to the Master and told him my
experience. The Master asked me: "What is your original face?"
When I was just about to answer, the Master drove me out and
closed his door. From that time on I gained a subtle improvement
every day. Later I realized that the whole difficulty was because I had
not stayed long enough with the Master to work on the subtle and fine
part of the task. But how fortunate I was to meet a really good Zen
master. Only through him was I able to reach such a stage. Not until
then had I realized that if one exerts himself in an incessant and
compelling manner he will gain some realization from time to time,
and strip off his ignorance at each step of the way, . . . like stripping a
pearl. The more you strip it, the brighter, clearer, and purer it becomes. One stripping of this kind is superior to a whole incarnation's
work of another."
Nevertheless, every time I tried to answer my Master's question, I
was always told that something was still lacking in me.
One day in meditation, the word "lacking" came to my mind, and
suddenly I felt my body and mind open wide from the core of my
marrow and bone, through and through. [The feeling was] like old
piled-up snow suddenly melting away [under the bright] sun that had
emerged after many dark and cloudy days. I could not help but laugh

out heartily. I jumped down abruptly from my seat and caught the Master's arm with my hand and said to him: "Tell me, tell me! What do I lack? What do I lack?"

The Master slapped my face three times, and I prostrated myself before him three times. The Master said: "Oh, T'ieh-shan, it has taken you several years to get here!"

KAWWANA: THE STRUGGLE FOR INWARDNESS IN JUDAISM (MEDITATION AS A PREPARATION FOR PRAYER)

Hyman G. Enelow

All religion is rooted in emotion, whether it be awe, fear or love, it originates in a sentiment that comes from, and goes to, the heart. Founders and reformers of religions have recognized this fundamental truth. The difficulty, however, has lain in preserving the spirit of inwardness. It has been the common fate of religious ideas, no matter how vital or genuine at first, to lose their inner meaning and force in the course of time, and religious institutions are wont to drift away gradually from the spirit that created them, and continue in sheer mechanical fashion.

Judaism has not escaped this common experience. It would have been a miracle if it had. The danger . . . lurked in the talmudic insistence on the minutiae of performance; it jeopardized the inwardness of religious life. But even before the talmudic age, the peril of perfunctoriness was not absent. The tendency to perfunctoriness is an ancient characteristic of, and menace to, religion, and Judaism has formed no exception.

(It has been asserted) that the formalism of the Jewish teachers, laying stress as they did on accuracy of performance, was far from true piety. There could hardly be any question of true piety where prayer, the central feature of the religious life, was bound in the fetters of fixed forms. Prayers that were made the subject of regulation could not help becoming a mere matter of outward performance. The activity of the rabbis could not help degrade prayer into mere ostentation and hypocrisy.

However, it is an error to assume that the minute regulation of the

---

*Kawwana is spelled in many ways in an attempt to be phonetic with the Hebrew. It is most often seen as kavannah, though the reader will encounter it spelled variously as kavvannah, kavvana, kavana (rare) as well. The Encyclopedia of the Jewish Religion (Werblowsky) spells it kavvanah. The reader will note that different contributing waters in this book will use various spellings. Ed.

religious life was in itself antagonistic to spirituality and inwardness, or that it necessarily had that effect among the Jews. It is also an error to ignore the positive efforts put forth by Jewish teachers to safeguard the inwardness of the religious life. The real significance of Judaism has lain in its never losing sight of the ultimate object of all religion, and its constant effort to maintain the spiritual character of its institutions and precepts. When some teachers declared that the laws and commandments were given only for the purpose of purifying and sanctifying Israel, they really summed up the perennial attitude of Judaism. It has always kept up a struggle for the conservation of inwardness.

The struggle for inwardness in Judaism is reflected in the history of the doctrine of kawwana. Kawwana is a thoroughly Jewish doctrine. Both the word and the idea belong to Judaism. Indeed, there is no one word in any other language, certainly not in English, connoting all that the term kawwana embraces. It may mean intention, concentration, devotion; it may mean purpose and the right spirit; it may mean pondering, meditation and mystery. The word kawwana connotes all these things, for the reason that it kept on gathering significance from the religious experience of the Jewish people. The doctrine of kawwana is thoroughly Jewish, and in its history we catch a glimpse of the struggle for the maintenance of inwardness in Judaism.

The fulfillment of religious duties requires kawwana, for it means sustained devotion throughout prayer. The mystic interpretation of the kawwana has come to play an important part in the later kabbalists; namely, intensity of devotion and pondering of the words of prayer and of their mystic content. In time, kawwana came to designate devotional temper in the best and purest form, for prayer could not be a fixed task but a real yearning and supplication.

Kawwana is applied not only to prayer, but also to other religious duties. In the philosophic literature, it came to signify pure devotion. The Jewish philosophers assigned to prayer an important place in the religious life, but they laid stress on the right mood and preparation to purify the hearts and to teach the people how to put kawwana into the exercise of their religious duties.

No religious performance has any value unless it expresses an inner desire. Religious duties must proceed from the heart's desire. The foundation and pillars of all religious performance rests in the inner intentions of the heart, in the kawwanoth. If there is a blemish in the kawwana, the performance is useless. The duties of the heart are endless, whereas those of the body are limited.

From *Studies in Jewish Literature* (George Reimer, Berlin), 1913.

The emphasis is altogether on the superiority of inner devotion to outward performance, of the heart to the body. It is a laudation of kawwana. Prayer is particularly important for the purpose of stimulating the spiritual life. When the duties of the heart are involved, it is necessary to turn one's heart away from all thought and cares of the world and to direct it all toward God alone. The body must be freed from all occupations appertaining to this world or the next, and the mind from all thoughts that might separate him from the subject of prayer.

Having removed every sort of physical impurity, he should set his heart upon whom he would address in his prayer, and upon what he seeks in it, and how he means to speak it. Moreover, he should realize that the words of the prayer are but a shell, while the inner sense is the kernel, the prayer is the body, and the sense is the spirit. Mere bodily performance is just a motion of lips.

But if a man, while praying, has had his mind on worldly themes, and then winds up his prayer with the meditations of the heart, it is sheer shame and hypocrisy. He asserts what is not true. Let a man examine his mood. If he can concentrate his heart, let him pray. If he cannot, let him not pray.

All value is denied in the outward acts of religion, if devoid of kawwana. Lacking the proper intention and inner sense, they might as well be left undone. Judah ha-Levi, in the Book of the Kuzari, often dwells on the spiritual prerequisites and their inner appreciation of prayer. The preparation for prayer in the life of the devout man (Hasid) lies in the mastery of one's desires and faculties which is the essence of the ethical life. The Hasid must be like a prince. He must have full control over his realm, undisputed master of all his powers, leanings, appetites, so that he might reach the divine degress which is above the intellect.

The Hasid regards such hours of prayer as the heart and fruit of his time. He will long for such occasions of approach to God, for then he resembles most the spiritual beings, and is farthest removed from animality. Prayer of this nature is the food of the soul and does for the soul what meat does for the body. Its periodic recurrence serves to keep the soul bright, pure and strong, and protects it against the perils and coarsening influences of everyday toil and amusements.

But above all, Judah ha-Levi accentuates the need of joy in prayer. The value of divine praise is according to the joy that goes with it, and it is a duty while praying to put aside everything that might impair the spirit of serenity and joy. Kawwana doubles the delight of prayer. The Hasid must take to heart the idea of each prayer, and try to realize its kawwana—what it contains and implies, to realize their inner contents and the religious obligations that spring from them. And he should reflect at the same time that God's greatness is just as manifest in the ant and the bee as in the sun and stars, if not more so, because of their delicacy.

Ha-Levi reverts time and again to the idea of joy, freedom and kawwana as the highest qualities of the religious life. When deed and intent perfect each other, they bring on reward. But where deed lacks kawwana or kawwana lacks deed, all value is lost. Maimonides regarded those moments as most precious when a man is alone and, free from cares and interruptions, has the opportunity of meditating on divine themes and acquiring not only love but passion for God. The fulfillment of religious precepts has but one object, namely to accustom us to occupy ourselves with divine themes and free us from the anxieties of the world. For then we hold undisturbed converse with God.

If, however, we pray with motion of our lips and our faces to the wall, but really think of our business, if we recite the Torah with our tongue, while our heart is occupied with the building of our house, we are like those of whom the prophet said, thou art near in their mouth, but far from their heart. Kawwana is the one thing needful to get into the presence of the King. Absence of kawwana thwarts the efficacy of prayer. A prayer without kawwana is no prayer. If a man prays without kawwana, he must say it over with kawwana. He must pray until he becomes calm. He must pray until he has regained quiet. Let him wait three days, if necessary, in order to recover composure, and then pray.

Kawwana means to empty one's heart of every care and regard oneself as standing before the Shekhina. It is proper to compose oneself for a while before prayer, in order to prepare one's heart, and then pray in a spirit of serenity and supplication. Religious contemplation should precede prayer. Insist on reverence at the beginning of prayer, and then composure. One should not rush through prayer as if one were glad to have it over, but one should prolong every letter, in order to put kawwana into the heart with every word uttered.

Pray with kawwana. Refrain from conversation before the hour of prayer, but engage in meditation that will fill the heart with humility. It is the foundation of prayer. Be not content with recital of fixed prayers. After every benediction, add some personal supplication;

thus the heart is brought more genuinely into the service. If you can add nothing of your own, find some pleasing melody, and say your prayers to whatever melody you like best; supplications in a melody that makes the heart weep, and praise in one that will make it sing. Singing both expresses and augments prayer.

Not outward signs of devotion count, but those within. Let the eyes look downward and the eyes upward. During the recital of special supplications, it may be well to cover the face, and it may be well to close the eyes in moments of particular devotion, but it is not natural for the human heart to continue in devotion if the eyes are shut for any length of time. Only in short prayers the eyes may be closed. What is necessary during prayer is quiet and equipoise. Where there is much storm and heat, as Elijah learned, God is not present. The Shekhina will be found passing by such a prayer.

Reverence befits prayer and splendor of supplication is kawwana, and the crown of benediction is love, and diadem of wisdom is humility, and the result of humility is fear of God. Prayer without kawwana is like a body without a soul. This adage likely emanated from the school of R. Judah he-Hasid. No matter how the question of the unity of the Sepher Hasidim be decided, whether it all came from the hand of R. Judah or not, it is certain that it contains passages that suggest the complex and cryptic mysticism of the school of the Zohar. This is displayed particularly in the exploitation of the idea of kawwana.

Kawwana is interpreted as a meditation on the mysterious correspondence existing between the lower and higher regions, man and deity, a favorite idea of the Zohar. The essence of this idea is that every object on earth has its correlate in heaven, and that by doing of religious acts man affects in one way or another the celestial dominion, and that the purpose of kawwana is to realize, by means of concentration, the mystery of these correspondences, influences and effects.

Kawwana came to signify in the Zohar, and with the later mystics of the school of Lurya, not mere devotion in the ethical and spiritual sense, but rather appreciation of the mystic value of religious acts, and particularly of prayer, ecstatic contemplation of the cosmic mysteries, absorption in the occult significance of every religion duty and practice, and more especially, concentration on the mystic value of the Divine Names.

Everything has its kawwana: benedictions, study, holy seasons and fasts; indeed, every incident of life. However, the kabbalistic construction of the kawwana involves considerable play of the imagination. There is much fantasy in it, and some poetry. The erotic element in it is striking, grotesque and quite often repellent. One wonders to what extent it mirrors the sexual morality of those times. The subject of sex certainly is common in medieval Jewish literature. During the periods of gloom and persecution, it is not hard to see what solace the people must have found in the fantastic flights of the mystic kawwanoth. Kawwanoth were the wine of consolation and the apples of sustenance. But as far as the idea of kawwana was concerned, it had lost its purity. Every religious act came to signify some special mystic and metaphysical object, which it was the duty of man to fulfil, no matter how little he understood it. Absorption in the kawwanoth was represented as possession of twofold virtue; illumination of the soul and effect on the celestial order. But the celestial effect became the chief consideration, and the Kawwana was turned into a grotesque play with letters, words and ideas. It assumed magic significance. Even the best of the kabbalists were not free from this fault.

All religious performances and especially prayers, came to comprise supernal objects and metaphysical mysteries, occult kawwanoth, and one was supposed to refer to kawwana, or recite it, whether or not one understood it, or whether or not it had any meaning at all. An endless number of kawwanoth were composed and put into prayer books. As for the special prayer books of the kabbalists, the kawwanoth became so numerous as to outweigh the prayers and obscure their simple meaning.

Thus the kawwana which began as a means of quickening the religious life and increasing its inwardness, had itself deteriorated into a perfunctory and insenate performance. Indeed it formed a hinddrance to true devotion, so that those interested in the maintenance of of the devotional temper now were constrained to fight against the new species of kawwana, or rather against the superstitions and foibles with which the word had been impregnated by the kabbalists.

No matter how many voices made themselves heard against this abuse, it persisted. Kabbalistic aberration usurped the place of true devotion. Menasseh ben Joseph Benporat in 1828 complained of the condition of devotion among the people; "What is needed above all the prayer is true kawwana, devotion. In our time people imagine that mere reciting is enough. Everybody thinks he has a right to add what he pleases, and prayer is regarded as a sort of charm. People rely on the kabbalistic fiction that angels wind crowns out of the implicates of prayers and benedictions, and remain indifferent to the real object of prayer."

But the writer, who lived in a small town in Russia, was suspected both of sympathy with Hasidism and Reform Judaism. In this particular respect he certainly shared an ideal common to the leaders of Reform Judaism. One of their chief objects was to rescue the religious life, and especially the worship of the Jew from perfunctoriness and aberration, and to reintroduce the true idea of kawwana as a means of increasing genuine devotion and inwardness, to restore kawwana to the synagogue, to revive the true meaning of the word and idea of kawwana, and to preserve the inner beauty and power of Judaism. And insofar as they stood for renewal of devotion in the synagogue, there was a close relation between Hasidism and Reform.

The Naught In Zeno

by Hidenori Tashiro

In occidental philosophies, particularly in mysticism, God is frequently termed nothingness. That is something which can never be made an object of consideration, which can never be grasped by means of conceptualization. Occidental mysticism derives for the most part from Neo-Platonic philosophy. Its profound influence is felt in the so-called Pseudo-Dionysius, who became an important source for subsequent Christian mysticism. German theology distinguishes between three stages of the way that takes man to God: 1. purification of all worldly desires; 2. enlightenment brought about by God: and 3. unification of man with God (*unio mystica*). The last mentioned, however, only signifies an absolving of the human will into the eternal will of God, with God and man remaining substantially overagainst each other as before.

The concept of nothingness is often found in contemporary European philosophies as well. Nothingness plays an important role in Hegel's philosophy. Heidegger and Sartre treat of it also, even if in different ways. The "All-comprehending (das Umgreifende) in Jasper's philosophy likewise refers to the concept of nothingness or the non-objectifiable. Yet the nothingness of Western philosophies is nothing other than that to which is attributed a relativity, which hence is somehow made an object of consideration. Even the nothingness of occidental mysticism ultimately refers to God's absolute being, and functions as an attribute of God. In distinction from all this, the notion of nothingness has undergone a unique development in oriental philosophies. Besides Lao Tzu's philosophy, Zen Buddhism proffers various and typical assertions which point in the direction of absolute nothingness. In content, the *koan* of the Rinzai school, for example, consist primarily of depictions of the actions or words of outstanding Zen masters that spring from the source of nothingness.

But what is real nothingness? According to Zen Buddhism, true nothingness must be pure and absolute, real only in an absolute, single subject. In no case can it be objectified. It is nothing other than the whole universe as the one and only subject. One might describe the basic traits of this nothingness by dividing it into three phases: body (*tai*), form (*so*) and function (*yu*). With regard to the body or substance of absolute nothingness, one can say that it can never be made an object of reflection. That is, it totally and logically refuses objectification. For this reason, in practicing Zen, one must not be bound to an objectified enlightenment (*satori*) either, for this would mean that one has not been completely dissolved into the nothingness that can never be objectified. Absolute nothingness is the entire universe as the subject overagainst which nothing stands any longer.

One recognizes the form of absolute nothingness in the manifestations which leave behind no definite trace. One can attain to the substance of absolute nothingness only through rigorous practice (*shugyo*), in which one surrenders himself to the way of nothingness by thoroughly negating himself. The function of absolute nothingness consists in the spontaneity of all actions; even if they are enacted by one personally, they take place of themselves. When lived, absolute nothingness culminates in the realization of a totally free creation, for it is the true *causa sui*. The principles of absolute nothingness take effect not just negatively, but actively as well. All our actions, and all manifestations of the universe, should therefore spring from absolute nothingness.

By way of a total pulverization, absolute nothingness negates everything, hence all objectified notions, including pantheism. Yet something genuinely new and actually true could arise only from the ruins created thereby. Let us clarify a bit further. A monk once implored Joshu, a famous Chinese Zen master, to tell him "the meaning of the Patriarch's (Bodhidharma's) coming from the West." The master replied, "The oak tree there in the garden." The true sense of this answer totally escaped the monk, since he had expected some sort of clarification of an inner reason. Hence the monk tried once again: "Master, do not show us by pointing to external objects." Joshu said, "I do not show you by pointing to external objects." So the monk asked anew, "What is the meaning of the Patriarch's coming from the West?" Joshu answered as before: "The oak tree there in the garden."

Thus goes one conversation in a *koan*. What is the oak tree? What is its relation to the meaning of the Patriarch's coming from the West? As is known, in practicing Zen, at least at first, the practitioner strains to become one with the object in question. When the goal in the practice of the above case, for example, has been achieved, then the practitioner has finally and indeed ideally become one with the oak tree. The opposition between oak tree and practitioner vanishes. The meaning of the latter is totally absorbed, i.e., taken up, in that of the former. Then there is only the oak tree as absolute subject (*samadhi*). The entire universe-subject is therefore the same as absolute nothingness, because it is no longer amenable to objectification....

The nothingness, or naught, of Zen Buddhism is not something empty, but infinitely full, from which all objects are born. Thus one says that in nothingness there are flowers, the moon, towers, all kinds of people and things. And since the universe, as subject, is one and only, it can never be objectified, placed over-against. This nothingness is not something overagainst being; that is, it is not a relative nothingness, but rather single, pure, and absolute. Absolute nothingness can be attained only by way of thorough subjectification. Rinzai called the person born of this "the true man of no rank." Yet it is something positive, not negative, something from which everything in nature and life springs forth, something that undergoes a genuinely free creation. Absolute nothingness is *causa sui*.

The self can be totally active only when it is taken up, absorbed, in the spatially and temporally infinite universe as subject. One should be aware, therefore, that even in Zen Buddhism one can attain the ideal only when human self-conceit is eradicated from the bottom up. One's true actions and conduct unfold only when self-negation is consummated.

Self-Extinction
in Zen and Hasidism

Jacob Yuroh Teshima

1. Buber and Suzuki

Martin Buber rebuffed the patronizing attitude of the German-Jewish intellectual, and opened up the entire Hasidic face and view of life to the world, doing it despite the scorn held by the German intellectuals for the Hasidism of the Eastern Europeans. To the German "enlightened" circles, the Hasid was considered illiterate, fanatically attached to traditional orthodoxy filled with Kabbalistic superstitions.[1] For instance, Rabbi Israel, the Baal Shem Tov, the founder of Hasidism, was ridiculed by rabbinical authorities as a transgressor, as a dispenser of white magic in his writing of amulets to protect one from harm. But he proved to be a charismatic healer in modern terms, and his success as a "white magician",[2] based on the premise that every individual in Judaism had the capacity to make a special petition to heaven, that function limited only to those with faith, helped spread Hasidism despite opposition by the rabbinical community.

Hasidism filled the void between the Jewish people and the scholars, with their masters particularly becoming deeply involved in the daily life of the people, an involvement that gave pride and comfort to their followers. The true life of Hasidism was that of synthesis; of the life in the synagogue, the Beth Midrash, as well as the daily life in the home and in the street. Consequently, there are two kinds of literatures among the Hasidim: that of the Torah study itself and the other of Hasidic life around their masters, both being non-exclusive of each other. The former belongs to the genre of exegesis, and contains Kabbalistic interpretations of the Torah aimed to express the Hasidic ideology as well as rabbinical and halachic issues. The great contribution given by Buber was his retelling various stories of Zaddikim, (who celebrated the life with Hasidim in joyful chant, dance and miracles), to the Western Europeans. But Hasidic exegesis and homily were systematically ignored by him as if they were not a part of the rabbinical legacy. Hasidism teaches that only the true Zaddik can maintain contact between God and himself. The average man is so busy engaging himself in secular life that his only alternative is to keep himself close to the Zaddik through whose virtue man becomes eligible, somehow, to cleave to God. Buber, in his Hasidic Tales, explained Zaddik as a *helper*.[3] But authentic Hasidism claims and commands that Zaddik is not only a helper but an essential intermediary between God and man.[4] Many inaccuracies such as this were one of the points that angered the methodical historian Gershom G. Scholem in his critique of Buber.[4'] Yet, if Buber were to introduce the image of Zaddik as the only intermediary between God and man, then eventually his German contemporaries would not welcome the inspiration of Hasidism, such monopoly of virtue seemed to be against the spirit of German intellectualism in the early twentieth century. The fact remains that in Hasidism the Zaddik is the only intermediary. It may seem a chauvinism to the liberal modern Jew, but the efficacy of the Zaddik office and the noble idea of the holiness of Israel have proven a great consolation in Eastern Europe because of the inhumaneness of history.

There are comparable qualities in Zen: the two aspects of intellectual speculation and its day-to-day practice. Daisetsu Suzuki's Zen was practical Zen rather than purely speculative, the latter being too profound for outsiders to understand without a knowledge of the details, dogma and historical background. Suzuki presented and emphasized the practical-cultural value of Zen to the Westerners in terms of philosophy rather than systematize and analyze its doctrines and development in terms of history, and by doing so, he succeeded to stimulate their large interest to the world of Zen. Yet many critical scholars of Zen are not happy now because of his neglect of the historical analysis, and have been attempting to present Zen in the same manner as Gershom Scholem wanted to present Hasidism.

2. Nothingness

The dichotomies within themselves were a striking parallelism between Zen and Hasidism. The latter was involved in community, and Zen basicly maintains a monastic life. Both used the concept of "Naught" as a key to achieve their goal. Buddhism discovered that the entire universe is in transition. Being is in transition. Shakyamuni Buddha understood that there is no solid state of any doctrine. The content of his enlightenment was the fluidity of the cosmos. It lacks a fixed frame. The river of that understanding was coined in the term Nothingness. The only Absolute is Buddha/Buddhahood which is the very subject of the enlightenment, namely, the pure and unattached self. Zen seeks to achieve only this, by transcending the frailty of being. And in this point differs Zen from other Buddhist schools regarding conception of the world. To most Buddhist schools, the frailty of being is strengthened by the grace of Buddha and the hosts of the universe are supported by *His* mercy, and Shakyamuni Buddha is considered as the exalted and deified One like Jesus Christ in Christianity; while, to the Zen students, Buddha is never identical with any divinity but the super-self which is hidden behind the being, and the being is generated in the sea of Nothingness like numerous waves taking place on the surface of ocean. Being was made out of nothing. The idea looks similar to the Jewish concept of the creation *ex nihilo*. Zen is far more radical than Judaism, however. It says that nothing is being and *vice versa*. It completely denies introducing the idea of *a* Creator in explanation of the generation of beings. It insists on a most atheistic attitude, although it does not deny the freedom of others to maintain a theistic view. A Jewish professor once became furious when he heard from a celebrated Japanese Zen master, "We believe that everything is Buddha. Stones and trees are Buddha, and you too are Buddha." It was a mistake of the Jewish professor to take the term Buddha as identical with God. Lien-Chi (d. 867), one of the most influential Chinese Zen masters, said, "There is no substance to everything in the universe, no essence to their status; there are only tentative names and the names are no more than expedient,"[5] and "definitely is there no Buddha, no Law, no way to be disciplined and nothing to be understood!"[6] Zen considers both being and nothing as void. Everything out of the realm of reality is fiction, fantasy, dream and mortal. The monism of Zen deals only with reality, i.e., the self. The duality of Hasidism relates everything from man to God.

Compared to Zen, Hasidism understands that God is eternal and infinite. On the other hand, it deduced from the idea of creation *ex nihilo* another thought that God is Naught: God created being out of nothing, therefore, the Naught should be absolutely more real than any being, and the Naught out of which the whole universe is created is essentially to be identical with God himself because He was the only substance before creation. The idea could be explained in the expression: $\frac{1}{\infty} \doteq 0$. Namely, when God, who is the *only* reality in the universe, is understood as *infinite*, he is surely not a sort of object which can be counted as 1,2,3,—because his infiniteness never means multitudeness of himself; rather he is something *like zero* which cannot be counted but still unified and undivided. Naught (*Ayin*) and Infinite (*Eyin-sof*) are the two reverse sides of the same coin, and they are simply beyond one's intellectuality. To the Hasid, Naught is the Superbeing, while to the Buddhist it is a sort of cosmic process. Buddhism denies the somethingness of the universe and tries to reduce all being into non-something-thingness. In the primitive sense, Shakyamuni did not have the notion of eternal *being* in space and time. Even *Nirvana* is merely the eternal *state* of calmness and lack of suffering. In contrast with this, Hasidism attempts to reduce all being into super-somethingness. Perhaps the quality is identical, but the process is entirely different.

3. Need of *Satori*

In Zen, they have no assumption that there is an everlasting being like One God in Christian terms. They grasp the Absolute in the sense of psychological essence rather than metaphysical substance. Their realistic approach concluded that man is present in a passing state as a part of universal metamorphosis. If one seeks to achieve great harmony, Zen urges the reduction of oneself to the level of Nothing, for being (including human being) is a phenomenon of non-existence. There is nothing if the very notion of existence is discarded, but the understanding of nothing or being nothing is the goal. And this has presented a problem to the reason, since despite the discovery of being nothing, reason still functions. This enigma and paradox is the starting point of Zen.

Theoretically, Zen followers know that man as well as everything is nothing. Yet this knowledge is not yet *satori*, because the informed knowledge is a mere expediency and the mind still continues to operate as the old self. The notion of the self is indispensable to manage various aspects of human life. Without it a man is no longer man. It naturally tends to protect one's own interests primarily for survival. But its strong tendency of attachment has been a great obstacle in Zen as long as it resists to surrender before Nothing. The *satori* itself is the very experience of reducing that anguish of mind down to the level of nothing, and then results the flush of enlightenment, the freedom in Zen.[7] Only after the mind is freed of the agony, the entire person can realize what the reality is, and participate in the process of universal phenomena without attaching this or that, and freely command himself to do compassion, love, teaching and coming to the aid of others.

4. Effect of Enlightenment

According to Dogen (1200-1253), the founder of the Japanese Soto school, one brings all of the cosmos and the universe into Buddhahood at the very moment of the enlightenment.

"If, even a moment, a man sits on *zazen* in a perfect state of concentration and expresses the essence of Buddhahood through silent pure-minded sitting, then, all the hosts of the universe suddenly get the *satori*. Consequently, Buddha and Tathagatas increase their pleasure in themselves and the way of enlightenment enhances its grandeur. Furthermore, all the universe including hells and purgatories, all of them, are immediately purified throughout their heart and body, and materialize the world of great freedom. At the manifestation of the authentic quality, every being realizes the true enlightenment and every creation jumps into the same event experienced by Shakyamuni under the bo-tree, preaching at the same time the message of Buddha with profound wisdom."[8]

This experience, however, is not the end. Man in Zen has to continue to maintain probing the experience in depth. In this aspect, Hasidism has a similar approach. According to Rabbi Dov Baer, the Great Preacher (d. 1772), and his student, Rabbi Levi Isaac, for example, the renewal of cosmic vitality and even the course of history is possible through man's return to the Infinite God in contracted heart, in self extinction. "Man should keep himself in contact with the Naught so that he can bring everything together (to renew them)."[9] This statement contains twofold conditions: to be in touch with God and to diminish his self. To disregard oneself is the primary condition in order to attain the presence of God. and "whenever the people of Israel achieve the dimension of Naught, then everything gets the same dimension and our righteous Messiah will come."[10] This moment is crucial because the virtue of man's return to God releases the exiles of all creation seeking to be redeemed, and releases the holiness of their being up to the hand of the Creator. Not only Zaddik but also every Jew must, therefore, encourage himself to reproduce those moments of the unity. The moments are precious, yet they do not last. After the moment, the Jew has to fight again to reproduce another moment of flush until there will be almost perpetual brightness in the whole universe. And in the same manner, the Buddhist must continue his efforts to deepen the essence of *satori*, which is urgently needed for the world to end its darkness of illusion.

5. Problem of Zen

The problem of Zen is the ego which creates the veil of *Maya* (illusion) and the uncertainty of life. If there were no ego, there could be no problem. No problem in stones. They are peacefully in harmony with the universe. Only man is a problem in trying to achieve a harmonious life with his environment. It is the annihilation of man, the self-extinction, that is the goal of Zen. Lien-Chi taught his disciples:

> Do not misunderstand! There is no being to be called out either within or without. Hearing my words, then you think that there is nothing. Yet this thinking is also wrong. Throw even the desires to obtain an answer, and wholeheartedly pursue *zazen*! The current illusions, hence, will perish and potential ones also will never occur.[11]

However, it does not literally mean the extinction of the entire self. The self to be extinguished is the so called superficial consciousness, whose primary concern is existence and survival. Zen aims to establish the autonomy of the true-self who is in one's depth consciousness. The calmness of *zazen*/Meditation is not the goal. Lien-Chi says:

> It is quite obvious that either the body or the land of Law is nothing more than a reflection of heart. Friends, you must realize who is *the hidden man* manoeuvring these reflections. He is the very source to the variety of Buddhahood and the ultimate goal of way-seeker to return. Neither your limbs hear the lecture nor your organs understand the discourse, so nor the empty air comprehends the address. Then what does follow the teaching? It is one who unmistakably stands before you, showing no appearance but distinguishingly by himself, *this man* does understand the content of teaching.[12]

6. Problem of Hasidism

The problem of Hasidism is in the corporeal self which unceasingly enslaves man to the chain of earthly desires, though he is expected to perform the holy task, namely, to serve God and to sanctify the life. There are constant conflicts between the corporeal self (*yetser hara'*, evil impulse) and the spiritual self (*yetser tov*, good impulse). This view is very old in Judaism since the days of the Second Temple.[13] Judaism, like Zen, does not believe that human nature is evil. Humanity itself is a creation of God, and therefore good. Even evil impulse is eventually good, for without its desires a house cannot be built, a family cannot be produced and no engagement in business is possible. How to use appropriately these desires is a serious assignment to the Jew. Being influenced by the Zohar and Lurianic Kabbalah, Hasidism, however, was convinced that corporeal desires actually originated out of the evil (*kelippah*, bark, shell)[14] which acts against the divine cause. It is a bark in which the divine spark has been captured since the early stage of the creation. The Hasid is, therefore, asked not only to extinguish his corporeal desires but also to release the spark from the evil bark at the same time.

While Zen adopted *zazen*/meditation as the only means of solution, Hasidism had to mobilize every possible means to conquer the enemy at all occasions: study of Torah, fulfillment of precepts, good deeds and, above all, prayer. The difference is partly due to their social backgrounds: monastic life and community life. Although the seclusion is ideal to a mystic, the Hasid who lives in secular community cannot concentrate on certain means. But by *kavvanah*, by devoted intention, can he concentrate most of his activities including eating, drinking and marital affairs. This must be the intention: to ennoble all of nature.[15] By study and good deeds, human nature can be disciplined in the preparatory stages. It is these good deeds that stimulate heavenly mercy. But the fulfillment of self-extinction is only possible through an intense and deep devotion to God, namely, through devoted prayer. Rabbi Israel, the Baal Shem Tov, always prayed with a great deal of intensity so that often he was in trance for many hours. His successor, Rabbi Dov Baer, commented on prayer:

> In prayer, one should pour his entire strength into the words, and thus go through letter to letter with great intensity until he loses his corporeality ... then he will not hear any more even what he recites ... and finally, he enters into the dimension of Naught where all of his physical strength has ceased to function.[16]

At the peak of self-extinction, the Hasid encounters the presence of God. Because of the overwhelming superiority of the divinity, the human ego is totally oppressed to the point of nothingness. The nothingness at this stage is a total extinction which does not allow any intellectual reflection. Rabbi Levi Isaac described it as following:

> There are those who serve God with their human intellect, and others whose gaze is fixed on Nothing. . . . He who is granted this supreme experience loses the reality of his intellect, but when he returns from such contemplation to the intellect, he finds it full of the divine and inflowing splendor.[17]

7. The "I" in Hasidism

Hasidism is a unique religion in the West in that it is aware of the fluidity of the ego (*ani*) and the Naught (*ayin*). Although both Hasidism and Zen aim to reach self-extinction, there is a decisive distinction: at self-extinction, the Buddhist becomes a part of the universe and cosmos and the Buddha. But to the Hasid, still there remains a demarcation between the subjective Infinite, God who is the eternal subjectivity, and the created object. The gap is so tremendous that some of the Hasidim incline to consider that the genuine ego belongs to God alone and the human I is just a reflection of the divine ego, otherwise it is a null and void.[18] This is in contrast to Buber's view according to which "man becomes an I through a You", and the more he encounters the eternal You, the more clearly crystallizes his I in the consciousness.[19] According to Hasidism, the more he faces the presence of God, the more he diminishes his I. Abraham Joshua Heschel, a contemporary Jewish thinker and son of a celebrated Hasidic family, who was once appointed by Buber as his successor in Germany, expressed his Hasidic view against Buber regarding the subject:

> In prayer the 'I' becomes an 'it'. This is the discovery: what is an 'I' to me is, first of all and essentially, an 'it' to God. If it is God's mercy that lends eternity to a speck of being which is usually described as a self, then prayer begins as a moment of living as an 'it' in the presence of God. The closer to the presence of Him, the more obvious becomes the absurdity of the 'I'. The 'I' is dust and ashes. 'I am dust and ashes,' says Abraham.[20]

This understanding of the smallness of the ego in Hasidism is that which brings one to the idea of total helplessness of mankind. From this point on, if man wishes to achieve greatness, it is indispensable for him to return to God, to the state of self-extinction in God's presence. Only through this process can man mobilize the power of the Almighty for his own task to recreate everything and to achieve the elusive greatness he continually seeks.

8. Epilogue

The idea of self-extinction is probably a most desirable subject in ethics and morality as well as in religion. From the ethical point of view, it is felt as a sort of endless pain to man to maintain its implementation. There is pain of conflict at any subject which is imposed on man by force, even by the force of his own highest ethos. But Zen and Hasidism have found it as a goal available to man to attain, because they consider self-extinction as the gate through which one can return and reunify oneself with the source of the ultimate reality. Return is an authentic wish and aspiration of man's soul. It is a spontaneous act of man, therefore pains are no more pains. And as we have seen above, Hasidism and Zen, despite their similarity, differ from each other in details. The self-extinction results in independence of man from life and death in Zen, but in submission of man to God in Hasidism. The more careful clarification of other aspects in both religions is awaited.

NOTES
1. Many of Jewish intellectual movement (*Haskalah*), who were close friends of the Medelssohns of Berlin, became zealous advocates against Hasidism to censor Kabbalistic and Hasidic books in Austria, Poland and Russia throughout the 19th century. The details of antagonis is available by Raphael Mahler, "Hasidism And Haskalah" (Hebrew), Merhavya, 1961.
2. See, "Baal Shem" in Encyclopaedia Judaica, Jerusalem, 1971, vol. 4, col. 6f.
3. Martin Buber, "Tales of the Hasidism: Early Masters", New York, 1947, pp. 5f.
4. Cf. Samuel Dresner, "The Zaddik", London-New York-Toronto, 1960, pp. 113 141.
4'. Of Scholem's criticism of Buber, see the former's article "Martin Buber's Hasidism—*A Critique*", *Commentary*, November, 1964, pp. 31-39.
5. Lien Chi, "Rinzairoku, (The Collection of the Sayings of Lien-Chi)" (Chinese and Japanese), edited and interpreted by Sogen Asahina, Tokyo, 1966, p. 77.
6. ibid., p. 80
7. Cf. Heinreich Dumoulin, "A History of Zen Buddhism", Boston, 1963, pp. 273-281.
8. Dogen, "Shobo-genzo Bendo-wa", in "Dogen" edited and interpreted by Touru Terada and Yahoko Misuno, Tokyo 1970, vol. 1, p. 13.
9. Dov Baer of Mezhirech, "Maggid Devarav leYaakov" (Hebrew), at the section 96.
10. Levi Isaac of Berditchev, "Kedushath Levi", at the second half of the section

Bereshith. (See at the section (5) of "Kedushath Levi: Hasidic Exegesis on Pentateuch".)

11. "Rinzairoku", p. 90.
12. ibid., pp. 41f.
13. Cf., Solomon Schechter, "Some Aspects of Rabbinic Theology", New York, 1909, pp. 242-292.
14. Cf. Gershom Scholem, "Major Trends in Jewish Mysticism", New York, 1941, p. 280; Isaiah Tishby, "Doctrine of the Evil and the Kelipah in Lurianic Kabbalah" (Hebrew), Jerusalem, 1960.
15. One of Dov Baer's students, Elimelech of Lyzhansk (d. 1787) taught, "You should give your devoted intention to every worldly affair which you do, either eating or drinking and the rest of corporalities, for the heaven's sake to release holy sparks, for example, out of the food by taking it in holiness and purity."—"Noam Elimelech"(Hebrew) at the end of the section *Toledotn*; *See also* the commentary of Levi Isaac on the verse Joel 2:20, collected in "Kedushath Levi *Hashalem*" (Hebrew), Jerusalem, 1964, pp. 287f.
16. Dov Baer, ibid., at the section 97.
17. Levi Isaac, ibid., at the end of the section *Phekudy*. (in "kedushath Levi *Hashalem*", p. 176) This English translation was borrowed from Scholem's "Major Trends...", p. 5.
18. Levi Isaac, ibid., at the end of the section *Shemoth*; (in Kedushath Levi Hashalem, p. 90).
19. Martin Buber, "I And Thou", introduction and translation by Walter Kaufmann, New York, 1970, p. 80.
20. Abraham J. Heschel, "The Insecurity of Freedom", New York, 1966, p. 255: About his life, *see* F. A. Rothschild's introduction given to Heschel's anthology "Between God and Man", New York, 1959, pp. 7f.

THE VIRTUE OF SITTING

Akihisa Kondo

Anxiety—and its attendant states of self-dissatisfaction, emptiness, meaninglessness—is not the discovery and exclusive possession of the twentieth century; it is as old as the human mind itself. For Dogen, founder of the Soto Sect of Zen Buddhism in Japan some 700 years ago, anxiety is a reflection of the uncertainty of human existence. When this anxiety is consciously and acutely felt, moreover, there commences the flow of the Bodhi spirit that leads to enlightenment. Anxiety, then, accordng to Dogen, is the driving force to enlightenment. Without it as a spur we are left to flounder in a shallow, insecure life, eternally caught in the vicious circle of ignorance. Anxiety when accepted, therefore, works as the striking of a match in the dark, giving us a revealing glimpse of our impasse and at the same time igniting our desire to break out of it.

For most people ordinary daily life is a streamlined facade of so-called happy living, a life filled with competitiveness, jealousy, possessiveness, arrogance, humiliation, hate, love, aggressiveness, success, failure, and what not. At every turn our psychic energy is distracted and squandered in pursuit of this or that aim. We are trapped in the endless, blind, vicious circle of these drives. And because we are busily pursuing them, we do not have time to listen to our inner voice.

This voice comes from the depths of our real self. It may take the form of conscience, aesthetic feeling, creative thinking or activity, or just the warm, soft inner suggestion to return home. Whatever the form, it is the expression of something deep and basic, far beyond these forms. At the very moment when we hear and accept it we are actually affirming our real self. If we look deeper we find that listening to it is our unconscious act of faith—faith in our real self. Further, it is an unconscious act of our real self that leads us to have faith in it and

to listen to its voice. However powerful and overwhelming our ignorant drives are, the Real Self is always working in and through us. But
we do not have pure faith because our minds are too much pre-
occupied with other strong beliefs: in success, prestige, money, intellectual superiority. What we need is time and space so that, free from
all interruptions and distractions, we can at least once a day collect
our psychic energy and concentratedly bring it into direct contact with
our inner, most powerful resources. In order to feel vividly this kind of
pure faith we need to empty our mind, to liberate it from all false
values, and to experience directly our real self in its wholeness.

Psychoanalysis in its recent development has clarified the nature of
the blind drives which haunt us within the unconscious, and has
exerted its efforts to helping people realize specifically by what drives
they are driven. Horney called this kind of help a disillusioning process. She believed that when we become disillusioned of the idealized
image of ourselves that handcuffs the development of our real self,
our real self has a chance to grow . . . How ignorant human beings are
of themselves of the blind drives that are hindering them from listening to the voice of their real self ultimately come out of their idealized
image that is illusory. From the Zen point of view, this is a fine step in
discerning how grievously illusory are our ideas about ourselves and
our life . . . Especially as regards coming closer to one's self, the Zen
way is specific and positive . . .

In Zen practice, although the need to discern the illusory nature of
our concepts, ideas, and emotions is considered important, concentration of sitting is stressed. It is sitting with a single mind. What
does this mean? Those in the Zen temple will never make answer to
one who wishes to know before experiencing it. What they say, if
anything, is simply, "Just sit!" This is meaningful,because they know
from their experience that one can know the meaning of sitting only
by actually practicing sitting. The answer must come out of oneself,
by one's own experience. Single-mindedness is just single-mindedness and leaves no room for interrogation. It is a sheer act of faith in
oneself. It implies, therefore, total respect toward the real self. "What is
real self?" is not to be intellectually understood, it is to be experienced.
Zen regards sitting as the way in which to experience this Real Self.
Enlightenment, the realization of the true self, comes out of the
practice of sitting, out of the "sitting" state of mind, and this cannot be
vicariously understood. This single-minded state, it must be pointed
out, is not confined merely to static sitting, so called, but must carry
over and be strengthened in all our dynamic activities.

Dogen's advice about sitting is substantially as follows: Avoid distracting contacts and activities. Don't eat too much or too little. Sit in a quiet place on a thick rug or mat, with a pillow under your seat and your legs crossed in half-or full-lotus position (or sit in a straight-back chair with your feet flat on the floor). Keeping the back straight, breathe naturally from the depths of the lower part of the abdomen. Don't think about good or bad, yes or no. Become concentrated but not in thoughts.

When we sit as he advises, all our psychic energy that has been scattered as a result of our pursuits and internal conflicts is collected into a unity again. Of course at first, since our mind has been accustomed to functioning distractedly, sitting is felt to be a constriction of our activities. We become impatient and irritable, build up conflicting ideas, and feel desperate. Zen practice has been called the strenuous way to enlightenment, and it requires considerable effort; therefore we shrink from it. But this point is the test of our determination. Will we follow our old easy futile way of life or enter upon the path to liberation? This is the crossroads. If we truly realized the futility, meaning·lessness, and emptiness of our past way of life, our determination to seek emancipation will be stronger. In this connection I wish to point out the meaningfulness of Dogen's assertion that the consciousness of the Bodhi-Spirit as the propelling force for practicing Zen must be acutely experienced. If we continue to practice while fighting all kinds of temptations to escape, we come to experience a calmness that is charged with vitality. This comes about partly because our psychic energy is no more wasted in futile drives and partly because it has become unified. Nor is this all. Every part of our body and mind is filled with vitality. Actually we are not aware of mind apart from body or body apart from mind; only a total feeling of fullness exists. In this stage we are no longer separated from our sitting, so to speak. At this time, according to the school of Zen followed, some will concentrate on a *koan*, others will just practice sitting. Whatever the method, the result is the same: in place of the separatedness experienced before, more and more we enjoy oneness in ourselves. Our total being is strengthened as a consequence. We feel in ourselves tremendous stability, fullness, and harmony. We feel alive. So Dogen says, "Sitting is the gate-way of truth to total liberation."

This is the virtue of sitting that is called the power of sitting. This power or virtue achieved through sitting is not restricted in its functioning to the time of sitting. Once it is achieved it mobilizes and expresses itself every moment, and is strengthened through its functioning at all times. This may be called the dynamic functioning of the state of mind developed in sitting. It is, of course, different from the state of so-called enlightenment. Nonetheless in the steady deepening and strengthening of the practice of sitting there is enlightenment ever fulfilling itself. Enlightenment, then, is the fruit of sitting practice and not its goal. Actually, from a strict Zen point of view, in the very single-mindedness of the sitting and in the very life in which it functions, the real self is expressing itself most strongly and naturally without any consciousness on the part of the individual himself necessarily. In this sense only can we say there is enlightenment. According to Dogen, "There is enlightenment in practice and practice in enlightenment." To be sure, there are different expressions of experiences corresponding to differences in personality. Yet when one lives in the fullness of this kind of sitting, seriously absorbed in the problem of his true self, it is not astonishing that he can suddenly become enlightened at any time, since his real self is always expressing itself and only his consciousness is unaware of it. Emyo sought instruction from the Sixth Patriarch, who answered, "All right, I will teach you. At the very moment when you do not think good or bad, right or wrong, what is your original face?" Emyo was suddenly enlightened.

As a student of Zen I have personally profited a great deal. But as a therapist of neurotic patients I am greatly indebted to Zen teaching for their recovery. Perhaps, therefore, the following brief observations relating to my therapeutic experience with patients will not be inappropriate.

In addition to interview sessions, I strongly recommend patients to practice sitting as Dogen suggests. Inevitably at first it is almost unbearable for them. Some complain of physical pains and strains. Some complain of irritability and the great difficulty of keeping a motionless posture. Others say they feel more depressed and lonesome. Still others complain that they are haunted by stabbing ideas and fantasies and frustrated by their inability to achieve a tranquil state of mind. And some see only meaninglessness in this kind of practice. These protests add up to one general complaint: the method is ineffective and only leads to an intensification of the symptoms. This is quite understandable. In the first place, since they are accustomed to resorting to measures that achieve a pseudo-solution of their problems, they have an established pattern of activity. Sitting alone prohibits them from following their accustomed way of life. They feel frustrated because they can not follow their usual pattern of scattering their energy, which they take to be natural activity but which actually is an escape mechanism to avoid facing their problems. So they feel constriction. Secondly, when the dispersion of their energy in external activities is blocked, they have no other way to turn except inward. They now must see the inside of themselves. Again, in order to avoid facing their actual problems they start to juggle various ideas or fantasies. Nevertheless, especially for the shallow and aggressive patients, now comes the chance to experience themselves inwardly. Willynilly they see the problems they suffer from and hate to face. Because they hate to see the problem they hate the way they are brought to see it—that is why they think the method is ineffective. They feel their sufferings intensified because they have to see the problems causing their sufferings, the very problems from which they are trying to escape. In my interviews with the patient, of course I pay respectful attention to his complaints, as well as to the content of his ideas, fantasies, and emotional experiences, and I try to help him elucidate their meaning. But I suggest continuing to practice sitting, and advise him not to pay much attention to his ideas and fantasies, stressing only the importance of sitting itself. If the patient feels it difficult to sit more than fifteen minutes, I do not urge him to sit longer, but strongly advise him to sit regularly and devotedly every day. Usually patients concur in these instructions and begin to feel they can get along in their sitting. Not infrequently a patient reports that he does not know why, but he feels his irritability or anxiety considerably lessened. From the therapist's side it is very impressive that the patient, as he practices sitting steadily, begins to show, unconsciously, more intensive concentration in working on his problems in the therapeutic session. In other words, through the patient's practice of sitting his psychic energy has begun to become assembled, unified, and available for constructive work. I don't say that the patient after sitting for a period of time becomes enlightened. What I say is that he is helped considerably to become charged with more psychic energy and vitality. His dreams show a more constructive picture and his posture begins to show more stability. Often patients say, "When I sit I feel I am rooted and full of sap, where before I felt helplessly buffeted by every emotional wind or storm." Or "I feel as if there is a bubbling fountain within me. I don't feel tired or frustrated any more." It is noteworthy that in these self-expressions images of water or trees abound.

I believe, from my experience, that any teaching is ineffective fundamentally, whether it be psychoanalysis or psychotherapy or Zen, unless it helps a person feel, experience, and become confident of his fundamental resourcefulness, his real self, his Buddha-nature, his inborn freedom and security, his uniqueness and universality, from the inside of himself and by himself. Neurotic or normal, we are all human beings. As human beings we share the same fate. The neurotic's case is merely an extreme one. But as Buddhism teaches, basically we are all alike in our ignorance of ourselves and in our capability of becoming emancipated from such ignorance through self-realization. Buddhism from the very beginning of its long history clearly recognized the nature of human existence and sought to emancipate human beings from their suffering. Zen, however it may be understood, has this aim.

I have tried to show how Zen intends to bring us to self-realization through sitting. This is a practice leading to single-mindedness, first, by assembling our psychic energy into a unity, and second, by strengthening it through constant practice in our daily living, leading to a stage where we are fully charged with strong vitality and power, where we sit and act with stability and security—in other words, the stage of no-mindedness. It is always a matter of chance when the Self will come to its own realization in our consciousness. The enlightenment experience comes about through the ripening of sitting, just as a fruit or a flower appears as the natural result of the growth of the tree. The roots of such enlightenment have been nourished for a long time in the rich soil of sitting.

It is almost routine to talk about enlightenment. It is the ultimate in the practice of Zen and surely it is important. But how important is it to talk about enlightenment all the time when for those who are enlightened it is pointless and for those who are not, incomprehensible, and frequently a hindrance in that it agitates their already too greedy preoccupation with enlightenment? It is my belief that, enlightenment or not, sitting is strengthening. How much so is something one has to experience for himself . . .

After a number of interviews I asked a patient of mine who was very much concerned that she was an illegitimate child (and who had been sitting according to my instructions), "Who were you before you were an illegitimate child?" She looked puzzled for an instant, then suddenly burst into tears, crying out, "I am I! Oh, I am I!"

From *Chicago Review* (The University of Chicago), 1958

The Zen Cave

Paul Wienpahl

One of the earliest references to Ch'an or Zen Buddhism in the modern literature of the West occurs in Pierre Bayle's Dictionary with his long entry on Spinoza (2nd Ed. 1702). The reference is not by name. Bayle, indicating that Spinoza's philosophy is not new, compares it to the outlook of a "certain sect of Chinese theologians." No mention is made of zazen, or meditation, but it is clear in the reference that the sect was Ch'an. In 1906 one of the first books by a Zen Buddhist appeared in the United States: *Sermons of a Buddhist Abbott* by Soyen Shaku Roshi. However, it was not until 1927, when D. T. Suzuki published his *Essays in Zen Buddhism* (First Series), that anything appeared on the matter which was going to have an important impact. Nor did these essays and other writings by Suzuki have a wide-spread influence until the so-called "Zen boom" of the 1950's. The boom was an entirely literary phenomenon, which led Zuigan Goto Roshi to compare its effect to that of a firecracker. For the noise called no attention to the heart of Zen Buddhism: the practice of zazen, a way of meditating that requires total involvement of both the body and the mind of the practitioner.

During the 1960's this situation drastically and rapidly changed. A few individuals had gone to Japan to study Zen Buddhism. There they had found that all they had read of *satori* and the mysterious Zen-way had been highly misleading. They had been taught zazen and had practiced it long months and years, learning that there was very little reference to *satori* in the Rinzai and Soto temples. They returned to tell us of this, one of the most important messengers being Phillip Kapleau with his *The Three Pillars of Zen* (First Ed. 1965). The seeds they sowed fell on fertile ground. For those with an interest in Zen Buddhism who had remained at home had realized that there must be more to it than the fine-sounding words in the books. When they learned that there was something enormously realistic and practical, a physical practice of great power, they seized upon it. By 1976 a list of the names of Zen Centers throughout the United States, in which zazen is actively pursued as the basis of Zen study, fills a typescript of 8 x 11 sheets over an inch and a half thick.

This development leads naturally to questions that have received little public attention. We hear a great deal about the benefits of meditation, particularly in the popular forms such as Transcendental Meditation. What, however, if any, are the excesses possible with it; and is there a danger of being enslaved by it? The purpose of this article is to discuss some answers to these questions. I shall limit myself to Zen Buddhist meditation, zazen, with an occasional reference to a Western Christian form commonly called "contemplation."

I think that the question concerning possible excesses can be simply and directly answered by stipulating at the outset that there can be excesses in the performance of any activity. After my brother had learned to play the piano, he began to practice so excessively that his fingers attained a tendency to spasm so pernicious that the condition extended to his back and eventually rendered him incapable of playing the instrument. He now teaches musicology. It is reported that at one time Hakuin drove himself so hard that he suffered "meditation sickness." Another report has it that seven of his disciples died from the sickness. However, this sort of thing is, as indicated, not peculiar to the practice of zazen. Common sense warns against it, and it cannot be styled an excess of meditation.

Turning next to the question about a danger of being enslaved by meditation, we must note first that there are impediments to meditation which are generated within its practice. In one of its forms, Zen meditation or zazen, the student is taught to sit quietly in a certain manner and endeavor to empty his mind of all thoughts. There is a large number of aids for this, of which the most important is the teacher. There are also particular ways of breathing, counting breaths, and perhaps eventually the use of koans. However, almost immediately the impediments to the process appear. The practitioner may notice that it is very difficult to sit still for even a short length of time. His nose itches and he wants to scratch it. Later the legs begin to ache—the back, and so on.

With a little diligence these impediments are overcome and the student learns to sit quite quietly for relatively long periods. Then come the more serious difficulties and with them real dangers in zazen. Suddenly the student may find himself asking: "What the hell am I doing this for? So what, so you sit quietly. Meanwhile you look pretty damn silly sitting here day after day like an old fakir. Talk about being free. Talk about being enlightened. I'm just becoming a slave to another habit."

It is not that he cannot sit now. It is that somehow he does not want to. This is a sufficiently strong impediment that it nearly works. It nearly makes the student stop zazen. Indeed, unless strong measures are taken, it may make him stop it. He may think that by stopping it he gains his freedom. He finds himself thinking that breaking with the teacher, leaving the temple, and going home is an act all on his own. And making the break brings with it a feeling of exaltation. Then if he is lucky, or rather if his teacher is very good, something will be said or done that enables him to return to the practice. He has taken one step. Now he takes another, returning to zazen knowing that he is free in doing so.

There are more subtle things which can happen later on in the process which can distract the student even more dangerously from his work than one of the kind just considered. For these do not drive him from zazen. A variety of them sends him even more deeply into it. These are the phenomena of visions, hallucinations, revelations, and illusory sensations which in Japanese are called *makyo*, or "devil objects." Hearing voices, seeing Buddhas and Bodhisattvas, getting penetrating insights into things read that had been puzzling are not limited to those practicing zazen. Warnings about similar phenomena are given in Christian mystical documents. St. Theresa of Avila in her autobiography called them visitations by the Devil, even those that involved union with her beloved Christ. The anonymous author of *The Cloud of Unknowing* devotes Chp. 45 to "a word of warning" about them; and says, "for I truly tell you that the devil has his contemplatives as God has his." If you want to read about *makyo*, one of the most sensible discussions of them is that by Yasutani Roshi (see, for example, *The Three Pillars of Zen*, pp. 38-41).

We get more deeply into the matter in another section of his book in which Kapleau reproduces "Yaeko Iwasaki's Enlightenment Letters to Harada-Roshi and His Comments." Toward the end of these (p. 287) Miss Iwasaki, dying of tuberculosis but continuing with her zazen and deepening her enlightenment, writes: "I have come to understand clearly the single-minded love and respect I feel toward you. Already I have rid myself of the smell of enlightenment." Harad-Roshi's comment is: "Not quite. You are even now emitting the awful smell of enlightenment." Later (p. 298) Miss Iwasaki closes a letter: "Tears of gratitude and joy well up in me when I think that I have accomplished the practice of Zen from first to last without strain, and that I can receive your eternal guidance." It may be noted that Dogen said, "Meditation *is* enlightenment."

Harada-Roshi's comment is longer: "An ancient Zen saying has it that to become attached to one's own enlightenment is as much a sickness as to exhibit a maddeningly active ego. Indeed, the profounder the enlightenment, the worse the illness. In her case I think it would have taken two or three months for the most obvious symptoms to disappear, two or three years for the less obvious, and seven or eight for the most insidious. Such symptoms are less pronounced in one as gentle as she, but in some they are positively nauseating. Those who practice Zen must guard against them. My own sickness lasted almost ten years. Ha!"

We have here another form of "Zen sickness." It may be likened to what a Christian would call spiritual pride. It might then be said not to be a danger in zazen or contemplation, since many Christians come to suffer from this sickness without having become serious contemplatives. However, that it is, in the form to which Harada-Roshi refers, a danger typical of zazen may be seen in what has been called the "Zen Cave."

I first heard of this from Ruth Fuller Sazaki (it is rarely mentioned in the literature) when she told me that passing the first koan is crucial and requires the greatest effort. She then likened the way of Rinzai Zen to this: there is an absolute over there beyond the phenomenal world. Or so we think, and there is the Buddhist metaphor of getting to the other shore. The first major step is to jump over the phenomenal world to it. Then gradually, in further koans, the student moves back to the phenomenal world and sees that it is the absolute. The absolute is not something beyond and behind. The so-called phenomenal world is simply an aspect of the absolute. However, there is danger of getting caught in the "Zen cave", as it is called; that is, in making the first large step, liking the calm and quiet found in it; and staying there, feeling a disgust for the phenomena. Even if the student makes considerable progress, he may get stuck in the cave and fail to take the step out of it. That is, he may come to prefer the school (the temple) for the world for which it is the school, the monastic life for the workaday world.

Zen Buddhism has been aptly described as the religion of tranquility. However the description can be misleading, for it encourages an old and oft-repeated charge that the practice of zazen is a quietistic practice and that it leads to retirement from the world. This charge has been made so often and with such justification, that some of the developments in the history of Zen Buddhism have been moves made both to counter-act it, and that which gives it a basis. For the fact is that those who come to Zen may slide into mere quietism; that is, into the Zen cave, which makes them exhibit Haradi-Roshi's "sickness".

Thus in his *Essays in Zen Buddhism* (Second Series), when he came to discuss "The Growth of the Koan System" (pp. 83-91), D. T. Suzuki indicated that in the eleventh century when the system arose there were "two tendencies" at work "undermining Zen": "the doctrine and practice of absolute quietude" and "the habit of intellection." Suzuki refers to the latter as Zen Buddhism's "most deadly enemy." It is the habit of thinking that wonderful things are hidden in words and phrases and those who have it try to learn many words and phrases. This prevents them from ever having "the experience of Zen," for it takes them away from zazen. Such people either do not know or forget that the words are only "the finger pointing at the moon, and come to mistake the finger for the moon."

The metaphor is Daie's (Taï-houeï, 1089-1163), one of the greatest figures in Ch'an Buddhism, who relentlessly combatted quietism. Suzuki also quotes him on the first of the tendencies. "Blindly following the instruction given in the sutras where words are said to hinder the right understanding of the truth of Zen and Buddhism, they reject all verbal teachings and simply sit with eyes closed, letting down the eyebrows as if they were completely dead. They call this quiet-sitting, inner contemplation, and silent reflection. Not content with their own solitary practices, they try to induce others also to adopt and practice this wrong view of Zen. To such ignorant and simple-minded followers they would say, 'One day of quiet sitting means one day of progressive striving.' "

According to Suzuki one of the greatest developments in Zen Buddhism, the koan exercise, was introduced to combat these two tendencies, that of quietism being of special interest to us. We have no concern with the koan exercise. I refer to its introduction only as one of the moves that have been made to counter the most serious danger that awaits those who practice zazen.

There are often good reasons for being critical of meditation because the Buddhists sometimes misused it and because sitting in meditation itself, when not properly used, can be self-defeating and a crucial practice. There is a great danger in it.

A danger with sitting in meditation is that one can become attached to it, to the process of sitting formally in meditation (whether in a meditation hall or in one's own home). But the roots and the tree, knowledge and action are one. Sitting in meditation can be talked about as separate from everyday actions. However, in reality they are not two things. When formal meditation and everyday living are taken to be two diverse things, a mistake is being made. Meditation, then, should extend into everyday actions. Hence the need for the teaching that we must extend our innate knowledge.

We have here further insight into the nature of the Zen cave. One gets into it and perhaps cannot get out because meditation can result in subtly deepening the dualism which it is in part designed to dissolve. A way of talking about the goal for which it is designed is to say that it is to bring about non-dualism, or the awakening from dualism. Generally the latter is seeing things as really distinct from each other. Ultimately this consists in seeing God as distinct from the world, for example, or mind as distinct from body. The making of these distinctions stems from really distinguishing more particular things from each other: this tree from that, this person from that, and I from thee. An aspect of the Zen cave is distinguishing meditation from everyday living, becoming attached to the former (and all that can go with it, such as the quiet monastic life), and retreating from the latter. The Zen cave, then, is a form of dualism, which paradoxically assumes the guise or non-duality of taking oneness to lie in one of the polarities.

This is brought out in the history of the Oxherding pictures, widely known for their formulation of the levels of realization in Zen. These are now a sequence of ten illustrations annotated with comments in prose and verse, illustrating the developing stages of Zen realization through pictures. Earlier versions of five and eight pictures exist in which the ox becomes progressively whiter, the last painting being a circle. This implied that the realization of oneness (i.e., the facement of every conception of self and other) was the ultimate goal of Zen. But Kakuan, a Chinese Zen Master of the twelfth century, feeling this to be incomplete, added two more pictures beyond the circle to make it clear that the Zen man of the highest spiritual development lives in the mundane world of form and diversity and mingles with the utmost freedom among ordinary men, whom he inspires with his compassion and radiance to walk the Way of the Buddha" (*Three Pillars*, p. 301).

In their earlier culmination, in the eighth picture of a white circle (or void), they left the matter in the cave. The ninth picture of returning to the source in life (a picture of the branch of a tree) and then of the tenth (the man happily on his way to the market-place) take us out of the cave. The addition of these pictures stems from the same criticism of meditation. You are not there, on the Way, when you are stuck in the cave. There are further steps to be taken.

There is a far more recent example of the concern with the Zen cave in another important development in Zen Buddhism. I refer to the attempt to transplant it in the West, a move with many ramifications of which one of the most important has been the writings of D. T. Suzuki. It might be said that he brought a knowledge of Zen single-handedly to the West; first with his *Essays in Zen Buddhism*, beginning in 1927, and then with his many other writings which continued into the fifties. It was a prominent feature of these writings that they obscured the importance of zazen and emphasized that of *satori*, with the result that Zuigan Goto Roshi compared the so-called "Zen boom" of the fifties to the explosion of a firecracker.

This fact was mainly due to Suzuki's concern throughout his works to combat both the charge of and the tendency to quietism. For this reason he stressed those aspects of the history of Zen Buddhism that deal with efforts and the development of techniques for combatting quietism: and he stressed the aspect of insight or intuitive understanding (*satori*) in the practice of the Zen Buddhist to show that it is anything but mere sitting when it is properly carried out.

However, he stressed the matter of insight so greatly that, as far as Western readers were concerned, the pendulum swung in the other direction and the importance of zazen was overlooked.

Thus, if one turns to the indices in Suzuki's books, one finds very few references to zazen or to meditation. In the *Essays*, for example, there are only thirty pages, out of more than a thousand, devoted to explicit discussion of zazen. And in a chapter on the zendo or meditation hall in the first volume, there is no mention of what the hall is primarily used for: meditation. Furthermore, there are dozens of stories of how this or that man became enlightened by something that a master said or did, perhaps a single word or blow; and yet there are few references to the facts that all of those who became enlightened were at the time practicing zazen, that they continued to do so after the insight came to them, and that they got further insights.

The result of this stress for the unknowing reader was the impression that the insights (*satori*) are what count and that these came about solely because of some tricky saying or violent action by the master. Indeed, in the long chapter called "Practical Methods of Zen Instruction," these verbal tricks are discussed at length and classified, giving him who is not aware that they presuppose zazen the idea that short lectures, pithy remarks, and blows are the only methods of Zen instruction. In actuality they are preceded by instruction in zazen and are accompanied by the constant and unremitting practice of it.

In sum, zazen was at first neglected by the Western interest in Zen partly because the leading interpreter of Zen was concerned with refuting the charge of quietism (he avoided discussion of the basis for it).

That zazen does not eventuate in retreat from the world when practiced properly and with great care is attested not only by innumerable references by Zen teachers to the student's "everyday life" but also by the custom in Zen temples that requires everyone to work. There is an old saying among Zen Buddhists that a day of no work is a day of no eating.

To deal with the charge of quietism Suzuki emphasized *satori* or sudden awakening. Perhaps he over-emphasized it, for his books gave people the impression that miraculous things can occur with meditation. A story about Bankei is apt in this connection. It has been related that Bankei was once interrupted as he talked to his students by a Shinshu priest. " 'The founder of our sect,' boasted the priest, 'had such miraculous powers that he held a brush in his hand on one bank of the river, his attendant held up a paper on the other bank, and the teacher wrote the holy name of Amida through the air. Can you do such a wonderful thing?' Bankei replied lightly: 'Perhaps your fox can perform that trick, but that is not the matter of Zen. My miracle is that when I feel hungry I eat, and when I feel thirsty I drink.' " (Quoted in *The Matter of Zen*, Paul Wienpahl, p. 42.)

Like all forms of mysticism Zen Buddhism is noted for the paradoxes which cluster about it. The koans in Rinzai Zen Buddhism abound in paradoxes. Joshu said, "*mu*" (no), when asked if the dog has Buddha-nature. The Buddha had said that all sentient creatures have Buddha-nature. The great danger in zazen or Zen meditation, that of being enslaved by it or getting into the Zen cave, is of such force that it has produced its own paradoxes. In bringing Zen Buddhism to the West Suzuki caused its heart to be overlooked at first because he took such pains to avoid its being branded as quietism, which brand can only be applied to it because of the main pitfall in meditation. The practice, the essence of a great way of teaching, has repeatedly been overlooked or slighted because of a danger in it so great that it cannot be overlooked or slighted.

A last word, however, is necessary. It may well be unfair to refer to the Zen cave as I have. For the danger in meditation may arise not because of meditation, but because of the extraordinary difficulty there is in awakening from dualism and discursive thought to nondualism and direct or intuitive knowing. Thus, any technique that might help to bring this about might contain within it either the danger of attachment to it or some other equally pernicious pitfall. Therefore what I have called the "Zen cave" may not be the name of an illness that is peculiar to meditation.

III

CAN A JEW PRACTICE ZEN AND/OR BUDDHISM AND STILL REMAIN A JEW

If God is the lord of the whole world and creator of the multitude of beings, then why has he ordained misfortune in the world without making the whole world happy; for what purpose has he made a world that has injustice, deceit, falsehood and conceit? Or, (is) the lord of the world unrighteous in ordaining injustice where there could have been justice?

The Buddha
Jataka, VI, 208

Some Gurus not Inimical to Judaism

Zalman Schachter

On one of my journeys to Chicago, I was to meet with a group and conduct a meditation session. I wanted to buy some incense sticks, and as this was in the early 1960's, before head-shops, I knew of only a few outlets for joss sticks. Certain that I could always find some at the Vedanta Society, I called the Ramakrishna Vivekananda Mission and introduced myself. He said: "You Jews are such a spiritual people." I was puzzled by this and asked him how he meant that. "Everywhere I go," the Swami replied, "Bahai, Vedanta, Subud, Zen, Theosophical Society . . . they are full of Jews!" I was filled with both joy and dismay at this, for I knew it was so. The more spiritual the Jew, the more difficult it seems for him or her to find a place in the synagogue. This is largely so because the synagogue projects images of God, *Torah*, and the Sabbath which it celebrates through an entire liturgical structure, while appearing to allow little room for the celebration of spirit. It is no wonder that Jews drift to other places in search of a celebration more appropriate to them.

An unrequited longing

"Rationalism" has infected most of modern Judaism. Even modern Orthodoxy, in its response to the challenges of Reform, assumes the stance of rationalism. Jewish mysticism, it has been said, is fine for those who are deeply immersed in the *halakhic* life and, as such, have reached the plateau attainable by the normative means of piety. Having "filled their belly with *Talmud*," and reached the age of forty, they are deemed capable of entering into the mysteries of Judaism.

But for those unqualified, other ways are suggested: *Kashrut, T'fillin*, Daily prayer, *Shabbat* with the emphasis falling on the letter of the law. Then on the other side comes the Rationalist Reformers, who dispose of the "empty rituals," but who have nothing of substance to offer in their place. It is no wonder that so many are leaving in the midst of such polarization; leaving to nurture the tender shoots of youthful insights in what appears to be more fertile soil.

For there is no denying the current interest of Jews in mysticism. Even current secular Jewish literature shows an involvement in mysticism at one level or another (consider Elie Wiesel, I. B. Singer, Franz Kafka). It is a part of a general education to know the ideas and principles of Eastern teachings, in one form or another, which now pervade contemporary culture. Still the Jewish establishment is mainly unprepared to meet the new demands that this new consciousness calls for. Having been trained at a time when Dewey and Whitehead were in vogue, they have difficulty in discussing Tielhard de Chardin, Buckminster Fuller or D.T. Suzuki in a Jewish context.

Some attempts at fulfillment

The lives of our Jewish leaders, filled as they are with the demands of synagogue activities, coupled with their own interests and training, do not lend themselves to contemplation. High schoolers are enquiring about mysticism. It would be difficult to find a rabbi conversant enough with the Jewish counterparts of, for example, Tarot, I Ching, or astrology, to be able to discuss them with the young seeker.

There are a few (one might call them revolutionaries or reformers) who are insisting that there is a Jewish expression to spiritual needs. One finds people chanting the Sh'ma like a mantra. In an *Esalen-like* growth center, people wrapped in *talitot* sway in rapture and chant from a *Siddur* (most using English text) and dance, with great joy to greet the *Shabbat. Chavurot* are giving courses in the texts of Jewish mysticism, which are received with great interest by their members and the community outside. At Shlomo's House of Love and Prayer in San Francisco young people want to learn and to meditate. Many of them have come from other communes where the exciting rumor of Jewish mysticism had reached them. In New York, Rabbi Gelberman conducts services and gives counsel and instruction according to his insights in *Chassidism* and *Kabbalah*.

From *Sh'ma*, (Port Washington, New York), 1974

One man's guide to eastern mysticism

I do not consider it to be dangerous for persons of Jewish background to experience and explore Eastern Mysticism provided they check it out for technique and content. The older the system, the better the results. The process of a soul's way to G-d is often initiated by an excursion into the realms of the Eastern Religions. Of the forms of Yoga available, Hatha Yoga is surely no problem. But Bhakti Yoga may become a problem, especially as it relates to forms like KRSNA consciousness since the followers of Bhaktivedanta are asked for exclusive devotion and must deny all other religious ways. Satchitananda is a warm teacher appreciative of the Jewish way and encouraging people to find themselves in Judaism. Ramakrishna—Vivekananda people are generally helpful to Jews, as are Yogananda's followers. Zen can be helpful, especially the way it is taught by the San Francisco Zen Center; and Tassajara, Roshi Baker, is a very caring man. Wali Ali of the San Francisco Sufis, himself a Jew and the disciple of the late (Jewish) Sufi Sam Lewis, and Yogi Bhajan are friendly, and encourage their followers to deepen their Jewish experience.

I see the greatest problem in the fact that once the spiritual progress is initiated in the Jewish Seeker he, in order to integrate the experience into his life finds no place where he might do so with other Jews. I feel that a crash program in which interested rabbis and Hillel Directors would participate is called for.

The opportunities for helping are immense. If we reject these Jews, we reject the finest, most sensitive and spiritual persons of our age.

Beyond the Torah's Limits

Chaim Zvi Hollander

The article "Some gurus not inimical to Judaism" (Sh'ma 4/74) by Rabbi Zalman Schachter left me incredulous and profoundly distraught. Incredulous, because some years ago I was elated by an encounter with a deeply committed Jew who impressed me as having a rare gift and facility for kindling the flame of *Yiddishkeit* within the sensitive young people of our time: He was Zalman Schachter. Today Zalman Schachter is overtly recommending excursions into Eastern religions, albeit for the purpose of becoming a Jew with a "celebrated spirit". Profoundly distraught, because the essence of the message must be identified as inimical to the basic principle of Judaism, and thus it constitutes *hassata vehadakha*, the equivalent of a lure to engage in *Avoda Zara*, or forbidden religious service. My term "forbidden religious service" according to the *Halacha*, does not refer exclusively to service of pseudo-gods or "independent" forces of nature. The term also relates to the worship of the G-d of Israel in an exotic manner which lies outside the framework of *Halacha*. See Nachmanides re the tragedy of the golden calf, Exodus 32. He and other *Rishonim* (pre-*Shulkhan Aruch* legal authorities) explain that the act of worshipping the Golden Calf was nothing more than a deviationist form of worshipping the Almighty—deviationist in terms of the newly accepted *Halacha*; however to the innovators it was a familiar and effective way of celebrating the spirit and achieving rapport with the *Shechina*. Also see Ibn Ezra on Deuteronomy 12:30: "Guard yourself from following after the nations of Canaan and don't be tempted to inquire about their gods and say "How do these nations worship their gods and then I'll do likewise'." Comments Ibn Ezra: "I'll do likewise—in the service of my own G-d."

Zalman Schachter's incredible advice is a direct contradiction of the Almighty's request that we not seek out and explore the spiritual modes of the *Goyim*, even if it is for the purpose of enhancing our own spiritual experiences in the service of our G-d.

Gurus are not for Jews

We have had a long personal relationship with the G-d of Israel—called Jewish History. Throughout our history even a hint of compromising our love and exclusive worship within the unique framework of *Torah* tradition and *Halacha* was shunned. The annals of our history are full of the records of thousands who willingly were martyred so that their unique concept of G-d and His service would not be tainted in the least by the introduction of foreign concepts and methods of worship. There is a callous disdain for this need to preserve Judaism from inroads of extraneous theology or methods of worship in Schachter's notion that "Some gurus are not inimical to Judaism" and his idea that the young and spiritually sensitive should be encouraged to experiment with the spiritual disciplines of the ancient Eastern religions. There is a deprecation of all that is sacred to Judaism in the casualness of the suggestion that the "Bhaki Yoga may become a problem...since the followers of Bhaktivedenta are asked for exclusive devotion and must deny all other religious ways". Schachter advises that "Zen can be helpful, especially the way it is taught by the San Francisco Zen Center...." Assuming that San Francisco Zen is helpful and that it, hypothetically, is not banned by *Halacha*, the advice suggests a total lack of concern for the distinct possibility that unhelpful sorts of Zen and Yoga would encumber the unwary and uninitiated.

There is yet another grand fallacy in the article. Zalman Schachter seems to say that it is indeed possible for one to enter the mysteries of Judaism before having "filled one's belly with *Talmud*" and before having reached the age of forty. To know Jewish "mysticism" is to know the mysterious and hidden meaning of the *Torah* and G-d, but it is patently absurd to think that a mysterious meaning can be fathomed without the full awareness of the meaning of the mystery which lurks in the lower level of comprehension. Preceding the turn-on stuff there is a hidden meaning of the *Torah* at every level of comprehension.

Only Torah mysticism is valid

The greatest mystery is uncovered by the second grader who begins to see a pattern of Providence in the *Torah*. It is mysticism whenever a *parasha s'tumah*—a "sealed chapter"—unfolds; when a student unlocks the meaning of a passage in the *Tanach* or *Talmud* and is able to reconcile an apparent contradiction. There is no other meaningful mysticism. See the well-known verse of the *Sh'ma*, Deuteronomy 11.13: *"Vehaya im shamoa tishm'u el mitzvotai*: and it shall be if listen you will listen to my commandments". The double form "listen you will listen" is interpreted in the *Talmud* (*Sukkah* 46): if you will listen to the old you will hear the new. The idea is axiomatic—the new is a deeper dimension and an expansion of the old; there must be a continuum and progression of knowledge and spiritual experience. It is misleading to young people to dangle notions of ecstatic mysterious revelations without a grounding in the "old".

There is an implied blessing and attractive advice in Zalman Schachter's pronouncement that he doesn't consider the exploration of Eastern mysticism to be dangerous. In fact, according to the writer, "The process of a soul's way to G-d is often initiated by an excursion into the realms of Eastern religions." I confess my ignorance and plead guilty to my inability to discuss Teilhard de Chardin or D. T. Suzuki in a Jewish context. I also am hopelessly unable to discuss the Jewish counterparts of Tarot, I Ching or astrology. Of one thing, however, I am certain: the sampling of certain Eastern religions, regardless of the motive, is categorically and unequivocally a forbidden act.

Under other circumstances I would be wary of such dogmatically fundamentalist declarations. However when a clear license is proffered to a sensitive and thirsty but nevertheless Jewish young person, it is necessary to define the statement for what it really is. Our young people must know that there is no *Torah* authority which agrees with the exciting advice of Zalman Schachter. The *Halacha* is implicitly clear: The practice of any religion other than Judaism is, for a Jew, an act of *Avoda Zara*, and subsequently one must be prepared to offer one's very life rather than be persuaded to engage in the practice, no matter what the motive. The guru business and excursions into the realm of Eastern religion is the sort of thing that the *Halacha* forbids and categorizes as *"Yehareg v'al Yaavor*— let him choose to be killed by the coercer but let him not violate the precept of *Avoda Zara*."

Rabbi Zalman Schachter should expand the theme of chanting the *Sh'ma* like a mantra and even the notion about meditating and learning in Shlomo Carlebach's House of Love & Prayer in San Francisco. The rest of his suggestions are not for Jewish ears.

A Response: We Must Save Jews and Their Spark

Zalman Schachter

I read Rav Hollander's statement, and given his assumptions, he is right in his indignation and outrage. Imagine me going into a *Yeshiva* meeting *bakhurim* involved in their committed *Torah lishmah* studies, and me advocating that they dance around the *bimah* and chant *Hare Krishna*. (Did you notice *Krishna* in the *Megillah?* The first name in sentence I:14, a good name for a counsellor of the king who reigned from Hindu to Kush) then according to his assumptions he would be right in bringing down the full wrath of the laws dealing with the religious seducer.

I am not speaking to the *bakhurim* at the *Yeshiva*, whose Jewish commitment is clear and firm, but to the many Jews who went their way to explore the Far Eastern religions first. They discovered in their meditation that their Jewish souls burst forth from their inner being and, having attained a certain higher than usual level of consciousness, they check this out with me and look for ways of "getting into the Kabbalah". This is a different universe of discourse.

Many baaley t'shuvah returned from the near east. When you ask me to write an article dealing with the latter Jews and their trips and options, I just won't write from the space in which Rav Hollander and I would carry on *our* dialogue.

Many of the young men and women who today designate themselves as *baaley t'shuvah*, and are among the *Hasidim* of Lubavitch and Bratzlav, as well as those who flocked to the Bostoner Rebbe and Rav Freifeld's *Yeshiva*, Rav Goldstein's *Yeshiva* in Jerusalem, and others, came from worlds which were charged with the consciousness of the Far East and drugs. They came home to

From *Sh'ma* (Port Washington, New York), 1974

Judaism not as a result of the attitude of Rav Hollander, but of the attitude that "opened the door for the returning ones."

Many a parent concerned (not during the early years when they could have sent their children to dayschools, and when they could at home have lived according to *Torah* and *Mitzvot* but) upon becoming alarmed when their children have begun meditating and chanting or moved to an Ashram, need to be reassured that they need not ban their children from their homes, but instead need to be guided to establish some form of intensive and celebrative *Yiddishkeit* in their home so that their children will feel closer and share their higher "head space."

There are two kinds of souls

So my statement deserves to be seen in the context in which it was made. *Vekhakarta vedarashta hetev* (you shall diligently investigate) is part of the same law of *Mesit umadiakh* (one who lures people to apostasy.)

But I don't want to avoid the other element of his criticism, which will stand as a barrier between us. As I wrote in TRADITION— Spring 1961, there are two kinds of souls and the *hacham* type with his detachment cannot stand side-by-side with the *baal t'shuvah* type who seeks depth, fervor and involvement. Matters of inner temperament are not given to be sorted out by verbal means. As an empirical suggestion how he might best get an idea of the dynamics involved, he might try the following:

Given that Rav Hollander would make a three-day silent retreat and still his mind sitting vis-a-vis G-d in quiet surrender, and then from the perspective of one of our straying young people, go and visit a *shul, beth hamidrash*, and honestly check his responses, he might find a great deal that calls for improvement and for more esthetic style.

I too make the kind of *klappey khuz* (for public consumption) statements which are nothing but pious PR. But what about the gnawing dissatisfactions with callousness, smugness, insular thinking and quixotic prooftext jousting against the windmills of reality which are the unvoiced criticism we have *klappey pnim* (amongst ourselves)? They too call for incredulity and distress.

If Rav Hollander were to work with young Jews in the Bay Area who are presently involved in other ways for a year's time, I would like to reopen the dialogue with him away from prooftexts. We might meet on common experiential ground.

Concerning Zen
A Halachic Responsum

Chaim Tzvi Hollander

Dear Mr. Heifetz,

I am writing in response to your letter seeking Halachic clarification with reference to Zen Buddhism. I agree with you that your question is a vital one and it should be confronted. Your phrasing was "Can a Jew practice Zen and still remain a Jew, or is Zen merely a technique applicable to many life situations, and thus not anathema to Jews?"

First with regard to your phrasing of the question, I would say a Jew remains a Jew regardless of whether or not he practices Zen, even if it should be Avoda Zara. The gates of T'shuva are open to him. One's mistaken notions do not effect a release from one's duties and responsibilities as a Jew. The term "Din v'Cheshbon", judgment and reckoning, promised us in the heavenly court[1] is interpreted by the Gaon Elijah of Vilna: When one will be judged for a misdeed one will also be held accountable for failing to do a Mitzva at the very moment one was engaged in the misdeed. The prophet decries the idolatrous sins of our people in the early years of their settlement in the land of Canaan, "And the B'nei Yisrael continued to do what was evil in the eyes of G-d. They worshipped Baal, Ashterot, the gods of Aram, the gods of Zidon and Moab and the Ammonites and Philistines, and they forsook the Almighty and did not serve him".[2] They failed to serve Him! No Tefillin, Zizit and charity while engrossed in the metaphysics of Baal worship! Until the last moment the Almighty waits patiently, willing to receive everyone as soon as a fresh breath of reality and truth has penetrated the abyss of confusion.[3]

You have succeeded to overwhelm me with your discovery that Nyanaponika, a leading Buddhist of Ceylon, is Jewish, and the

statistics that 50% of Zen people in San Francisco and 33% of them
in Los Angeles are Jewish. A veritable epidemic. A few weeks ago I
also confronted this epidemic of defection to oriental religion. I met
the leader of a Krishna Temple who casually referred to fact that he
was Jewish. I also met another man who was a functionary in a
Buddhist Temple, whose name is Epstein. These encounters and
your statistics depress me. I see in this phenomenon the curse of
Leviticus, the "Tochacha": "Your sons and daughters will be turned
over to another nation while your eyes see this, and you will be
powerless to stop it..."[4] I'm pessimistic about the prospect of re-
versing the growing tide of our best children turning to a strange
foreign nation to discover the meaning of their lives. I write to you
with abiding faith that the words of Torah will burn their way
through the maze of oriental transcendentalism into which so
many of our best kids have strayed and there remain, wandering
about, seeking their ray of light.

A tragic scene is portrayed in the Sifra:[5] Elijah was walking
among the starving and bloated survivors of Jerusalem's destruction when he came upon a young boy, swollen with hunger and
lying in a pile of rubbish. He said to the boy, "Have any others of
your family survived?" The answer was, "I am the sole survivor of
3,000 members." Elijah asked, "Shall I teach you one lesson by
which you shall live?" "Yes", said the boy. "Then say Sh'ma Yisrael
Hashem Elokenu Hahsem Echad". "No", screamed the boy, "That
is unmentionable for me. My father did not teach me that." Then
he took an image he was clutching and pressed it to his heart,
embracing and kissing it, until his abdomen burst and the graven
image together with his corpse fell to the ground. This is the tragic
meaning of the verse "I shall throw your corpses upon the corpses
of your pagan idols".[6]

In the Krishna fellow, I saw the reincarnation of this boy in
Jerusalem; the hollow, sunken, emaciated face, shaven head and
baggy gown—clinging to the drab monastic life in the Krishna
temple, clutching to his heart the Bhagavad-Gita. He was a wasted
person, thrown upon the corpse of his Avoda Zara. To him and
others we speak and hold out hope of reunification with their
families and the family of Israel. It requires the reciting of the
Sh'ma.

The question whether or not Zen in particular is Avoda Zara, a
"pagan" form of worship, can be answered by first examining the
halachic definition of Avoda Zara, and subsequently analyzing the

essence of Zen. Fackenheim [7]formulates some provocative questions relevant to Judaism's view of idolatry. Why does Judaism take idolatry seriously since idolatry is the worship of nonexistent deities and only the "foolish thralldom to empty phantoms?" Why should the G-d of Israel be jealous about idolatry when this is a worship of no-gods? Finally Fackenheim protests "that it should fascinate some benighted ancients we might understand; that its lure should extend to moderns as well as ancients seems simply laughable. Imagine the evil inclination that says to a modern man, first 'steal your neighbor's money', then, 'seduce his pretty wife', and finally, 'prostrate yourself before a graven image'. What to the rabbis was the ultimate in evil fascination and the most devastating sin comes to us as a ludicrous anticlimax."

Maimonides, one of our greatest formulators of Halacha, speaks about the essence of Avoda Zara:[8] "In the days of Enoch mankind began to err in such a way as to repudiate wisdom itself, and this was the error: they said since the Lord Creator created these stars and planets through which to guide events on earth, and He placed them in the heavens and attributed honor to them, and they are His servants who serve Him, they should therefore be praised and glorified and given honor; and this is in fact the will of G-d. Just as a king wants his courtiers to receive honor, thus does G-d desire. When this idea came to them, people began to build temples to the stars, offer them sacrifices, praise and glorify them, and prostrate themselves before them in order to receive through them the favor of the Almighty, according to their mistaken view. This was the essence of Avoda Zara. It was not that they said there is no G-d besides this star—but their foolish mistake is that they imagine this service to be G-d's will."

We learn from this that man, who inherited the tradition of Adam and Noah, was expected to understand fully the nature of the Creator, because of the tradition first perceived by Adam and Noah via direct prophecy and subsequently transmitted to their progeny. To such an extent was this tradition clear that when man forgot it he was deemed guilty of betraying a fundamental condition of his very existence. These precepts were later reinforced through the Revelation at Sinai some 2448 years after Creation.

The main point here is that Avoda Zara is NOT belief in the stone face. Even when there exists a deep and abiding faith in the Creator, one may not allow oneself the luxury of innovating better ways of reaching and beseeching G-d. Maimonides further develops the rationale:

And not only is the turning toward the Avoda Zara in one's mind forbidden. Every thought which can cause the rooting out of any principle of the Torah must not be entertained in one's heart because the mind of man is limited and not all men can discern the full truth. If man were to be drawn after the thoughts of his own mind he would surely destroy the world because of his limited intellect. Sometimes he would explore the routes of worshiping the constellations and other times he would meditate about the one-ness of the Creator: is He or is He not, what is above, what is below, what was before and what is beyond? Sometimes he will meditate about prophecy: is it true or is it not? Other times he will reflect about the Torah itself; was there a Divine revelation or was there no such thing? Man will likely not know the appropriate measure (of the truth) in order to determine what in fact is the truth and thus he will become a "Min", an apostate. It is with regard to this matter that the Torah admonishes and states 'You shall not be enticed by your hearts and your eyes', that is to say one should not be distracted by one's limited mind and imagine that he can arrive at the truth through the medium of his mind alone. Our sages have interpreted 'after your eyes', that is "Minut", apostasy.[9]

To some extent there is a natural ability to fathom the concepts of G-d's service, as did our patriarch Abraham, but for us there is a tradition. We learned the specific do's and don'ts of how to serve G-d at Sinai and it is not possible to improve or modify those divinely revealed precepts.

We discern here that the whole problem of Avoda Zara is primarily one of forsaking the belief in the revealed truths and the rooting out of any elements of Torah. The main thing is that the G-d of Israel, the Revealer of Sinai, is forsaken. The blessings which He has bestowed are unrecognized. G-d is not jealous in the sense that He needs or cares about our worship. His anger reflects the reality that the individual who has ignored the unmistakable source of his blessings is not worthy of those blessings.

The adherent to Avoda Zara is like a boy who was riding comfortably on his father's shoulders while the father trudged through fire, water and wilderness, and then suddenly asks a passer-by, "Have you seen my father anywhere?" The devastating sin of

Avoda Zara lies basically in the nonrecognition of our Father and His will. This aspect, of non-recognition, is no less devastating today than in any other age.

There is, however, a difference. Today no one has any sort of fascination for serving G-d in better ways. The Yetzer Hara for Avoda Zara has long been removed from mankind. Ezra the Scribe, according to our Talmudic tradition, exorcised the "Yetzer Hara" shortly after he returned to the land of Israel from Babylonia with the second wave of settlers.[10] What had previously been a fierce passion for serving G-d, so fierce a passion that it sometimes overflowed into irregular channels, was reduced to phlegmatic nonchalance. The inclination to Avoda Zara was tamed by diminishing the passion for serving G-d. Today the most devout and fiery Chassid would seem apathetic when compared to an ardent Avoda Zara worshipper such as Ahab, and Manasseh. The Talmud relates that Manasseh once appeared in a dream to a great sage who had talked frivolously about him. He chided the sage, saying "If you would be living in my generation you would lift up your robe and run, not walk, after me to satisfy the Avoda Zara passion."[11] So although we have lost the flame, there remains a simmering glow within us. This enables us to sense a Divine presence in our lives, and it is what makes us culpable should we fail to recognize the Divine blessings which permeate life. Today our evil inclination will not say to us: Bow to the graven image; but it says "Steal your neighbor's money, seduce his wife," and finally "Forget about G-d who has given you the power to do all these things."

It is now evident that the atheist and the agnostic are included in the framework of Avoda Zara. We have seen from Maimonides' formulation that the essence of Avoda Zara is not the act of service to the graven image, but rather the negation of the will of the Creator, for this will cause one to root out one of the principles of Torah. It is evident that the total negation of G-d as the primary, everpresent and infinite Creator is no less Avoda Zara than the cry of "Eli atta," "You are my god," in the presence of a graven image. In both situations G-d is negated and reduced to inconsequentiality. The only practical difference between the two acts is that in the latter the Jewish courts in an autonomous Torah society are empowered to administer punishment. The atheist and agnostic who disavow G-d cannot be punished because no punishment is meted out without the performance of a specific physical act. Only the Bet Din she Ma' lah, G-d's own court, can deal with spiritual felonies and transgressions in the realm of thought and consciousness. As long as no act is performed in the service of a deity, the atheist can escape the punishment prescribed for Avoda Zara; however, the scope of his transgression against the Creator is not mitigated. The atheist and agnostic remain the antithesis of a Jew, who cut themselves off from the stream of Jewish social, religious and communal life, in this world and the world to come. Again the illuminating words of our great sage and teacher, the Rambam:[12]

> The following will have no share in the world to come, but will rather be cut off from the world to come and judged for their great transgressions forever: the "Min", the Apikores, the one who denies the reality of Torah. Five are classified as "Min": one who says that there is no G-d and that the world has no caretaker; one who says that there is a G-d and caretaker but that they are two or more; one who says that this Lord has a physical form; one who says that this G-d was not the first cause of all things; and also one who worships a star or planet and similar things, believing that these could be intermediaries between himself and the Master of the universe. Any of these is considered a "Min".

The atheist and agnostic is thus classified together with the pagan idolator, and even precedes him in this classification.

The literature which deals with the halachic status of the Meshumad, the apostate, generally includes the agnostic and the atheist, as well as the Avoda Zara practitioner. One issue related to the problem of defining Avoda Zara has to do with the commandment of saving a life. It is well-known that the Torah demands that life be saved at all costs and even at the expense of all other Mitzvot with the exception of Avoda Zara, adultery and murder, in which case one must not transgress but offer his life to sanctify the name of G-d.[13] With regard to idolatry the rationale is that existence is meaningless if one cannot deny Avoda Zara, because the confirmation of G-d's rule is the totality of Jewish existence. Now does the edict of "Yehareg v'al yaavor", submit to death rather than transgress, pertain only to Avoda Zara involving a specific act of worship which is punishable by the Bet Din, or does this Mitzva of Kiddush Hashem also pertain to one who contemplates embracing a doctrine of atheism or agnosticism?

One impeccable halachic source is a ruling by the sage Reb Chaim Brisker, z. l., who ruled that one must expose himself to the possibility of death rather than submit to a study of apostatic doctrine which may lead him to become a "Min". Evidently Red Chaim z.l. understood that the entry into apostasy or "Minut" lies within the category of Avoda Zara, albeit without the attendant halachic penalty.[14]

The aforementioned sources have explained the sense of Avoda Zara, and have shown that "K'fira", or denial, is identical to idolatry in terms of moral culpability and self-inflicted spiritual damage.

Do Buddhists deify the Buddha? Does Zen deify anything? Suzuki apprises us:" . . . this admiration of his (Buddha's) personality later developed into the deification of his being, and all the evils moral and physical were supposed to be warded off if one thought of him or his virtues."[15]

At least a significant portion of Buddhists agree with another statement of Suzuki in which he describes the religious ramifications of Buddhism: " . . . The process of deification thus constantly went on until, some centuries after the death of the Master, he became a direct manifestation of the Supreme Being himself—in fact, he was the Highest One in the flesh, in him there was a divine humanity in perfect realization. He was Son of G-d or the Buddha and the Redeemer of the world. He will then be considered by himself independently of his teaching; he will occupy the center of interest in the eyes of his followers. The teaching is of course important, but mainly as having come from the mouth of such an exalted spirit, and not necessarily as containing the truth of love or Enlightenment. Indeed, the teaching is to be interpreted in the light of the teacher's divine personality. The latter now predominates over the whole system; he is the centre whence radiate the rays of Enlightenment, salvation is only possible in believing in him as saviour."[16]

It is clear that those Zen masters who are influenced by this divine aspect of Buddhism, if only on a subconscious level, will inevitably transmit to their disciples certain elements of Avoda Zara. Halachically speaking, the slightest degree of Avoda Zara constitutes transgression.

There are, however, many Zen masters who profess that pure Zen in deity-free. These, then, will not become involved in Avoda Zara on an active, halachically-liable level. However, their teaching, if successful, leads directly to a posture of "Minut", denial, which makes one morally as culpable as if one actually worshipped an image, and therefore is clearly proscribed for a Jew.

Theravodus, the formulator of Hinayana Buddhism, categorically denied the existence of a soul, G-d and Creator. Bahm expresses amazement at the ingenuity of the numerous subtle distinctions which add up to the startling phenomenon of a religion without a soul-or a G-d. He writes: "Theravadins are also atheists; existence required no creator, and the doctrine of impermanence eliminates an enduring G-d as well as an enduring soul. Salvation is attained as nirvana when an illusory ego gives up its mistaken attachment both to a world mistaken as real and permanent and to a soul mistaken as real and permanent. The law of karma, or of causality (or "dependent origination"), explains how such illusions arise and why several rebirths of consciousness may be needed before it can free itself from bondage to its illusory existence."[17]

Consider further the unavoidable conclusion which must be drawn from Bahm's distillation: A Creator is perfectly dispensable. "Zen is high religion. It brings yea-saying to a pinnacle. It needs no G-d, no church, no future heaven, because it finds its goal immediately at hand. Zen is not atheistic, because Zen is not against anything. Whether thoughts of G-d or thoughts of no G-d present themselves, its yea-saying response is the same. Zen, as universal, can adapt itself to the forms, ceremonies, beliefs, and circumstances of any other religion, to any form of government, as well as to any occupation. Zen has no need of creed, but in Zen one can assent to a creed more efficiently. Zen is not forward-looking, but one may say "yes" more quickly and fully to his propective fate when in Zen.[18] Can there be any doubt in a Jew's mind that it's impossible to recite the "Shema" when saying yea to the suggestion of no-G-d?

Suzuki's view is also that Zen in particular dismisses the notion of G-d and relegates it to the realm of a human creation. What is Zen? That is a good question and it has been asked for centuries. One thing is certain, it is not rational, it is inconceivable and it is totally devoid of intellectuality. Neither does it have an emotional appeal. Yet it has and continues to captivate and enthrall millions. One succinct passage of Suzuki contains a key to understanding Zen: "Zen never explains but indicates, it does not appeal to circumlocution, nor does it generalize. It always deals with facts, concrete and tangible. Logically considered, Zen may be full of contradictions and repetitions. But as it stands above all things, it goes serenely on its own way. As a Zen master aptly puts it, 'carrying his home-made cane on the shoulder, he goes right on among the mountains one rising above another.' It does not challenge logic, it simply walks its path of facts, leaving all the rest to their own fates. It is only when logic neglecting its proper functions tries to step into the track of Zen that it loudly proclaims its principles and forcibly drives out the intruder. Zen is not an enemy of anything. There is no reason why it should antagonize the intellect which may sometimes be utilized for the cause of Zen itself."[19]

The essence of Zen deals only with concrete facts. It is a method of becoming aware of the finite phenomena of the material world. In doing this Zen rips away every vestige of awareness of G-d and any notion that the soul is a portion of the Divine within us and is an infinite, timeless entity. Assuredly there will be upheavals in the soul of a man who undertakes the difficult mental discipline of achieving a non-mind. But rather than finding the meaning, purpose and the way of living, one will feel the undertow of Zen pulling the soul of man out from under and he will sense the wrenching away of man's eternity. Can there be any doubt that whatever Zen is, purports to be, achieves, or purports to achieve, it does not need any help from G-d whatsoever. For that matter, G-d's being or non-being makes no difference since He obviously doesn't exist— and besides, Zen is too busy sitting and meditating.

The Min-Apikores philosophy of Zen is formalized by Suzuki: "We are all finite, we cannot live out of time and space; inasmuch as we are earth-created, there is no way to grasp the infinite, how can we deliver ourselves from the limitations of existence? This is perhaps the idea put in the first question of the monk, to which the master replies: Salvation must be sought in the finite itself, there is nothing infinite apart from finite things; if you seek something transcendental, that will cut you off from this world of relativity, which is the same thing as the annihilation of yourself. You do not want salvation at the cost of your own existence. If so, drink and eat, and find your way of freedom in this drinking and eating."[20]

It was stated that "Zen is not an enemy of anything." This should read "of anything physical." Zen does not launch frontal attacks on the notion of G-d, soul, the world to come, reward and punishment. It is much too busy finding out the real meaning of the stream and the mountain. Zen doesn't attack G-d; it merely waves away the notion of G-d as inconsequential, nonsensical stuff—a troublesome notion which can only disrupt the quietude of man and urge him to be dissatisfied with an existence that offers no nourishment for his G-dly image. A serene wave of the hand places Zen above all else.

"It doesn't challenge logic, it simply walks the path of facts, leaving all the rest to their own fates."

Is Zen or is it not a religion? Many writers have defined religion in such a novel manner so as to accommodate Zen very nicely into the family of major religions, although G-d is exorcised from the scene. The result is a notion to the effect that "Zen is a religion that transmutes the dread of duties yet undone into persistent awareness that the 'Kingdom of Heaven' is already at hand.[21] Zen, in other words, is Minut and Apikorsut. Centuries of devotion to the Zen idea by idealistic masters have had the cumulative effect of tinging Zen with a religious flavor, whether or not it really is a religion. Its longevity is a reflection of the potency of its promise to give salvation to its adherents. This promise is basically that man really will have no trouble if he will only not allow his bothersome Neshama to nag with those nasty symptoms of eternity. Such a "non-belligerent" posture is nothing less than Sh'mad—apostasy. Suzuki's litany of what Zen abhors leaves very little room for speculation as to whether or not Zen is inimical to Judaism; "As nature abhors a vacuum, Zen abhors anything coming between the fact and ourselves. According to Zen there is no struggle in the fact itself such as between the finite and the infinite, between the flesh and the spirit. These are idle distinctions fictitiously designed by the intellect for its own interest. Those who take them too seriously or those who try to read them into the very fact of life are those who take the finger for the moon. When we are hungry we eat; when we are sleepy we lay ourselves down; and where does the infinite or the finite come in here? Are not we complete in ourselves and each in himself? Life as it is lived suffices. It is only when the disquieting intellect steps in and tries to murder it that we stop to live and imagine ourselves to be short of or in something. Let the intellect alone, it has its usefulness in its proper sphere, but let it not interfere with the flowing of the life-stream."[22]

Without challenging, it proceeds to obliterate everything remotely spiritual.

Can one just take a short casual trip into Zen — remove the kernel and spit out the chaff? The real state of no-mind demands a total commitment to the discipline. There can be no halfway measures and once having sensed the difference between the one life and the other, it becomes very difficult to return. Suzuki compares the impact of Zen's casual utterances with deadly poisons that when they are once taken in "cause such a violent pain as to make one's intestines wriggle nine times and more."[23] Indeed the conversion from spiritual man to Min is not accomplished without a violent psychic upheaval. The new awareness,the third eye of Zen which sees only the meaning of now and here and exorcises the before and after, is enough to make the famous "sweat break out all over your back." Indeed there must occur a Satori when one wrenches oneself out of eternal existence. There must be a sense of exhilaration and movement, a momentary sense of release. However this movement is not upward; it is toward disintegration.

There is a popular maxim in the Talmud: "Go out and learn." I have gone out, and talked to lay practitioners and teachers of Zen. I wanted to corroborate or refute the printed reports with the living practice of Zen. I received some forthright responses from individuals who had no axes to grind. They corroborated and confirmed the published rhetoric. They believe with perfect faith that there is no G-d, no Creator, no reward, no punishment, no life after death, no commandments, no Divine will, no Revelation. There is only the great enlightenment of Nirvana or a Satori, and with this the attainment of perfect peace and a sense of unity with the cosmos.

Zen purports to deal only with the concrete, with the now and here, that is with "facts". If in fact, Zen would inculcate a true respect for factual data, not only would it open the third eye but also a fourth and a fifth.

There is also a Fact of History, which a truth seeker must recognize unless he chooses to live in a world of phantasy. These facts are as tangible as the stream and the mountain, although they exist only in the realm of knowledge and memory.

History contains many fables and myths, not more and not less than the mythology which is churned out by many stimulated contemporary minds. But historic facts are the foundations of the present-day reality structure. Zen master Epstein did have a grandfather named Epstein He was tormented by the Czar. He did pray to the G-d of Abraham. Grandfather Epstein did study the law of Moses, the Mishna of Yehuda HaNassi, the Talmud of Akiba and the commentaries of Elijah of Vilna. Zen master Epstein is a Zen master today because the Almighty Creator guided Grandfather Epstein through the Czar's snares and miraculously delivered him to Chicago. Undoubtedly some of our Zen-infatuated brothers and sisters are children of families who were burned in the Holocaust. Auschwitz and Dachau are still smoldering before our eyes and their eyes. Can we ever relegate this fact 'into a state of no-mind? Zen would say "Don't challenge," there is nothing, there is only the mountain, meditate upon it, learn the secret meaning of life from it, eat when you're hungry, dress when you're cold. We must point our finger to the Past and reflect on the truth that the past exists as a concrete reality.

That historical reality tends to become muted is also a real fact of life, but this malady has a cure: ask someone who was there, someone you know and trust, and live with the knowledge you've learned. "Ask your father and he will tell you, your elders and they will confirm."[24] Your father can and will verify the events of one generation past. Check out your father, too by asking an elder who lived two generations ago; then you will know, as if you were there, and the past will be the present.

Jewish belief in the "Lord your G-d who took you out of the land of Egypt" is not a construction of a troubled mind. It is not an exciting hypothesis. We were all subjugated in Egypt and walked out in the year 2448 after Creation, and we were all, at least three million of us, present at Sinai that year to receive the Torah through Divine revelation. Today we are in the year 5736, amere 3288 years later, and since Sinai we have maintained a meticulous record of an uninterrupted chain of Torah transmission from father to son and teacher to student.

When we were subsequently exiled to many lands, in no place of our dispersion has there ever arisen a doubt about the fundamental Halachot of Torah. We universally agree about the dates of our festivals, their meaning and the manner of observance. This thesis is presented to the king of the Khazars through the words of the "Chaver" in Yehuda Halevi's "Kuzari":[25] "G-d did not address the people of Israel at Sinai with the words 'I am the Creator of the world and your Creator.' He addressed the people with the words 'I am the G-d you worship who has led you out of the land of Egypt.' Now in the same style I spoke to you, O King, when you asked me about my creed. I answered you as one who knew these things first from personal experience and afterwards through uninterrupted tradition, which is equal to the former."

There are standards by which reality is measured. Judaism's standard is the reality of the Revelation at Sinai. The experience of Sinai was absolute and no phenomenon can be significant if it attempts to diminish any aspect of this Sinaitic revelation. To illustrate this idea consider the dilemma when a prophet appears and delivers a message of a new, Sinai-repealing doctrine. He is in fact suggesting that a new reality has superseded the previous Sinai —reality. If this man should demonstrate the ability to modify nature, suspend gravity, or split the sea, and with these awesome credentials demand in the name of G-d that we repudiate even a nuance of our Sinaitic experience, this man is a false prophet and must be repudiated. This concept is lucidly formulated by Maimonides in his "Epistle to Yemen". It is instructive, relevant and readable in the translation of Boaz Cohen.[25]

The special prayer recited on Tish'a b'Av contains the lamentation "Libi libi al Chal'lehem"—"My heart, my heart goes out to their slain ones"[26]. The Hebrew word for empty space is "Chalal". Our Torah is such a splendid heritage of beauty and truth, and its paths are so exceedingly pleasant, and yet some have chosen to cultivate "empty-mind" according to the admonition of the Zen teacher. They strive for true condition, true opinion, true enlightenment, and hope to enter the great Bodhisattva way and save all people from their suffering. In doing so they have become true "Chalal", empty and devoid of beauty and truth.

Judaism has a different exhortation about empty-mind and clear-mind. It is the passage in Deuteronomy 4:39—"And you shall know on this day, and place this knowledge upon your heart, that G-d (YKWK) is the All-mighty in the heavens above and upon the earth below; there is nothing else." Judaism says empty your mind of any notion that there is anything but the Creator, and do not allow this knowledge to slip away from your consciousness. After this reflection the mountain of Sinai will once again become the mountain.

NOTES

1 Ethics of the Fathers (Pirkei Avot) Ch 3:1
2 Judges Ch. 9
3 Maimonides Codex, Hilchot Tshuva 3:14
4 Leviticus 28:32
5 Sifra Ch 26:30 and Bab. Talmud, Sanhedrin 63A
6 Deuteronomy 26:30
7 Fackenheim, E., Encounters Between Judaism and Modern Philosophy, 1973, p. 178
8 Maimonides Codex, Hilchot Avoda-Zara Ch I:I
9 ibid, paragraph 3
10 Bab. Talmud Yoma, 69B and Sanhedrin 64A
11 Bab. Talmud, Sanhedrin 102B
12 Maimonides Codes, Hilchot Tshuva 3:5. 6, 7
13 Bab. Talmud, Yoma 82A: Sanhedrin 74A: Pesachim 25A

14 Birkat Shmuel: Boruch Ber Lebowitz, Kiddushin Ch 27, paragraph 6
15 D. T. Suzuki, Zen Buddhism, p. 37
16 ibid
17 Archie J. Bahm, The World's Living Religions, p. 113
18 ibid, p. 120
19 Suzuki, ibid, p. 10
20 ibid, p. 14
21 Bahm, ibid, p. 216
22 Suzuki, ibid, p. 9
23 ibid, p. 20
24 Deuteronomy 32:7
25 Yehuda Halevei, The Kuzari, Schocken, New York (1968), p. 46
26 Moses Maimonides, Epistle to Yemen, American Academy for Jewish Research, 1952, translation by Boaz Cohen,

For They Bow Down To Emptiness and The Void

Zalman Schachter

Dear Harold:

You write that you read the exchange between Rav Hollander and myself in Sh'ma, and that you are now disquieted since you have been doing zazen for the last year and a half and gained much benefit from it.

You point out further that in the past, if someone had said to you 'zazen is against Halakha,' you would not have cared. As you have from time to time told me you saw in Halakha the skeleton of an outworn parental tradition which, so you experienced it, betrayed you at your Bar Mitzvah. When we talked about this we decided not to look upon whom to lay the blame. The parents and teachers were no less misguided than you. But we left this and spoke of your soul's awakening, first through chemical aid, then through communal experience, encounter and sensitivity training, and finally through the aid of many variants of Far Eastern religions and some profound love relationships; ultimately with meeting your beloved Roshi, Ananda upon his atman (how else can I say Alav Hashalom?).

You told me of your becoming a lay devotee who "sits" every day, practices "Beginner's Mind" during your daily pursuit and seeks your Roshi's (your late Roshi's successor's mondo) counsel from time to time. And yes, I need to add that our friendship began at a weekend at . . ., when out of curiosity you wanted to see what an Aquarian Hasidic Shabbat was all about. You began to read Jewish books, The Jewish Catalogue, Jewish periodicals and Sh'ma among them when this exchange occurred. You made, I recall, a great effort to attend the Torah Dharma Day at Berkeley.

You told me that you were glad to hear a Zen prior, Sufi Shaikh, and 3H Sadhu, all of Jewish birth, discuss their journey. Especially when it was (in a somewhat pained and humorous way) admitted that almost all the seekers of Jewish extraction had experienced the intrusion of "schmaltz," warm Jewish bhakti images in either their own Bhakti, or making talmudic insight connections in Jnana, or other Jewish intrusions into their emptying.

They concurred that repressing the Jewish stuff brought about an inner drying up, and so they reopened themselves to the Jewish stuff, to varying levels of Jewish involvement. Now you wonder is Rav Hollander right? Then what are you to do? You trust me enough to be able to help you and I intend not to betray that trust.

As Rav, I have to agree with Hollander in his general view, though not in his extremist formulation. As spiritual guide, (let us grant that I write now from that place), I disagree with the most basic of his premises.

I trust that the movement of a soul toward G-d, enlightenment and self-realization, is not under the category of routine service for a Jew, but under the category of T'shuvah, turning toward G-d. Halakha is not the body of law that knows about this. Spiritual direction by living persons is. This is what Hasidism has taught me.

In the movement of T'shuvah, we are told of two things: one is the T'shuvah done out of fear; the other is the T'shuvah done out of love; his intentional sins are reckoned as merit.

By no stretch of the imagination can I think of the Jews I have met at encounter groups in ashrams, zendos etc., as people driven to return to G-d out of fear. A deep love and longing motivates them and nothing could be farther from their mind than either the hope for monetary gain, social prominence or the fear of punishment, human or divine.

The one important category under which I can think of them from the Torah perspective, is that of Baaley-t'shuvah—out of love.—The process of their movement toward G-d is not ours or Hollander's or anyone else's to predict. The process I am talking about is G-d and the soul finding their most fruitful interaction for the growth of the soul, and for that soul's participation in the building of the divine kingdom here on earth.

I must tell you of an occurrence that touched me profoundly: I was at Naropa Institute (Boulder, Colorado) last summer. While I taught a course in Jewish mysticism there, my father, of blessed memory, passed on. I did the shiv'ah in Boulder. Reb Allen Ginsberg participated in the minyon. He read Psalm 49, the one to be recited in the house of the mourner, as if he had written it. I led the alenu, and as I came to the words, "for they bow down to Emptiness and the Void," the teachings in Chogyam Trungpa's yeshiva in Boulder and the words emptiness and void (hevel wariq) made an altogether different sense to me than they have ever before.

You call it kensho, don't you? That is, when the inner and outer, the upper and lower, the momentary and the eternal all coalesce together, and regular reality comes back just so. Once emptiness and void had been freed from a bad value judgement on my part, and seen in the same perspective as King of Kings, the Holy One, blessed be He whose highest attribute is NO-THING, I was once again in touch with the one aim of all religions.

I wished I had an eternity to reflect on this, but Kaddish came up, and I had to put my super-WOW into the words of bechayeychon uveyomechon, and was once more connected with the here and now, and with my Jewish expression of it. With it came the rhythm of kaddish in the morning, kaddish in the evening, the seven days, the thirty days of mourning, the high holy days, and the most delightful time punctuator: the Shabbat.

Suddenly, I am aware that the discussion of this matter has translated itself to another plane, one in which the categories of the Sh'ma exchange are insignificant. What is significant is that there is a mountain, and we are all climbing it, and we all want to get to the top, and we all call that mountain and the path leading to it by different names, and when we get to the top we get to see what we are, always were and will be. Then we get our orders to go down and fix this place, our mother earth, to establish the kingdom of Him, whom we call the Almighty, and get to live the heavenly days right here on this planet.

To get this to happen we have to be spiritual empiricists. So what works is what's true. Behind the discussions such as Rav Hollander's and mine, the following slip stands back of the argument. It concerns the nature of the man whom G-d had created in his image. The means we use to create such a perfect man is the path. The view of G-d one holds, and hence the view of the perfect man made in his image who is led on path, that path being Halakh, the Tao, the Dharma etc. .

But is this *etc.* not Avodah Zarah? An alien form of worship? No Halakhic objection could be raised even from the Hollander camp to the worship of an anikonic infinite G-d. To call the encounter with the Void the worship of a heathen god is absurd. First there is a mountain. Then there is not the mountain. Then there is. This is not religion. And even if it were religion, how could anybody forbid this, least of all, G-d?

So there is in that Zen part a portion that is a religion; that has customs, ritual, images and forms, a hierarchy, a liturgy, etc., and as much as you can participate in it, it is universal. And as much as you cannot participate in it, because it is Japanese, ethnic, located in a different kind of space, and appearing under archaic forms, it is Avodah Zarah.

If Avodah Zarah is not the category under which you can be supposed to sin, sitting for endless hours in the presence of a void, not doing anything, there remains only the category of having wasted time from the study of Torah.

However, I do not think that you would have difficulty convincing the heavenly tribunal at the final judgement that you were *not* wasting time, investing, perhaps, in no-thing. If you ask whether it is okay for you to adorn Buddhas, light incense sticks, chant mantras, etc., from what I know of Zen and its aims, yes. But from what I know of the Hara Krishnites and their aim, no. What I'm saying is, that from what I know of the attitude that Zen has to the function of the sacramental acts and their meaning, I know of nothing objectionable, given a lucid understanding of Zen aims by the strictest Halahkist. On the other hand, I.S.O.N. (Hare Krishna), besides participating in every single aspect of what the Pentateuch considers idolatry, it also demands the total abnegation of any other religion, and demands that you give up Judaism. That is the basis for my decision that it is Avodah Zarah, idolatory.

In all this I am saying that some people have not made it to G-d, to realization, to Judaism, to Halakh, to T'shuva, through that way. So please G-d, we will yet talk about this, and meditate and davven together for more and clearer light. May you have luminous years ahead of you.

Harold—
In Zen all concepts are destroyed.
"If you meet the Buddha, slay him."
Self is destroyed.
The very notion of "existence" itself
is discarded.
How could "being a Jew"* be of
importance to one on such a
path?

Gary Snyder

*   or man,
    or Moslem,
    or woman,
    or black,
    or human,
    etc.

I V

THE OVER-VIEW

Commentary

I had the feeling that everything was being sloughed away; everything I aimed at or wished for or thought, the whole phantasmagoria of earthly existence, fell away or was stripped from me—an extremely painful process. Nevertheless something remained; it was as if I now carried along with me everything I had ever experienced or done, everything that had happened around me. I might also say; it was with me, and I was it. I consisted of all that, so to speak. I consisted of my own history, and I felt with great certainty: this is what I am. I am a bundle of what has been, and what has been accomplished.

This experience gave me a feeling of extreme poverty, but at the same time of great fullness. There was no longer anything I wanted or desired. I existed in an objective form; I was what I had been and lived. At first, the sense of annihilation predominated, of having been stripped and pillaged; but suddenly that became of no consequence. Everything seemed to be past; what remained was a fait accompli, without any reference back to what had been. There was no longer any regret that something had dropped away or been taken away. On the contrary; I had everything that I was, and that was everything.

C. G. JUNG
"Memories, Dreams, Relections"

Recorded and edited by Aniela Jaffe
Translated by Richard and Clara Winston
Pantheon Books, a division of Random House, Inc.

Zen and Hasidism

Martin Buber

I begin with a story, which proves quite clearly how a certain theme may be common to different religious spheres, but which shows us at the same time that the establishment of this common factor by itself signifies no great advance.

The story is told of Rabbi Aaron of Karlin, a favorite disciple of the Maggid of Mesritch, who died young. A fellow disciple, returning home from Mesritch, came about midnight to Karlin, and desired to greet his friend. He at once went to his house, and knocked on the lighted window. "Who are you?" asked a voice from within, and, certain that Rabbi Aaron would recognise his voice, he answered, "I." No reply came, and the door was not opened, although he knocked again and again. At last he cried, "Aaron, why do you not open to me?" Then he heard from within, "Who is it who is so bold to say 'I,' as God alone may do?" He said in his heart, "I have not yet learned my lesson," and returned immediately to the Maggid.

We know this story, and in a fuller version, from the literature of the Sufi sect of Islam, from the first part of the collection of mystic parables "Mesnewi" of the Persian poet, Jalal-ed-din Rumi. There is no mention here of the name of one of the great Sufis, everything remaining anonymous. A man knocks at his friend's door. The friend asks, "Who is there?" He answers, "I." The friend sends him away. For a full year the grief of separation burns within him, then he comes and knocks again. To his friend's question, "Who is it?" he replies, "Thou." And at once the room is opened to him, wherein is no space for two "I's," that of God (of the "friend") and that of the man.

Doubtless the theme does not originate with Rumi. In the opinion of Massignon and Paul Kraus its source is a saying of the mystic martyr, al-Hallaj, quoted by Solami. There God rejects the faithful one, who answers "It is I," but receives him, when he returns and gives the answer "No, it is thou, my Lord." And in that moment his desire for God becomes God's desire for him.

It is indeed possible that the appearance of the theme—in fragmentary form—in Hasidism may be traced back to Sufi influence, perhaps through Turkey in the Sabbatian era. So far as I know it cannot be proved. For us here the question is unimportant. For we have before us an inner connection not between Sufism and Hasidism alone, which would attest a special proximity between them. We find parallels not only in Indian Bhakti mysticism and in the Rhenish monastic mysticism of the Middle Ages, but also in a mystic system, which, unlike them all, bears no theistic stamp, the Chinese Zen-Buddhism, which we shall consider further. There it is told how a monk from another Buddhist sect, following the advice of a Zen monk, absorbs himself in inner contemplation. In the grey morning light he hears a flute playing, falls into an ecstasy, runs to the cell of his friend, and knocks on the door. To the question "Who is it?" he replies, "I." Whereupon the other rebukes him, "Why do you get drunk, and snort away the whole night on the street?" The following day he attains the "right attitude," and expresses it in these words, "Now no more do I have an idle dream on my pillow, I let the fluteplayer play whatever tune he wills." In the symbolic language of Zen this means that he no longer opposes the "I" to the Being, but experienes the Unity.

We may regard the theme as one common to mysticism generally, one in which its tendency to eliminate the barrier between I and Thou, in order to experience Unity, has found a pictorial expression. With regard to typology the comparison has not led us beyond the general sphere.

We come far nearer to an understanding of what is peculiar to Hasidism, if we compare some of its legends with legends of Zen, with just that sect, or more correctly with one out of that sect-group within the Mahayana, which held itself far from the theistic elements which had arisen in it. Here it is proved, that in comparing historical manifestations in the realm of mysticism, it is not always good to begin with a central religious content; it may be more fruitful to set out from life itself, from the relationship to concrete reality, and only finally to inquire after the central content, which it is true exercises a definite influence on the realm of the concrete too.

Zen's . . . most important characteristic is that it declines to make any direct utterance on transcendent matters. According to tradition Buddha himself refused to speak of the realm of the transcendent, and substantiated it by saying that such talk is of no avail in seeking the path of redemption. From this the Zen-school evolved the teaching, that man could not even think of the Absolute as such, let alone express it.

In a particularly authoritative writing of the Mahayana, the Lankavatara Sutra, it is said, "Ideas and judgments depend upon each other, they are unable to express the highest reality." This conforms utterly with the saying of Lao-tse, "The Tao, that can be told, is not the eternal Tao." In many formulations of Zen we can see the influence of Taoistic teaching, that truth is above antithetics. All conceptual assertion submits its object to the law of contradiction. It brings it down to the dialectic plane, where it is possible to place an antithesis in opposition to every thesis, and thus absolute truth is transformed into relative truth.

Therefore the Zen-school even refuses to recognize the opposition of concepts in classical Buddhism, that between Sansara, the "stream" of incessant being, and Nirvana, the running dry of the stream: in truth both are one. "The highest truth," it says in an early Zen text, "is not difficult, it only spurns choice"; that is, the rational urge to expound either "a" or "non-a" as the truth and not both at once. Hence the Absolute may not be apprehended through anything universal, instead it may be apprehended through the tangible and concrete, through something that we experience.

Zen teachers tell the story of how Buddha, when he desired to impart the full teaching, held up a flower, and smiled in silence; only one in the assembled throng, his disciple, Kashyapa, understood him and smiled too. The Zen-school traces its tradition back to Kashyapa, who received the mystery from Buddha. According to this, the import of this tradition cannot be to hand down spiritual values in abstract speech. But also all established methods of meditation appear merely as more or less questionable expedients and not as the way to the attainment of truth; indeed some even designate them as a disease. When the pupil asks about the transcendental, the teacher shows him, for example, his staff, as if to oppose the concrete to the universal. Or he raises his finger. Or he breaks forth into the cry, now famous in the history of the school, "Kwats!" Or, if notwithstanding he speaks, he speaks a verse. And sometimes he even strikes the disciple in order to transport him at once into reality, where the mystery, superior to all Yes and No, will be revealed, the mystery that cannot be transmitted except by letting it spring from the heart of the disciple under the influence of the teacher.

"Everyone," it is said, "should find the heart of the Buddha in his own heart." Not by turning away from reality, but only by surrendering himself to it, can man achieve salvation. In accordance with this, Zen cloisters are not places of contemplation for individuals, but fellowship settlements of landworkers; the work is the foundation of their life. Of the patriarch, who founded this way of life in the eighth century, it is told, that when the monks besought him to tell them the secret truth, he commanded them to go to work in the fields, and after their return (he said) he would speak to them. When they returned, he went to meet them, spread out his arms, and pointed at them.

Through the activity of his whole spiritual-corporal being man achieves intimate intercourse with concrete reality, in intimate intercourse with concrete reality man becomes capable of grasping the truth, and in turn the comprehension of the truth leads to the highest concentration of deed. Hence comes the determining influence exercised by Zen upon the military caste of the Samurai. The sword masters were accustomed, before they went into battle, to come to the great Zen teachers, and to learn from them the highest concentration. There they learned, as one of them says, that "those who cleave to life are dead, and those who defy death live."

I should like now to compare some Hasidic stories with analogous stories of the Zen school.

It is told of Rabbi Shmelke of Nikolsburg, that one of his disciples complained to him that "alien thoughts" were troubling him at prayer. The Rabbi told him to go to another disciple, Rabbi Abraham Haim of Zloczov, at that time an innkeeper, and to spend some time with him. For two weeks the disciple observed the habits of the master of the house. He saw every day how he prayed and how he worked, and remarked nothing unusual in him. It was only in the evening, after all the customers had departed, and in the early morning, before they arrived, that he did not know wherein Rabbi Abraham Haim busied himself. Finally he dared to ask him about it. The latter told him that in the evening he washed all the dishes, and as, in the course of the night, dust settled on them again, he washed them afresh in the morning, and he was particularly careful to see that they did not become rusty. When the disciple returned to Rabbi Shmelke and told him all this, he said, "Now you know what you need to know." In the writings of Zen we find the theme in a narrower setting. A monk asks the Superior of his monastery, a great teacher of the ninth century, to reveal to him the secret of the doctrine. The teacher asks, "Have you had your breakfast?" "Yes," he answers. "Then wash the dishes," the teacher says to him. And as he hears this, the disciple receives the inner illumination.

In the Hasidic story the symbolic character of the occurrence is emphasized, whereas in the Zen story it remains concealed, and in the literature the meaning of the saying is discussed; it remains however almost without doubt, that the washing of the dishes is here also a symbol of a spiritual activity. But in spite of the explanation given in the Hasidic story, it would be wrong to understand the doings as purely symbolic. It is really meant that a man should do whatever he has to do (as here the washing of dishes) with complete concentration, with the gathering together of all his being, with full intent, and without turning one's eyes from anything.

After the death of Rabbi Moses of Kobryn the Rabbi of Kotzk asked a disciple of the deceased, what had been the most important thing for his master. He answered, "Always what he was engaged in at the moment." And the Abbot of a Zen monastery is asked, "One of the first patriarchs has said, 'There is a word, which, when understood, wipes out the sins of innumerable aeons'. What is this word?" He answers, "Right under your nose!" The disciple asks again, "What does that mean?" "This is all I can say," replies the teacher.

Both answers, the Hasidic and the Zenic, are almost alike: the key to the truth is the next deed, and this key opens the door, if the deed is so done, that the meaning of the act finds its fulfilment here.

The teacher therefore is the man who does whatever he does adequately, and the core of his teaching is this: that he allows the disciple to take part in his life and so grasp the secret of the doing. Rabbi Mendel of Rymanow used to say that he learned the Torah from every limb of his teacher, Rabbi Elimelekh. The same thing, only from the other side, is said by the Zen teacher. When a disciple, who is serving him, complains that he has not yet initiated him into the wisdom of the spirit, he answers, "From the day of your coming I have not ceased to instruct you in the wisdom of the spirit." "In what way, master?" asks the disciple, and the teacher explains to him, "When you brought me a cup of tea, did I not accept it? When you bowed before me, did I not respond to your greeting?" The disciple kept his head hanging, and now the teacher explains further, "If you want to see, look straight into the object; but if you try to brood over it, you have already missed it."

Hence truth in the world of men is not to be found contained in a piece of knowledge but only as human existence. Man does not reflect upon it, he does not declare it, he does not perceive it, but he lives it, and receives it as life. In Zen and in Hasidism this is expressed in almost the same language. The "Song on experiencing the truth" of a Zen teacher about the year 700 begins with the verse, "Have you never seen a man, who is truth itself?" And Hasidism says just the same thing, when it applies the word of David "And this is the teaching of man" to a man who has become a complete teaching in himself. In almost the same language here and there the holiest teaching is rejected, if it is found in someone only as a content of his thinking. According to the Hasidic view it is dangerous "to know too much Hadisuth," because one can come to know more than one performs, and one of the Zen teachers reproaches his disciple with this failing, that he "has too much Zen"; "If Zen is spoken about," he says, "I am filled with disgust."

Here and there silence is held in honor. And here and there it is not intended to refrain from all expression, but only to renounce all abstract observations on that which is not given to abstraction. Here and there singing takes place, here and there folk themes are introduced in song and transformed into mystical ones. The Zen monk paints too, and his importance in the development of East-Asiatic art is great. The Hasid cannot paint, but he dances. All this, song, painting, and dance, means expression, and is understood as expression. Silence is not the last. "Learn to keep silence, so that you may know how to speak," says a Zaddik, and one of the Zen teachers says, "Talk is abuse, but silence is deceit. Beyond talk and silence there is a steep passage." One other feature must be added, however, which is common to Zen and Hasidism, and very characteristic of both. Sometimes with different variations profane conversation is engaged in by the masters of the mystery, conversation which deceives the outside listener by its apparent complete superficiality, yet which in truth is important word by word and full of hidden meaning.

Both in Zen and in Hasidism the relationship between teacher and disciple is central. Just as there is no other people in which the corporeal bond of generations has achieved such significance, as in China and Israel, I know of no other religious movement which has to such an extent as Zen and Hasidism connected its view of the spirit with the idea of spiritual propagation. In both, paradoxically man reveres human truth, not in the form of a possession, but in the form of a movement, not as a fire that burns upon the hearth, but, speaking in the language of our time, like the electric spark, which is kindled by contact. Here and there the main concern of the legend is what passes between teacher and disciple. In Zen indeed this is almost the only concern, whereas in Hasidism, which does not present itself in brotherhoods of isolated individuals, the community plays a great part; of course it too is to a certain extent made up of potential disciples, of occasional disciples, of men who ask questions, seek explanation, listen, and from time to time learn something they had not intended to learn.

But this is also the point at which the ways most obviously part. I should again like to quote a typical story from both movements.

To a Zen teacher of the tenth century there comes a youth from a distant land. The teacher closes the door in front of him. The youth knocks, and is questioned about himself and his desires. "I am able," he says, "to contemplate the foundation of my existence, and I desire to receive instruction." The teacher opens the door, looks at the visitor, and closes it again in his face. After some time the youth returns, and the performance is repeated. The third time the visitor pushes inside, the teacher seizes him by the chest, and cries, "Speak." As the youth hesitates, he rebukes him, "You blockhead," and thrusts him out. The door turns on its hinge, and one foot of the disciple is caught in it and breaks. He cries out, and in that very moment he receives the inner illumination. Later he founded his own school.

In Hasidism we hear also of the "severe" method, namely in relation to the sinner, who desires to repent. But here it is unknown in the relationship between the teacher and the questioning disciple. Characteristic of this relationship is the following incident. One of the disciples of Rabbi Bunam of Pshysha, Rabbi Enoch, tells how he longed for a whole year to enter his teacher's house and to talk with him. But every time he approached the house he could not summon up enough courage. Once as he walked around the field weeping, the desire came upon him with unusual strength, and compelled him to run at once to the Rabbi. The latter asked him, "Why are you weeping?" Enoch answered, "Am I not a creature in the world, and am I not made with eyes and heart and all limbs, and yet I do not know, for what purpose I was created, and what good I am in the world." "Fool," said Rabbi Bunam, "I also go around thus. This evening you will eat with me."

It would be wrong to think that the distinction here is essentially a psychological one, perhaps the distinction between pride and humility—in Hasidism humility is counted one of the chief virtues, whereas in Zen it is not mentioned. The decisive distinction is of another kind. I will elucidate this by showing how here and there a widespread theme is at work, which we find first in an old Egyptian tale, afterwards retold by Herodotus, and which reappears in much folk-literature. It is the theme of the master thief. It is told of a Hasid of the Maggid of Kosnitz, that following the latter's advice he became a master thief, and yet remained an upright man; the story tells of his cunning and his success. But the Hasidic tradition goes still further. From the mouth of some Zaddikim we hear jesting words, in which they take as a pattern for the service of God the bold thief, who puts his whole life into his undertakings, and when at first he doesn't succeed tries and tries again. The enterprise of the great thief appears here as the symbol of concentration in the service of God. It is worth noting here, that the thief and the sucking child are put side by side: from these two beings, the immoral and the amoral, the highest qualification, inner Unity, is to be learned. A completely different symbolism of the thief motif is found in Zen.

A teacher at the end of the eleventh century tells in his sermon of an old master thief, who undertakes to instruct his son in his art at the latter's request. He goes with him at night to the house of a rich man, together with him breaks into the house, and orders him to climb into a large chest and to hide the most valuable objects in it. As the son crouches down in the chest, the father pushes down the lid, bolts it, goes out of the room, alarms the inhabitants of the house, and goes away. The son has to conjure up all his wits to save himself. Finally he appears in a fury before his father. The latter listens calmly to the whole story, and then says, "You have now learned the art." So is the Zen teacher with his disciples. He makes nothing easy, he never intervenes, he forces them to venture their life, and thus achieve for themselves what one can only achieve for oneself. We have seen how truth, both in Hasidism and in Zen, appears not as content and property, but as human existence and as movement between the generations; this movement however from existence to existence signifies in Hasidism transmission, in Zen stimulation.

In Zen, and even more clearly before it in Taoism, which as we have said influenced it greatly, we find it asked from time to time, whether we are not dreaming that we are alive. Chuang Tse, the great Taoistic poet and teacher, asks himself, after he had dreamed that he was a butterfly, "Now I do not know: was I a man, dreaming that he is a butterfly, or am I now a butterfly, dreaming that he is a man?" An answer is not given here; in Zen such questions are answered by a stroke, which may be translated by the cry, "Wake up!" Not so Hasidism. A Zaddik is asked by his son, "If there are dead men walking about in the World of Delusion, who imagine that they are pursuing their customary life, perhaps I also still live in the World of Delusion?" The father answers him, "If a man knows that there is a World of Delusion, then it is a sign to him that he does not live in the World of Delusion." A yet more characteristic answer however comes from another Zaddik, belonging to a generation close to our own. It is given to a disciple, who asked how we may know that we are not living in the World of Delusion. The answer runs, "If a man in the house of prayer is called upon to take part in the reading of the Torah from the desk, then it is a sign to him that he does not live in the World of Delusion." The Torah is the measure of reality.

After the establishment of this fundamental distinction, we must consider afresh what seemed to us most clearly to be common to Zen and Hasidism, the positive relationship to the concrete. We have seen that in both the man in process of learning and becoming was directed to things, to sensible being, to activity in the world. But the motive force in each is fundamentally different. In Zen the intensive direction towards the concrete serves to divert the spirit intent on the perception of the transcendent from discursive thought. The direction is, although aimed against the usual dialectics, itself of a dialectic nature; it is not the things themselves that are concerned here, but their unnotional character as symbol of the Absolute, which is above all notion.

Not so in Hasidism. Here the things themselves are the object of religious concern, for they are the abode of the holy sparks, which man shall raise up. The things here are important not as presentations of the un-notional truth, but each of them as an exile of divine Being. By dealing aright with them, man meets the fate of divine Being in the world, and helps in the redemption. His activity with things is not like the activity of the Zen monk, something that only accompanies the seeing into his own nature, but it is permeated with independent religious meaning. The realism of Zen is dialectic, it means annulment; the Hasidic realism is messianic, it means fulfilment. Just as, linked with revelation, it heeds the past, so, linked with redemption, it heeds the future—both in contrast to Zen, for which absolute reality is only accorded to the *moment,* as this is the possibility of inner illumination, and before the moment the dimension of time disappears. Hasidism is, so far as I see, the only mysticism in which *time* is hallowed.

Of all manifestations in the history of religion, Hasidism is that in which quite clearly two lines meet, lines which it is generally assumed cannot meet because of their nature: the line of inner illumination and the line of revelation, that of the moment beyond time and that of historical time. Hasidism explodes the easy view of mysticism. Belief and mysticism are not two worlds, although ever and again in them the tendency to become two independent worlds wins the upper hand. Mysticism is the realm on the borderland of belief, the realm in which the soul takes breath between word and word.

Hasidism and Zen-Buddhism

Abraham Kaplan

I would like to begin by differentiating my approach to the subject I
have chosen to speak about, "Hasidic Judaism and Zen Buddhism,"
from one that is often improperly called ecumenical. There are people
who think that the ecumenical spirit is to say, "If you compromise
what you believe in and I give up something of what I believe in, then
maybe we can iron out the differences and meet together in something that none of us believes in."

I have no sympathy with this pattern of ecumenical spirit. I believe
that there are many differences among human beings; differences in
language, culture, age, sex, and I believe that these differences can
enrich our lives if we learn how to accept and understand them. I think
we will all be impoverished if we think that whenever we confront
differences, we must desperately try to remove them. I do not want to
say that Hasidic Judaism is only another form of Zen Buddhism. It is
not! I do not want to say that these two things are really indistinguishable. There are many points of commonality, but also many points of
difference. And I would like us to appreciate both.

There is another attitude which is very common when people
approach religions, philosophies, and cultures other than their own.
That is the attitude of incorporation or adoption, especially when such
things become a kind of fad. So, as you may know, Zen for some time
has been a fad in the United States, and many people are very
interested in what they think is Zen, but what is really something else.
There are also places where people have become interested in what
they think is Hasidism, but what is something else. So, I not only do

From *Japanese Religions,* (NCC Center for the Study of Japanese Religions, Kyoto)
1975

not want to tell you that Hasidism and Zen are the same thing, I also do not want you to feel that I would like you all to become Hasidim. And I do not want to sit before you and pretend that I am a Zen Buddhist.

My approach to these cross-cultural religious and philosophical studies is different both from what is mistakenly called ecumenical and what is mistakenly called adoption or incorporation. My approach is to encourage understanding of another religion and philosophy, so that we may each of us deepen and enrich our understanding and appreciation of ourselves. I will not tell you very much tonight about Zen, because you all know more about it than I do. I will tell you something about Hasidism in the hope that the more you hear about Hasidism, the better you may understand your own Buddhism; and I am interested in speaking with you and hearing about your Buddhism so that I will better understand and appreciate my Judaism.

The spirit of my approach is conveyed in a beautiful Buddhist story which could also have been Hasidic:

A blind man was guest at the home of a friend. When he was ready to leave late at night, he asked his friend for a lantern. The friend said, "But you are blind. How will the lantern help you?" He answered, "It will tell others that I am coming."

When he had gone on his way for a little time, someone bumped into him, and he exclaimed, "Couldn't you see my lantern?" The man said to him, "My friend, your candle has blown out."

We are all of us blind in these matters. We lend one another lanterns, and perhaps the best we could do for one another is to say, "My friend, your candle has blown out." I hope what I say tonight can be of help for each of us to relight our own candles.

The Hasidic master—I will tell you shortly what person he was— very often used to talk in parables and stories. Someone came to him and asked, "Why do you always speak in parables?" He said, "I will answer you with a parable: A man once built a new house and invited a friend to come and look at it. He showed the visitor through the whole house and the visitor said, 'Everything is very nice, but there is one thing I do not understand: the curtains over the windows.' And the man said, "Why are you puzzled by the curtains over the windows?' He said, 'If you want people to look in, why do you have curtains? And if you do not want people to look in, why do you have windows?' And he answered, 'Because one day someone whom I love and who loves me will walk by, and together we will draw the curtain aside.' "

So there is in Hasidism as, I believe, in Zen, a double level of communication, one in which there is still the curtain, and another in which the curtain has been drawn aside. To draw the curtain aside requires something not merely abstractly intellectual, but intimately personal. I will therefore draw the curtain a little away, hoping that you also will draw it, by sharing with you an experience I had some years ago when I was a professor at Columbia University in New York. It was the anniversary of my mother's death, which in Judaism is an occasion that is very much noted. I wanted to go to a synagogue that my mother might have gone to. As I come from a Hasidic background, I found a Hasidic synagogue in New York. At 7 o'clock I appeared to attend the service, and I was the only one there. The rabbi said to me, "Who are you?" I had been raised in the Hasidic tradition and knew the answers. So when he asked me, "Who are you?" I answered, "I am a Jew." He smiled and said, "And where has a Jew come from?" I said, "I came from a great distance." The rabbi said, "And why has a Jew come from a great distance to this place?" I said, "I came to pray." He said, "In that case, *shalom!*" We shook hands and he said, "What is your name?" And I said "My name is Kaplan and I come from Los Angeles," etc.

Starting with the question, "Who are you?" he asked as though in Zen one might ask, "What was your face before you were born?" That was the very first question. That was the question which God asked of Adam, "Adam, where art thou?" Not that God did not know where Adam was. He wanted Adam to ask himself where he was. But Adam ran and hid. Where have I come from?—From a great distance, as we all of us have come from a great distance, not a distance in terms of rebirth, but the vast distance that separates *avidya*, ignorance, metaphysically from enlightenment. And why have you come? That is the only reason that any man ought to come anywhere, to try to attain this kind of understanding.

Notice that I have chosen as a starting point a concrete episode in my own life in an encounter with another concrete human being. It is very characteristic both of Zen and of Hasidism that their teaching is not conveyed in abstract, general formulas, but in these concrete encounters among human beings. What you call a *mondo*, and what in Hasidism is called a *maasé*, a story or tale or anecdote, is really the same. Just as the teaching of Zen is associated with the personality of the *roshi*, so in Hasidism it is associated with the personality of the *rebbé*. And the *rebbé* is, like a *roshi* or a *guru*, not a priest, but a person who has an intensely personal relationship with his followers. And

Hasid means among other things a follower or a disciple. So Hasidism is the relationship between the *rebbé* and the Hasidim. The Hasidim share in the teaching by telling one another particular experiences that they have had in relationship with the *rebbé*.

Common to both Zen and Hasidism is a basic attitude of determination, of concentration, of tremendous investment of energy. In Rinzai Zen the devotee involves himself with certain insoluble problems, *koan*, as for instance to hear the sound of a harp without strings. The *mondo* is that when the monk asked the master, "Teach me to hear the sound of a harp without strings," the master said, "There, did you hear it?" But the monk said, "Alas! No, master." And the master said, "Why didn't you ask me louder?"

Judaism, especially Hasidic Judaism, asks, very loudly. That is, the attitude towards life is an attitude of intense determination.

A good deal of Jewish life throughout its history has consisted in finding some way around its difficulties. This is expressed in a Jewish folk saying: "If you can't get over it, you get under it." Hasidism had a simple teaching as follows: "If you can't get over it, you *must* get over it!" What is impossible only requires a greater effort and energy. In Hasidism this is called *kavana*, which literally means intention. But in Hasidism it has the meaning of intense determination. To do something with *kavana* is to do it with your whole heart. In fact, the founder of Hasidism once suggested that sin could be defined as whatever a man does not do with his whole heart. To live with your whole heart, with *kavana*, that is the fulfillment, and I think this is an attitude shared by Zen and Hasidism.

There is, however, also a difference in respect to this *kavana*. The difference is: what the Zen master is characteristically occupied with, and what is done with this *kavana*, is meditation, *zazen*, or yoga in its various forms. What is characteristically done by the Hasid with *kavana* is prayer. In the one case, the *kavana* is directed towards establishing dialogue with the divine. In Zen the object of *kavana* is to realize that you yourself are the Buddha. In Hasidic Judaism the object of *kavana* is to realize that God is speaking to you. God called, "Abraham, Abraham!" And Abraham answered, "Here I am." To be able to hear what is said, and to be able to reply, that is the essence for the Hasidic *kavana*. However, whether it is the Buddha nature you grasp or whether it is the capacity for an encounter with the divine, what is happening in both cases is something that could happen and should happen *all day every day*, and is not something reserved for rare or special occasions.

In Zen this is conveyed by the *mondo* of the monk who said to the master, "Master, I have been in the monastery for two years and you have not yet taught me anything of Zen." And the master said, "I teach you Zen every day. When you come and offer me my tea, I accept the tea. When you say 'Good morning,' I reply 'Good morning.' When you offer me the rice, I eat the rice. I teach you Zen every day."

In Hasidism the idea is expressed in this way: The Hasid said, "At the home of my *rebbé*, we did not look for miracles. We scooped miracles by the bucketful. We lived in miracles always. And, in fact, the only reason why I went to live with the *rebbé* was to learn from him how to tie my shoelaces." That is a statement which I believe a Zen monk might also have said. If only we knew how to tie our shoelaces with such *kavana* as to see into our nature or to establish dialogue with the divine, we would have attained the purpose of human life.

There is, however, a fundamental difference in the conceptions of the nature that one sees into. In Zen it is a universal nature that one sees. You become aware of yourself as a Buddha. But all Buddhas are one Buddha. There is no significant individuality that is looked into. Judaism, in common with other Western religions like Christianity, notably, and other Western philosophies, individualizes the human being, and the aim is to see into one's own individual nature.

The *rebbé* said, "When I appear before the heavenly court, they will not ask me why I was not Moses. They will ask me why I was not myself." Moreover, God does not need another Moses. He has one. But he needs me and each of you as the particular individual human beings that you are. And the just step towards *satori* or towards fulfillment, however defined, is to know oneself as the person that he is and to assume responsibility for the person that he is.

A man lived what he recognized to be a very foolish and wicked life. He wanted to start afresh and went to the *rebbé* to see if he could get forgiveness. But he was ashamed of how he had lived. So he said to the *rebbé*, "Rebbé, I had a friend who lived a very wicked life. But he is ashamed to come here, so he asked me to come instead." The *rebbé* asked what the friend had done, and he described his wicked and foolish life. The *rebbé* said, "I can tell you, your friend is a fool!" "Why do you say that, *rebbé*?" The *rebbé* said, "Because your friend could have come here himself and just told me that he was speaking for a friend."

In saying this, the *rebbé* was not scoring a point, but he was making the fundamental reply: As long as you do not know who you are and resume responsibility for the person that you are, nothing has been changed. Although you may deceive yourself, and possibly deceive me, nothing will be gained. It is impossible to fool God. You may fool other men, but if you fool yourself, you are nothing but a fool. If you do not fool yourself, you assume full responsibility for yourself. That means, you must know your own way.

One of the techniques that the Zen masters often used was to reply to a monk's question by repeating the question. The monk might have thought that in that case the secret lies in the repetition. But in that case he is not living his own life, but only imitating the life of the master. So the master said to the monk, "What do you understand by this: Let the difference be even one tenth of an inch, and it will grow as great as the distance between heaven and earth?" The monk, who thought he had learnt the lesson, said, "It means: Let the difference be even one tenth of an inch, and it will grow as great as the distance between heaven and earth." And the master said, "No, that is not right." So the monk said, "Well, how should I understand it?" And the master said, "Let the difference be even one tenth of an inch, and it will grow and grow as great as the distance between heaven and earth." The monk was only repeating what the master himself talked, he was not repeating, but was saying what he himself was standing for, and then it had a content.

There is in Hasidism almost exactly the same teaching. A *rebbé* is not a priest, but someone others come to because they respect his teaching and recognize that he has something to share with them. But as with the Zen master, it quite often happens that the *rebbé* confers the robe on a disciple to be his successor, often his own son. Once a *rebbé* died and was succeeded by his son. This son was beginning to do things his own way, and the congregation was very disturbed by this. So they came to him and said, "Your father was a very holy and learned man. How is it that you do things differently? How dare you depart from the way of your father?" The man answered, "I depart from the way of my father? Heaven forbid! I do exactly as my father did. He did not imitate, and I do not imitate." So, following the way of his father, he had to walk on his own path. No one else can walk the path for us. In order to walk that path, both Zen and Hasidism insist, we must simply put one foot in front of the other, nothing more complicated than that. As the whole art of the tea-ceremony was described by the Zen master who created it, the art of tea is simply this: you boil water, make tea, and drink it. So that is also the spirit of Hasidism: you simply move your life as it comes before you.

I will give you one of the most famous *mondo*, anecdotes, of Hasidism, which illustrates this freedom from dependence on words and rituals. It concerns the founder of Hasidism, Baal Shem Tov, The Good Master of the Divine Name, who lived as a spiritual leader in South-Eastern Europe about 200 years ago. The day after *Yom Kippur*, which is the most holy day of the Jewish religious year, Baal Shem Tov ordered his horses and carriage to be made ready and told the driver to set off in the direction of the forest. When they came to an inn in the middle of the forest, he ordered them to stop, and went into the inn, which was operated by a Jew. This man said, "Oh Rabbi, I have been wanting to see you. I have something terrible to confess." Baal Shem Tov said to him, "Tell me, what happened?" "Well," the man said, "I live here in the forest far away from other Jews. Once a year on *Yom Kippur* I would like to pray together with other Jews, but somehow I have not been able to do it. This year I was determined I would do it, and we all started off for the city. But when we had gone a little way, I remembered that I had forgotten to close the back door of the inn. So I sent my wife and children ahead, took a horse and rode back. While I was closing the back door, a customer came in the front door, and while I was serving him, another customer came, and another, and soon it was too late for me to go, and I saw that it was my destiny once more to be alone. I prepared to pray, and then discovered that the prayer-books had gone with my family. But I have never learned Hebrew.* I am an ignorant man and all I know of Hebrew is just the alphabet. So what I did was to stand up and face Jerusalem and I just recited the alphabet, alef-bet-gimul-dalef, a-b-c-d, and I said to God: Here God, here are your holy letters, you put them into the right words and put the words into the right order."

Baal Shem Tov put his arms around him and said, "It was revealed to me in a vision that on this *Yom Kippur* your prayers had opened the gates of heaven, and I came to you to find out how to do it."

His prayer was nothing more than a-b-c-d-e, but he was praying with all that he had in himself to give.

I must tell you also a Christian legend which is exactly in the same spirit, and which is one of the essential points of commonality bet-

---

* Jews pray in Hebrew, but for 2,000 years they have lived in other countries, as they did in the rise of Hasidism, and instead of Hebrew they spoke Yiddish, which is a dialect of German; Yiddish mixed with Russian and Polish and other languages. And Hebrew was the holy language that they used for prayers, as Latin is used by Catholic Christians, Pali by many Buddhists, and so on.

ween the major religions. It is the legend called "The Juggler of Our Lady":

A man who worked as a juggler in a circus decided to join a monastery which was devoted especially to the service of Mary, the mother of Jesus. While the other monks were able to recite the prayers and chant the hymns, he, having spent all of his life in the circus, was unable to share with them. But at night he would go down to the chapel. The abbot followed him one night to see what was happening. There, before the image of the virgin Mary, he performed his juggling acts, and the image looked down upon him and smiled. He was living as the person he was, with *kavana*, with dedication, simplicity, and directness.

The last point I want to put before you is the fulfillment of this intense, concentrated, simple, direct, honest, aware, responsible life, which characterizes both Zen and Hasidism.

The fulfillment is essential in both. Both have a very strongly pragmatic orientation. The Zen master was asked by the monk, "Master, what is the nature of the self?" And the master replied, "What would you do with that self if you had one?"

This is also very much the orientation of the *rebbé*. Rather than asking abstract metaphysical questions we must occupy ourselves with the concrete tasks of a moral life. It is, to take another image from Buddhism, like the task of herding the cow. Whenever the cow strays from the path, one must immediately pull her back. So the *rebbé* also said, "I myself do not sin, not because I do not have an evil impulse, but simply because I don't have the time." His time is devoted to herding the cow, we might say.

There is a story of a *rebbé* who could not sleep one night. So he went out for a walk on the city streets, and he met another man and said, "What are you doing out so late?" The man said, "I am working, *rebbé*." He said, "At this hour, are you working? Whom are you working for? What work do you do?" He said, "I am a nightwatcher." The *rebbé* was about to leave when the man said, "Excuse me, *rebbé*, you are also up late at night. For whom are you working?" The *rebbé* said, "How would you like to come and work for me?" The man said "What would be my duties?" And he replied, "To remind me! Your duty would be only to ask me: For whom are you working?"

Here is a man concerned for nothing more than his daily bread and a handful of rice, who was up in the night, and here is the *rebbé* for whom the whole meaning and value of human existence is at stake, and he may not be willing to give himself totally to the task.

This task of working for what really matters, is called *avoda*. That word in Hebrew really means labor or work. But it also means service, like the English word service, in expressions such as Sunday morning service, to give service to the country, etc.

There is a story of a *rebbé* who invited a rich man to come to visit him, because this rich man, for all of his wealth, was not engaged in *avoda*. He was not giving of himself. So he brought the rich man to the window and said, "Look out of the window; what do you see?" He said, "I see many people, *rebbé*." Then the *rebbé* took him by the hand and put him in front of the mirror. "Look here, what do you see?" The man said, "I see myself, *rebbé*." And the *rebbé* said, "Behold, in the window there is glass, and in the mirror there is glass. But in the mirror there is also silver. And when you add the silver, you will no longer see the others. You see only yourself." With the silver—it may be gold, or it may be the income of a hundred billion dollars from oil—whatever its source, you may no longer see others, but only yourself, and no longer capable of giving service.

Now, there is a difference here also, although both Zen and Hasidism agree in the task of serving others (as does also Christianity, for which also *laborare est orare*, "to work is to pray"). This is another element shared by the major faiths. But there is a very characteristic doctrine in Hasidism which comes from *Kabbala*, a system of mysticism in which the most extraordinary idea is that God needs man as much as man needs God. The relationship between man and God is a reciprocal relationship. It is not only man who seeks God, but God who seeks man. They are in need of one another. What Buddhism calls *duhkha* is the condition of separation, of exile of man and the divine from one another. So for *Kabbala* the most important book is the *Song of Songs*, which is a love poem, but which is interpreted as the love of the human and the divine for one another.

There is a story of the *rebbé* who was visited by his little grandson. The little boy was out playing, but came into the house and burst into tears. The *rebbé* comforted him and asked why he was crying. The boy said, "I was playing hide and seek with my friends. It was my turn to hide, and I waited and waited, but my friends had gone off and left me." The *rebbé's* own eyes burned with tears as he held the little boy closer and said, "God says the same thing: I hide and no one seeks me." So man and God play this game of hide and seek with one another. But God is always searching. Only we sometimes run off and leave the game. When we turn back to it, then we accept life for all it brings, as Zen does, and we accept our fellow men as also sharing in this same game.

A Zen master used to greet the monks and say, "Have you been in the monastery long?" The monk would say, "No, I have just come," and the master would say, "Have a cup of tea." He would ask another, "Have you been in the monastery long?" And he would say, "Yes, I have been here for several years." The master would say, "Have a cup of tea." So one day the assistant, called Inju, came to the master, saying, "Master, how is this? You ask a monk how long he has been here, but whether he says he has been here a short time or a long time, you just offer him a cup of tea." The master said, "Oh, Inju!" He said, "Yes, master." The master said, "Have a cup of tea!"

This is exactly paralleled by the *rebbé* who once listened to a dispute between two people to settle it for them. After one of them had stated his case, the *rebbé* said, "Yes, you are quite right." But the other one said, "Wait a moment, Rabbi, you have not heard my side of the story." Having heard it, the *rebbé* said, "Yes, you are quite right." So a disciple said to the *rebbé*, "How is this? This man said it is white, and he said it is black. This man said it is night, and he said it is day. And yet you tell them they are right. How is that possible?" The *rebbé* turned to him and said, "Yes, you are also right."

So the man who is engaged in *avoda*, in serving, serves his fellow man and loves his fellow man as a way of loving the divine. Whatever God sets before him, he accepts, as a guest accepts whatever the host sets before him.

But more than that, when the lover is united with the beloved, the experience is one of great joy. I think this is the most striking feature shared by Zen and Hasidism. I do not know of any other denomination in any of the major religions in which there is such a sense of humor, in which there is laughter and just joy in being alive and in sharing in this world and being the man that one is. I think that it is because of this joyous acceptance of life that Zen has had the enormous impact it has had on the various arts, and that Hasidism has also had a great impact on music and dance and theater.

I want to conclude, as I began, with a personal experience with Hasidism connected with this expression of joy. The teaching of Judaism is contained in the scriptures which are called the *Torah*, which has very much the same meaning as the word *Dharma* has for Buddhism. It means the law, the teaching, the doctrine. The *Torah* is the first five books of the Scripture, the Five Books of Moses, and is divided into fifty-two sections, one section to be read each week. At the end of the year, when the whole of the *Torah* has been read, one celebrates this as an occasion of great joy. That holiday is called *Simhat Torah*, "the holiday of the rejoicing of the Law." The *Torah* is written on a parchment scroll, usually quite large. Actually the Jews carry the *Torah* and dance seven times around the whole room of the synagogue. While they are doing so, they may also take a drink of wine or brandy from a bottle that is provided. There is a story that some one said to the Hasidim, "How can you, who claim to be religious, allow yourself to be drunk on brandy?" And they answered, "No, you don't understand. The brandy only brings us joy. It is the joy that is intoxicating."

A few years ago I went to a Hasidic synagogue in Jerusalem on the night of this festival and watched the Hasidim dance. One came up to me and gave me the scroll to carry, and said, "Come and dance!" Although I am a philosopher and professor, I have a principle that if the *Torah* is actually thrust into your arms, you must take it. So I took it and danced around the room. When I returned, I gave it back to him. He said to me, "Why are you abandoning the *Torah* so quickly?" I said, "I am not abandoning it. It is just that I am tired." "Oh," he said, "but if you are tired, I must give you of my strength." Thereupon he bent down and picked me up onto his shoulders, holding the *Torah*, and then we began to dance around the room. That was *simhat*, joy; it was *avoda*, service; it was a *kavana*, with one's whole heart. And for me, most of all, it was a memorable symbol and actualization of what in Buddhism is known as the Bodhisattva—ideal of strengthening those who are weak, and having a feeling that we are together in this enterprise. This is something that is of particular importance to me as an Israeli, when now in the world we feel sometimes almost alone, and, even though we are alone, hoping somehow to find the strength to hold to the *Torah*.

INNER WORLDLY MYSTICISM: EAST AND WEST

Whalen W-L Lai

The beginning of the twentieth century witnessed the activities of two creative spirits: Martin Buber from within the Judaic tradition in the West and D. T. Suzuki from within the Japanese Buddhist tradition in the East. Both figures, each in his own way, were looking for the dynamic spirit lurking behind the deadwood of the formalized religious traditions. Both were seeking for a counter-thesis to the rationalistic worldview of the Enlightenment which had by then left its impact on the Judaic tradition and had also spread to the East, challenging as well as undermining the long-cherished worldview there. The two figures were forced to review their cultural past within the context of an emerging world culture. It was Martin Buber who gave the world the book *Ich und Du* (I and Thou) in 1922 and uncovered the Hasidic tradition for the Jews and the rest of the world. It was Suzuki who, after trying to introduce the East to the English-reading public, found his vocation in 1927 when he published the first collection of *Essays in Zen Buddhism* to become *the* modern spokesman of Zen for many a Japanese and the Western world. Both were at home in the world of mystical thought, and could speak from experience. Buber freely referred, in his early writings, to Zen, to *Lao Tzu* and *Chuang Tzu*, the Taoist mystics. Suzuki found a kindred spirit in Eckhart and Boehme. How ever much their personal (and therefore modern) experiences might color their interpretations of the religious reality, they were the ones who brought to life again their own mystical heritage. Cosmopolitan and international, they were the forerunners who made Hasidism and Zen known to the modern world. Any essay on Zen and Hasidism cannot but commence with their heritage. This is because it was under their tutelage that the two traditions (one might call them Neo-Hasidism and Neo-Zen) were perceived. And it will be out of their shadows that the mystical cultures of East and West should seek to move beyond. In the following essay, I would try to preserve the intention of a cultural 'I-Thou' dialogue—that is, on one hand to acknowledge the common ground between the two traditions and on the other hand to affirm the uniqueness of their individual contributions.

Martin Buber made much of the notion of 'dialogue' and was more ready to draw parallels between Hasidism and Zen. Suzuki was apparently less sensitivized to the Hasidic tradition, and the philosophy of the *I-Thou* probably could not fare well within the negative Madhyamika dialectics of "neither self nor other". The Zen counterpart to 'dialogue' would literally be *mondo*, 'questions and answers' between master and disciple, an esoteric exchange known only to the participants and the initiated. Therefore it would not seem inappropiate to begin here with an essay "The Teaching of the Tao", a preface Buber wrote to his translation of tales from *Chuang Tzu*. This would initiate us into a general discussion of the comparable elements in Zen and Hasidism.

The Absolute and the Unitary Life

"The Teaching of the Tao" was written in 1909 during Buber's mystical' phase when the 'ecstatic' experience of the exclusive and all-absorbing unity of his own self predominated. He was supposed to have moved beyond this solipsist mood to discover the more dynamic I-Thou inter-relationship later. Nevertheless, his delight in the 'unitary life' remained to the end and this essay—basically a subjective mystical discourse on another mystic—still provides one basic clue to the Zen/Hasidism dialogue: the fascination with the *Person*.

> The teaching (of the Tao) includes no subjects, it has only *one* subject—itself. . . .
> It stands beyond 'is' and 'ought', information (of Science) and command (of Law); it knows how to say only one thing, (that the unity of the Tao) must be realized in genuine life. . . .
> (It) finds its pure fulfilment in a central human life. Only in its decline that begins soon after this fulfilment does the teaching mingle with elements of science and law. Out of such intermixture there arises a religion. . . . Now belief and action are demanded: the One has disappeared.[1]

Intellectual historians of the modern West would recognize the elements of *Lebensphilosophie* in this appreciation of Chuang Tzu and

Taoism.[2] The adoration of "a central human life" in which the One fulfilled itself prior to its immediate corruption into a "religion" with creeds and imperatives can also be found in the sociology of a Max Weber (although Weber associated personal *charisma* immediately with *authority* and commands). Both Buber and Weber showed a distinct disenchantment with (and actually also by) the routinization and institutionization of that sacred spiritual gift (the original meaning of *charism*). One can also find similar sentiment expressed by another Jewish giant, the writer Franz Kafka. The terror of the bureaucratic machinery was given expert expression in *The Trial*, and, with a rare sardonic hope, in *The Penal Colony*. Given such an atmosphere in the European intellectual scene, it would therefore not be surprising to find Buber regarding "Law" and "Science" (the reference was clearly aimed towards Talmudic legalism and probably the Jewish enlightenment) as a "product of contamination",[3] a corruption of the "genuine life." At first glance, and considering the major Jewish interest in the *impersonality of justice and law*, this interest in an almost *cult of personality* (at the heart of the Christian faith in Christ, the *Logos* incarnate in "a central human life") seem somewhat inappropiate. However, as will be shown later, the ambivalence or love/hate relationship towards the Holy Man is at the heart of the Hasidic as well as the Zen tradition. Buber only revived an interest that had long existed within the Jewish faith. His targets, "Law" and "Science", were in another sense resurrected enemies of old.

In the East, a similar movement was afoot. It was also directed against the formalism of the Buddhist institution and the encroachment of rationalism from the Christian West. In Kyoto, a school of modernized philosophy based on Buddhist thought but drawing upon Hegelian dialectics was being formulated. Nishida was the foremost spokesman, but it was Suzuki, his classmate, who popularized Zen philosophy for the Western readers. In a comparable style, Zen was presented as being above law and science. In typical antithetical terms that mystified, Zen was seen as not a religion, not even mysticism, not even (any conception called) Zen itself. Zen was supposed to be focalized in a unitary experience called *satori* (enlightenment) and in a total lifestyle. The language of discourse used by Suzuki also had its modern 'comparative' ring.

> We may say that Christianity is monotheistic, and the Vedanta pantheistic. But we cannot make a similar assertion about Zen. Zen is neither monothestic nor pantheistic, Zen

defies all such designations. Hence there is no object in Zen upon which to fix the thought.[4]

The earlier quote from Buber can easily be applied to Zen, especially considering the fact that Taoism had close affinity with it. Just as Buber rediscovered Hasidism, Suzuki can actually be said to found his own school of Zen that has no lineage but likewise an intellectual, international, romantic and self-conscious favor. Like Buber too, Suzuki was scholarly as he was didactic, i.e. polemical—a mixture of subjective insight and objective appreciation, best to be denoted as "inspired". His presentation of Zen had that dramatized simplicity[5] that stripped off so much of the deadwood of the Japanese Zen tradition, a spiritual re-reading of a faith tarnished time and time again by ignoble associations. He helped to uncover roots of Zen (in his study on the *Lankavatara Sutra*), bring to notice minor traditions (*Bankei* Zen for example), applied his knowledge of *Religionswissenshaft* (admitting specific Taoist and Shinto contributions) but he also stood by the sacred tradition concerning the sixth patriarch, *Hui-neng*, against the sharper literary and historical criticisms of *Hu Shih*. . . . In one word, Gershom Scholem's uneasiness with Buber is no less Heinrich Dumoulin's discomfort with Suzuki.[6] The two giants, Buber and Suzuki, so highlighted Hasidism and Zen, showing them in their spiritual essentials in their pioneering new scholarship, that conscientious if awed disciples feel the need now to tone down the sharp contrasts. Despite their modern favor, with its natural nostalgia for a creative past, their presentation of Hasidism and Zen are not totally spurious and without historical basis. The focus upon the "Hallowed Life" was there in these two mystical traditions. The Zen and Hasidic tales provide Buber the point of contact for a mutual enlightening.[7]

Hardly any religious tradition would deny the necessity to live out a holy life, and in one sense both Zen and Hasidism reflected a transition towards popularized pietism in their respective mystical traditions (see later discussion). What is unique is perhaps the centrality of the master as the living paradigm of the hallowed life. . . . Hasidism brought the mystical *kavannah* (direction, intention) to the dining table. So too the Zen monastic rules insisted upon the pounding of rice itself as part of the Zen (meditative) discipline. If the passage of the Buddhist Dharma in the Zen tradition was from mind to mind, so too the long Kabbalah tradition in Jewish mysticism emphasized the esoteric mouth-to-mouth transmission of the tradition. Zen treasured silence; it found its paradigm of wisdom in the silence of Vimalakirti, the lay Bodhisattva, The Hasids, like most mystics, also valued at times quietude especially above literal or refined understandings. The word of a Hasidic master carried weight because the master was literally regarded at times as the mouthpiece of God. Similarly the Zen *guru* was traditionally seen as a living Buddha and his wisdom unchallenged and well-obeyed (except when the initiate reached *on par* status with the master). The Zaddik was popularly regarded almost as a demigod (like the Sufi saint) by his brotherhood followings; he, a holy man and miracle worker, was seen even as an intercessor between men and God. The reverence shown to the Zen master by the peasantry could match such fervor, and even for the more knowledgeable disciples, the living Buddha—the master—was the original reason for the absence of the Buddha hall in Zen monastic architecture (seldom followed now).

There are differences. Hasidism existed within the theistic framework where complete union with the absolute was generally not a [6] theologically sustainable motif. Better it is to speak of communion. The Hasids were literally the 'pious'. Humility was a virtue. "Clinging" onto God in a spiritually dependent mode was endorsed. Zen had generally been classified as a Buddhist sect that emphasized "self-power," that is, attainment of enlightenment by *self-effort* (despite the possible antinomy of the term). A certain sense of pride, or, rather, courage was necessary. Even the teacher was ultimately a means. Like the raft used to cross to the other shore, the means must be abandoned. *Agraha*, not-to-cling onto anything, was the ultimate stand of freedom from all attachment. The Zen priests paint, noted Buber, and went on to say, "The Hasid cannot paint, but he dances."[8] In seeing their mutual spontaneity, Buber could also have seen in there a difference. Zen priests took quiet delight in nature, in the hills and waters eventually reproduced in the landscape paintings. It was not characteristic of Zen masters to dance. The dance is a certain form of the celebration of life, tied up with the community and with the liturgical worship of the Jews. The dance was part of the Hasidic promotion of joy and its distaste for asceticism. The Zen tradition in its literal form, that is, as a meditative school, remained generally more sober, often introvertic (during training) and its ideal of happiness lay closer to a sense of *peace*, a delightful apatheia,[9] a quiet joy traceable back to the original inspiration to transcend 'sentiency'. Of course, individual masters had their idiosyncratic lifestyles; it was one new note struck by both mystical movements that the *individuality* of the personalities was allowed full expression. Rabbi Nachman, for exam-

ple, apparently went through an early ascetic period before he participated in a more natural joyous celebration. Later in his journey to the
Holy Land, he was supposed to act in strange manners as perhaps
befitting to the extravagant hopes of such an undertaking.
Bodhidharma, the legendary founder of the Zen tradition, was depicted (by later records) as an extreme ascetic who would cut off his
eye-lids to stay awake in meditation, but the Japanese Zen tradition
soon recognized that physical well-being was a pre-requisite to true
Zen discipline. Nor should one be deceived by the pantheistic ease
visible in Zen's naturalism, for a sentiment like "Everyday is a good
day" came probably out of the anxiety induced by a genuine concern
over "the great events of life and death."[10]

Nuances of differences notwithstanding, both Zen and Hasidism
did produce, especially in their creative or founding days, unique
personalities and remarkable lives.The sources for such pictures of
the masters are the Zen and Hasidic tales. However, the emphasis on
personality instead of teachings might be one-sided. Scholem justly
questions Buber's over-reliance on the Hasidic tales as the basis to
reconstruct the Hasidic movement. "This genre of legends,"
Scholem notes, "developed at the end of the eighteenth century,"[11]
coming much later than the more reliable sermons, lectures and
commentaries on biblical texts by the Hasidic masters. Buber's defense of his interpretation only showed the difference of temperament
between himself and Scholem and recalled the age-old issue familiar
among Christian scholars: the tension or dialectics between the
teaching *of* a person (Jesus' *didache*) and the proclamation *about*
that person (the Church's *kerygma* concerning Christ). The latter, like
the Hasidic tales, was usually told in a more *mythological* language,
and generally from the more popular tradition of the people. *Baal
Shem Tov* was a miracle worker as his name signified, and the glorifi-
cation of the life and person himself was a natural development that
finally led to the establishment of the Zaddik's semi-divine status and
cultus. Where to draw the line between the "Good Name" and his
teachings and how much of the continuity/discontinuity should be
underlined may never be resolved. As far as the present
Zen/Hasidism comparision goes, it is perhaps interesting to note that
in all probability the Zen "cult of personality" *at the expense* of the
scriptural learnings emerged only in time. Most of the Zen tales about
the various masters were fabricated later and the famous collections
of *Koans* came around the twelfth century A.D.[12] *Koan Zen* was possibly a reaction against a formalized exegetical Zen. Could not the

Hasidic tales also be a late attempt to revive the *simpler* Hasidic piety against both the rabbinization and Zaddikization of the Hasidic tradition? Seen from this wider historical perspective, Zen and Hasidism shared a common fate. Both actually had within their histories a Buddhological/Rabbinical and a more intuitive side. Even as 'esoteric' traditions (vis a vis the greater Jewish and Buddhist traditions), they contained within themselves their own 'esoteric' and 'exoteric' halves, the debates between which are only carried onto present-day scholars of different temperaments.

The attempts made by Buber and Suzuki to present Hasidism and Zen for modern men (themselves responsibly included) also raise another question concerning their interpretations. Compared with the cloistered mysticism of the Kabbalahist and the Buddhists monks prior to the Zen reform, both Hasidism and Zen were more ready to emphasize the immanence of the divine and the sacredness of the everyday. However, such "innerworldly mysticism" presents us with a paradox not unlike that of the Puritan's "innerworldly asceticism."[13]

The Paradox of Immanence

Buber presented Hasidism as "a joy in the world as it is, in life as it is, in every hour of life in the world as that hour is."[14] The phraseology, by a coincidence, would have delighted Suzuki for whom *as-it-is* meant the Japanese term "*sono mama* (Sanskrit, *tathata* or suchness). Zen was presented by Suzuki also as seeing the Absolute in the everyday, in the drop of a petal, in reality *as-it -is*. Both Buber and Suzuki tended to affirm the world as twentieth-century thinkers in a manner which in all probability was alien to pre-modern men of faith. Scholem criticized Buber for such earthly immanentalism by recalling the Hasidic motif of "lifting of the sparks"—the drawing upwards of the spiritual elements hidden in things to its destined height of unity. Scholem writes, cautiously as ever,

> The act in which all that is alive in individual things is raised to a higher level belongs only to the moment and may not last. . . . Or, as many Hasidic writers like to put it: It is necessary to reduce things to their nothingness in order to restore them to their true nature.[15]

I do not think Buber would disagree with Scholem at this point, especially when Buber, a one-time mystic, knew very well of the rarity of the mystical moments of union. *Via negativa* and *via passiva* were traditional mystical paths familiar to Buddhism as well as to Judaism.[16] Nor would Suzuki sharply disagree with the above quote when applied to Zen. By another coincidence, the language of "reduce things to their nothingness in order to restore them to their true nature" would strike a chord in any Japanese Buddhist. Mahayana philosophy long recognized that realities are empty (*sunya*) and Zen naturally insisted on seeing the nothingness (*sunyata*) of things *in order to* see them *as-they-are* (*tathata*, in their true concrete nature, *dharmata* and, in Japanese, *jiso*). If there is any basic disagreement here, it would be that both the dynamic Buber and the dynamic Suzuki would like to see the unity (*yihud* in Hasidism, *advai* or not-two in Mahayana) attained in the mystical insight to be 'lived out' in real life, that is, to bring the unity of vision into daily existence, while Scholem (in this passage here, not in his general evaluation of Hasidism) seems to be still arrested by the ideological issues of the 'more' proper understanding, because he is wary of the secularist dilution of Hasidic piety.

Ultimately, the contention lies with the matter of how much immanentalization of the perfected state is seen or regarded as possible in the here and now. The degree of "innerworldly mysticism" can be gauged by the commitment to historical time and to the reality of suffering or evil. It is generally agreed that the Messianic element receded in the Hasidic movement (see later discussion) and personal pietism came to the fore. Still, the Jewish commitment to history did not allow the Hasidic mystics to venture as radicaly into total immanentalism as some Zen masters would. Even Buber, justly criticized by some for his spiritual individualism,[17] held up the Torah as a measure against Eastern mystics (in this case, *Chuang Tzu*). "It (the Torah) is a sign to (man) that he does not live in the World of Delusion."[18] The world, the creation, is real and not (as he saw in *Chuang Tzu*) indistinguishable from a dream. Zen—said Buber—at heart annuls reality wheras Hasidism allows for true fulfillment. The latter hallowed time whereas the former only the moment. Naturally, Zen philosophers would disagree with such a criterion and càn twist the English language to argue that Zen alone can hallow time because the fullness of reality or Being coincides with the endless moments of our lives. The Western mystic who awaits for fulfillment in time (in the future) lives in a World of (to wit) Self-frustration. A good presentation of a Zen view on Being and Time can be found in the writings of Dogen, the foremost Zen master in Japanese history.

No distinction is made between name-and-form and void-
ness, between phenomenon and absolute reality. Dogen
explains: "All being is the Buddha-nature. A part of all beings
we call 'sentient beings'. Within and without these sentient
beings there is the sole being of the Buddha-nature." From
his view Dogen derives the equation of being and time. All
being is fused with time. Apart from time there is no being . . .
Time is the motion of absolute being.[19]

All realities are empty, void, yet absolute; each in its particulars is
immediately the universal (Buddha-nature). Being and temporal
becoming—irreconcilable in the Western Platonic outlook—fuse in
the unique eternity of Time-as-moment itself. As long as Hasidism
retains a theistic and historic framework, it would be difficult to find a
comparable statement on the fullness of time in every moment.

One basic inhibiting factor in Hasidism against such extreme immanentalism centered on the problem of Evil. The theistic religion in
general has to tend to this reality more than one where suffering or
ignorance (*dukkha*, *avidya*) is a more basic concern. It would not be
profitable to compare Hasidism and Zen on their divergent stands.
Instead I would rephrase the question structurally as one of "How is
the negative element integrated into the One?"

Here Martin Buber perhaps made famous a Rabbinic sentiment
that was retained by the Hasids. Man, said the Mishnah, Berakoth
section 9.5, must serve the Lord with all his heart—that is, with his evil
as well as good drive. Man cannot do evil with all his being (as Buber
often put it) because evil is the result of indecision, the lack of a
spiritual *intent*, a consequence of a divided soul or self. Elements of
Lebensphilosophie as well as the Hasidic *kavvanah* (intention) are
evident in Buber's rendition, but the following statement, though not
unchallenged, can convery the new ideal in Hasidic piety.

But ecstasy (in Hasidism) is not here, as, say, in German
mysticism, the soul's "Entwerden", but its unfolding; it is not
the self-restraining and self-renouncing, but the self-fulfilling
soul which flows into the Absolute.[20]

Not through ascetic self-denial but a strange sense of confidence
was the blissful state attained. The new psychology, as one might so
call it, involves an assimilation of the previously-regarded-as evil or
negative element in the total personality. There is a notable emphasis
on *will* and *intent* as the integrating mechanism. More will be said on

this in the historical comparison to follow. However, it is notable that the Zohar had already begun a more positive evaluation of the element of Darkness in the scheme of things. Hasidism inherited apparently this tradition after and despite the demonic overflow of the Sabbatai heresy. Similarly, in the *Hua-yen* school of Chinese Buddhism (which I regard to be crucial to the founding of the Zen tradition), the negative element in Mahayana—namely, *ignorance*— had also been given a place in the scheme of the "manifestation" and even "creation" of things by the Absolute Mind (Suchness, *tathata*) itself.[21] Ignorance was the 'partner' of phenomenal creation. This pre-Zen tendency led to a similar '*wholistic*' interpretation of reality, emphasizing not so much denial of the negative element but the completion of the whole. The self-fulfilling soul can also flow into the Absolute *without effort or assertion*, (the classical term is *muji*,[22] non-assertion, somewhat like the classical Taoist *wu wei*, non-action). Both Zen and Hasidism then seem to avoid the "weak" mysticism of Entwerden and develop the "strong" mysticism of *singlemindedness* and resolved the problem of the negative element (evil, ignorance) in a dynamic, daily fashion. Paul Ricoeur's study of the various types in the symbolism of Evil[23] can probably provide clues to understanding the above phenomenon.

The above section looks briefly into the general areas of similarities and differences between Hasidic and Zen mysticism. Yet to fully understand the dynamics of religious piety in these two traditions, as well as to provide a general background to the basic ideas involved, the following historical comparative analysis is pursued.

The Last Phase of Medieval Mysticism: Jewish and Buddhist

Hasidism and Zen represent two important last phases of medieval mystical movements, East and West. The term medieval is used in a rather general sense. Zen, begun in the seventh century, was the dominant and dynamic school prior to the classical renaissance of Confucianism in the eleventh century. Baal Shem also flourished some forty or so years before the Jewish enlightenment in Eastern Europe. Both turned towards the world (innerworldliness) in a popularist attempt to consecrate the everyday. Both inherited from a more complex and scholastic medieval mystical tradition as well as reacting towards the same. In the case of Hasidism, the predecessor was the Kabbalah and its offshoots. The Kabbalah was a Jewish gnostic text, and Hasidism inherited the Lurianic tradition of the Zohar. The central ideal there is the "lifting the sparks." Hasidism associated that with its own idea of *devekut*, cleaving to God, and both with reference to intimate day-to-day life and one's surroundings.

There is a great mystery: Why did God create the food and drink for which man longs? The reason is that these are full of sparks of Adam, the first man, which after his fall wrapped themselves up and hid away in all the four spheres of nature, in stones, plants, animals and men, and they strive to return and to cleave unto the sphere of holiness. And whatever a man eats and drinks is actually part of his own sparks which he is under an obligation to restore.[24]

In other words, every man is the redeemer of a world that is all his own. Restoration, *tikkun*, of the lost unity was achieved by *devekut*. "Luria is primarily interested in the exile of the souls and their sparks in the spheres dominated by the power of evil, the *kelipot*, whereas the Baal Shem and his followers emphasize the mystic connection between man and his immediate environment. In other words, the Lurianic doctrine has a more abstract tone, the Hasidic version a more concrete and personal one."[25] The development of this more privatized piety was also a natural response to the fiasco of the Sabbatai movement. The expected Messianic end led by Sabbatai and then the betrayal left the European Jewry disillusioned. Early Hasidism understandably neutralized the Messianic element, and its gospel of joyous devotion spread among the impoverished Polish Jews in Eastern Europe. The detailed spiritual flight of the Kabbalist through the ten zones which "requires extreme discipline and follows clearly charted routes"[26]—the very opposite of religious anarchism—was exchanged with the more immediate magical transformation of the real world of the worshipper. Hasidism was elitist Kabbalah turned into popular ethos, and should perhaps be seen alongside other pietistic movements in the seventeenth and eighteenth centuries in Europe, i.e., the Methodist and so on.

The Ch'an (Chinese for Zen) tradition also seems to be a 'privatized' mystical movement. The *Hua-yen* school to which Ch'an was affiliated[27] resembled the Kabbalah tradition in its interest in details. Instead of the ten zones of the Sephirotic world, *Hua-yen* mapped out the various stages (usually again ten in number) in the spiritual flight of the Bodhisattva. In its concern for details and rational steps, Hua-yen was also the opposite of religious anarchism. Zen turned that concern for philosophical categories into a concern for the concrete and the immediate. Not in the categories of refined scriptural understanding, but in the rocks and the waters was the principle of Buddha-nature to be found. Hasidism is known to have made the distinction between the two stages of individual and universal salvation, to assert individual redemption in exile and even to delay the coming of the Messiah until everyone attains his personal communion with the divine.[28] In one sense, the Zen tradition also abandoned a more literal, early eschatological' Mahayana ideal—the delaying of the attainment of nirvana for the Bodhisattva until all men could be ferried to the other shore. Personal enlightenment in Zen became such a key focus that perhaps that explained why it was condemned by the Tibetans in the Council at Lhasa for its individualistic lack of corporate compassion.[29]

Both traditions responded to their religious situations. The *kavvanoth* system of Lurian Kabbalah was abrogated by Nathan of Gaza, the first theologian of the Sabbatai movement, on the ground that it was no longer appropriate for the dawning of the Messianic age.[30] The Hasidic movement re-stressed personal piety and saw the real *kavannah* as the "breaking of the heart in humility and cleaving to God."[31] The Great Maggid R. Dobh Baer formulated it for the movement.

Thus the ancients employed in meditation the Kavvanah suitable for each thing. (But) now that we have no Kavvanah, only the breaking of the heart will open (the door) to everything.[32]

The Zen tradition was generally more stoic than emotional but it also anticipated and reacted in part to state persecution of the monasteries and the loss of learning and scripture in its call to "menial labour as part of Zen" and "transmission outside the scriptures."

Both movements were led by charismatic leaders who had a popular appeal. Considering thesfact that they challenged the ingrained scholar-authorities, it is not surprising that *Baal Shem Tov* and *Hui-neng*, the founder of the southern school of Zen, were depicted as far from being learned by traditional standards. *Baal Shem*'s Talmudic education seems to be second-handed and had ro have people read aloud to him from the books.[33] *Hui-Neng* was depicted as a southern barbarian, uncouth, being neither able to read nor write.[34] Such semi-legends endeared them to the people and underlined the limits of scholarly learning. If there seem to be little of new or original ideas in Hasidism that were not present already in the Kabbalah, then the so-called *Platform Sutra* of Hui-Neng contained also nothing new. In fact, certain license of interpretation of traditional ideas was evident in both movements.[35] Such plebeianization of 'higher learning,' however, led precisely to a flowering of local literature, colloquial genre and popular homilies.[36]

The Hasid was pious; the Zen master was meditative. One would appear to follow a liturgical revival while the other a monastic reform. In reality, however, their wider ramifications can be seen to dovetail into each other's areas of concern. *Hui-Neng* was a monk but an early inscription of his life spoke of him as "staying around merchants and laborers for sixteen years."[37] The Platform Sutra of *Hui-Neng* showed him to be having, in hyperbole, ten thousand monks, nuns and lay followers; and the prefect of Shao-chou, thirty officials from various departments and thirty Confucian scholars were in his audience.[38] *Shen-hui*, his famous disciple, is regarded by many scholars now to be the real engineer of the southern Zen movement. He definitely had many converts and was popular with the literati and officials of high rank; Confucian sympathy probably helped his cause against the northern Zen branch which was associated with the infamous Empress *Wu*. (The Empress, incidentally, claimed to be the future Buddha, Maitreya, incarnate. Her 'eschatological' rule faltered like Sabbatai's, and the southern Zen tradition could be seen as a reaction from the peripheral area.) *Shen-hui* had thousands of followers, many of whom were conceivably lay people.[39] Zen, like Hasidism, can also be considered to have "turned to the people with their mystical knowledge ... and instead of cherishing as a mystery the most personal of all experiences, undertook to teach its secret to all men of good will."[40] The *Platform Sutra* bears this out. *As it stands*, it has none of the Zen esotericism or mysteries that one now associates with *Koan Zen* of the Rinzai school nor any insistence upon *zazen* (sitting in meditation) or strict monastic lifestyle that one associates now with the Soto school. The *Platform Sutra* was basically a popular and even folkish tract concerning the life and teachings of *Hui-Neng*. Even the idea of the esoteric passage of the Dharma (Buddhist teaching) from the Buddha through Bodhidharma down to *Hui-Neng* was supposed to end: the *Platform Sutra* was thence to be the 'seal of Dharma'.[41] This work, the sole Chinese Buddhist treatise attaining eventually scriptural (*sutra*) status, was supposed to make the mystery open to all. *Shen-hui's* collected sayings went even further. *Zazen*, sitting in meditation, was given a free new twist of interpretation.

> By sitting (*za*) is meant that no thought is aroused; by Zen is meant that one sees one's nature (as Buddha-nature).

Therefore I do not urge people to seat their bodies, calm their minds and enter into *samadhi*, trance.[42]

People who came to *Hui-Neng* for spititual advice were simply told to take up the Bodhisattvic vows—to save all sentient beings, to cut of all passions, to study the scriptures and to achieve the Buddha Way[43]—and to seek out their innately pure soul or mind. *Shen-hui* was even more assuring in his teachings, since he regarded "natural knowing" itself to be informed by the same. It is said that the Kabbalist prayer was all restraint and the Hasidic prayer all movement. Although Zen did not generally go for ecstatic emotions, yet one can also see a similar transformation. Meditation before the Zen movement was strenuous; even the northern masters insisted upon vigilance and perpetual cleansing of the mind.

Daily to cleanse the mirror (mind) of any dust So that no defilements (dust) linger on it.[44]

Was the line written by *Shen-hsiu*, the northern master. Southern Zen removed the restraint, occasioning a confidence in the purity of the spirit. The mind is like a lamp and wisdom is its light, so said the *Platform Sutra*.[45] Zen too attained a kind of spontaneity comparable to the Hasidic prayer and dance by the time of *Ma-tsu*. One of *Ma-tsu's* famous dictums is "The everyday mind is Buddha itself." It is from *Ma-tsu* that the anti-scriptural and iconoclastic Zen tradition evolved. All later Zen traditions are to be traced to him and not to *Shen-hui*.

The above short summary of the early Zen tradition shows that this meditative school was at one time *not* a monkish movement placing its emphasis on *zazen* only and indulging in esoteric *Koans*, i.e. one-to-one master-disciple mysteries. At least, not those aspects alone. The Zen movement had actually a popular pietistic side. Its liturgical innovation might be the public grand lectures in which basic Buddhist doctrines were explained in simple terms to the people, who may then ask for private audiences with the master for clarifications. The Zen movement was a popularist movement, but unlike the Hasidic movement, it drew its social support largely from 'middle' and higher classes, not from the peasantry (although illiterate old women often figured in the stories and said to be full of folk wisdom of the Absolute). Zen prospered in literati, merchant, artisan, laborer circles, and at urban centers. For that reason, although *Hui-Neng* was equally a miracle worker like *Baal Shem*, Zen generally showed greater rationality and less spiritual extravagance. This outgoing Buddhist mystical school eventually turned inward again, as will be described later. The Hasidic movement was, in contrast to Zen meditation, more a pietistic movement. Despite its apparent similarity with the Islamic Sufi tradition—both being the 'esoteric' and yet the villagers' tradition standing against the public and learned legalistic streams of the Talmud and the Shariah, both also sharing similar social or organizational structures—the Hasids remained more 'devotional' than the Sufi mystics. The dance of the Hasid and the dance of the Dervishes were different. One celebrated in joy and worship, the others were caught up as a group in the ecstasy of a divine trance. The great Zen masters, in general more cerebral, were usually too haunted by the realities of suffering, the effects of *karma*, the paradoxes or ambiguities of Buddhist doctrines to ever participate in a similar effusion of emotions. The Hasids combined piety, clinging onto God, with mysticism, the concern for unity, seeing one leading to the other.[46] Chinese Zen masters eventually also adopted the Amida pietism, devotion to Amida the Buddha who presides over the Pure Land in the West. Yet even there, the masters generally moved on two levels, preserving the Zen unity to a higher realization (Dharmakaya) and the personalism of Amida faith to a secondary (Sambhogakaya) if equally effective level. If one is to look for a more appropriate oriental parallel to the one specific Hasidic element of "clinging" in divine communion, one would more likely find it within the *Jodo* (Pure Land Amidaist) figures in Japan than within Zen proper. All these are not to deny the mystical element in Hasidism. All these only show that Hasidism retained its ties with the Jewish tradition as a whole, such that community and worship remained central to the pious. The Hasids had a greater social calling, role and function to play. In almost all the cases, rabbinical training of some kind, scriptural studies, sermons and communal participations and leadership were a natural part of their life. Nor was the Messianic motif ever eliminated. In the end, these also explained the development of the Zaddik and his little oriental kingdoms. The hallowed life of popular mystics led to the worship of the saintly, while the communal duties that the pious assumed led to the founding of the spiritual fellowship of the leader and the led. The peasant basis of the movement allowed the inclusion of more and more magical elements than it would be possible within the more enlightened 'middle class' Zen circles.

If Hasidism lapsed into the later Zaddik developments, Zen also faced similar problems in a different setting. Both movements attempted the impossible, namely, to popularize what was once exclusive and cloistered contemplative lifestyles. Popular mysticism after all is a contradiction in terms, unless by that one means some form of 'pro-mystical sympathy' or some 'pantheistic sensitivity'. The Hasidic masters had what might be called an inner circle of followers, immediate disciples and an outer and wider audience and devotees. The Zen masters too had their immediate students and then a much larger lay following. An act or some sayings of the masters in both cases would conceivably be understood in different ways by the different people involved, as pietistic platitudes or as gems of profound wisdom. Speaking or writing for different audiences because of their popularist concerns, the masters too proved adaptive to the situations and roles demanded of them. Viewed by different people with different spiritual backgrounds, the masters appeared in different forms—the human, the divine, the anecdotal, the mythical and anything in between. The individual master's own inclinations also produced anything but homogeneity in the movements. Some Hasids were more pious like Rabbi Nachman, others more mystical like the great Maggid; some Zen masters were scripturalists and systematizers, like *Tsung-mi*, others followed the dictates of their whims like *Lin-chi* (Rinzai). A movement that emphasizes personality allows for much local or regional variations. Both Hasidism and Zen showed such tendencies. Such movements also had to tackle the problem of institutionalization and how to preserve the spirit behind the actual forms.

In the remaining portions of this essay, I would look a bit more into the tradition of the tales and especially into the history of Japanese Zen.

The Spirit and its Form

Buber in "Teaching of the Tao" talked of the degeneration of the Teaching into myth and later into legends. Yet even Buber worked through the Hasidic tales to what he perceived as the spirit of the early masters. The function of the Hasidic tales has been given as follows, in a retold tale itself.

> When the Baal Shem had a difficult task before him, he would go to a certain place in the woods, light a fire and meditate in prayer—and what he had set out to perform was done. When a generation later the "Maggid" of Meseritz was faced with the same task he would go to the same place in the woods and say, "We can no longer light the fire, but we can still speak in prayers"—and what he wanted done be-

came reality. . . . (Two more generations later, the sentiment became) "We cannot light the fire, we cannot speak the prayers, we do not know the place, but we can tell the story of how it was done." And, the story-teller adds, the story which he told had the same effect as the actions of the three.[47]

The days of the living master himself were gone. What was left was the record of those days and the supposed "power by association" of the stories themselves. Zaddikism had by then institutionalized the charismatic power and authority in its way, often through hereditary office. The tales might reflect a second path through which the magical reality of the Baal Shem was kept alive.[48]

Zen had undergone similar changes. By the twelfth century A.D. (and that is the time when Zen was imported into Japan), Zen had produced a popular culture, especially among the literati and through the arts. Zen wisdom was plebeianized and was "on the mouth of people" (word-of-mouth Zen, i.e. empty talk). Confucian gentlemen were doing their daily short quiet sitting but directing it apparently to non-Buddhist goals, turning it more into a kind of moral introspection of good or evil intent. Mysticism had gone 'soft', had been aestheticalized and become perhaps too diffused. As Scholem said to Buber, justly or unjustly, so too a strict Zen master like *Ta-Hui* could easily have said to the literati's adoption of quiet sitting: people had forgotten about the "necessity to reduce things to their nothingness in order to restore them to their true nature". Lovers of mountains and waters saw only the natural beauty of the mountain and waters—and did not go through the necessary *metanoia* of consciousness.

> Before enlightenment, mountains were mountains, waters were waters.
> During enlightenment, mountains were no longer mountains, waters no more waters.
> After enlightenment, mountains were mountains, waters were again waters.[49]

Popularized Zen produced adulterated Zen-like sentiments without the true spirit. It might be perfect for the Neo-Confucian revival where the concern was clearly more world-affirming, but that was not the true gnostic dream.

At the same time, the Zen monastic tradition—like the Zaddik development—was actually becoming more regimentated, partly as a reaction to laicized Zen on one hand, partly because of state

intervention. Interest in scholarship, especially the Buddhist philosophy of the T'ien-t'ai (Japanese, *Tendai*) school, was revived. Tales
of the masters, with magic and miracles, were circulating around. I will
overlook the (in Japanese) *Soto* school which emphasized sitting in
meditation with or without scriptural learning and look into the new
interest in the tales now used as *Koan* (public cases), 'mysteries' to
trigger off enlightenment in the student. Scholem is correct in seeing
a difference between a Zen tale and a Hasidic tale. The Hasidic tales'
"sense and meaning are immediately revealed and they transit something which can be transmitted."[50] Actually that applies to the *narratives* in the Platform Sutra concerning Hui-Neng, but what is new in
the new Koan Zen tradition of the Rinzai school is that the same
narratives were being used to *reproduce* the primordial experience
that accompanied the original event. The retelling of the Hasidic tales,
as cited earlier, usually has only a 'sympathetic' and 'didactic' function
although it claims actually to have magical efficacy. The Zen Koan
sought to accomplish the impossible—*to light the very fire again*. The
student could only be truly enlightened if he duplicated in his own
psyché the same lighting of the fire. In Zen vocabulary, the 'lamp' (of
enlightenment) must be transmitted intact from mind to mind, unbroken and uncorrupted by time. Without questioning the validity of
this practice one way or the other, one should nevertheless see this as
the key difference between the Hasidic tradition of tales and the Zen
tradition of tales. This might or might not explain the greater continuity in the living Zen tradition in Japan.

Both Hasidism and Zen represented a '*wholistic*' kind of mysticism,
that is, both tried to assimilate the negative element (evil, ignorance
and now doubt itself) into a total program of singleminded intent and
to bring this unity into the world of the everyday. To use Buber's
terminology, it was to bring the rare moment of the mystic union and
its experience into the world of the I-it, hopefully to transform every
moment into a possibility of the I-Thou that might point beyond to the
eternity of the Godhead.

However, it was built into the paradoxical nature of these two
immanentalist mystical movements that various forms of simplistic
solutions or resolutions of tensions could emerge. The forms might
be the diffused empty "word-of-mouth Zen," the renewed monastic
withdrawal of the monks in meditation, the secularized Zen aestheti-
cal sentiments. The forms might be the hereditary charisma of the
Zaddiks, the oriental monarchies they established and the popular
magic and superstition tied to the worship of such saints. Hasidism

could align itself to the rabbinical tradition. Zaddikism could join hands passively with the authorities. Zen too could keep abreast with the schoolmen in Buddhist thought and it had too often, in Japan, become politically supportive of the ruling power. These are the natural alternatives to any religious movement that seeks to be "innerworldly." The movement could also doubt its basic "inner-worldly" premise, and in the Koan Zen tradition we see a curious ability to keep Zen alive (Koan scholastics notwithstanding) by recalling the paradox of immanentalism.

Concluding Remarks

Zen and Hasidism are two late mystical traditions, one from within Judaism, the other from within Buddhism, that survived into the modern world. In their initial years, both produced a wealth of truly original types. Both drew upon an early more 'medieval' mystical tradition, and both went through the trauma of institutionalization. Both were revived and internationalized by two outstanding inspired thinkers, Buber and Suzuki.

Both mystical traditions were aware of a spiritual unity and pursued a singlemindedness of intention. The Hasid is he who does *mizvah* (commandments) with complete *kavannah* (intention). By cleaving to God, the divine sparks of the Lord (the *shekhinah*, the feminine glory of God immanent in the world; the "alien thoughts" so-called) were to be tamed and made to reunite with the hidden nature of God (the *En-sof*). The Zen masters also insisted on a singleminded attention to every minute activity, from moving a brush (in painting) to drawing the bow (in archery). In Buddhistic terms, Zen also sought to release the Buddha-nature, or, the hidden womb of the Buddha (*Tathagatagarbha*) so the self and the Other find union. Both traditions went out to the people and sought to retain their original identity through the inevitable transformations. Both acknowledged and took delight in the retelling of the mystique of the founding personalities. Zen developed a suprarational technique of doubt and enlightenment utilizing the stories of the masters. Hasidism told of the irrational power of the narrative: whoever tells tales of the Zaddikim is as if he were studying the mystery of the *merkabab* (the chariot of Ezekiel).

In the end, the Hasidic tradition remained faithful to history and to its theistic basis. The extravagance of the spirit, latent messianic hope, the reverence for the Zaddik are some consequences. In the end, too, the Zen tradition remained faithful to the Buddhist outlook. Zen is concerned with the attainment of enlightenment, gnosis. To find this transcendental wisdom, it dares even to break reason itself and doubts all premises so that it verges on an enlightened atheism. More contrast and comparison can be drawn. The scholar, I suppose, will dwell on the ideological differences. The more mystic-inclined will search out spiritual kinships. The two have never been mutually exclusive within the traditions or within the complex nature of man himself.

NOTES

1. Martin Buber, *Pointing the Way*, p. 34f, 33.
2. For a discussion on Buber's relationship to *Lebensphilosophie*, see Maurice S. Friedman, *Martin Buber: The Life of Dialogue*.
3. Buber, *opus cit.*, p.34.
4. From his *Introduction to Zen Buddhism*, as cited by Heinrich Dumoulin, *A History of Zen Buddhism*, p. 270.
5. See, for example, his selected works in Japanese, *Suzuki Taisetsu Shenshu*, vol. 2, on Zen Thought. His discourses on Knowledge without knowing, Mindless mind, etc. had a refreshing Taoist-like simplicity not available in the text book Zen of monastic trainings. There are other 'modern' Japanese Zen masters, like *Hisamatsu Shin-ichi*, but they are less known to the West due to the language barrier.
6. See "Martin Buber's Interpretation of Hasidism" in Gershom Scholem, *The Messianic Idea in Judaism*, also Dumoulin, *op. cit.*
7. Buber, *Hasidism*, pp. 190, 191.
8. *Ibid.*
9. In Japanese, the key terms are *anjin*, a composed mind, and *anraku*, peace and joy, which is however more restful bliss than ecstatic joy.
10. "Life and Death are matters of great concern" is the famous line the fifth patriarch spoke when he solicited a successor, see Philip B. Yampolsky trans., *The Platform Sutra of the Sixth Patriarch*, p. 128.
11. Scholem, *op. cit.*, p. 233.
12. These are the *Pi-yen-lu*, (The Blue Cliff Records) and the *Mumen-kuan* (The Gate of Nothingness).
13. The terms are from Max Weber, cf. his *Sociology of Religion*.
14. Scholem, *op. cit.*, p. 240.
15. Scholem, *op. cit.*, p. 242.

16. *See for example* J. G. Weiss, "Via passiva in early Hasidism" in the *Journal of Jewish Studies*, vol. 11/3 & 4 (1960), pp. 137-155. For the Buddhist use of the concept of Emptiness, *see* Frederich Streng, *Emptiness*.
17. Buber's liberal attitude towards the Torah and the Jewish laws is well-known.
18. Buber, *Hasidism*, p. 200.
19. Domoulin, *op. cit.*, p. 169f. Another key concept of time in Zen is *Zenki*, to which Dogen had devoted an essay.
20. Buber, *The Tales of Rabbi Nachman*, p. 10. *See* a discussion on this generalization and its problems in Weiss, *op. cit.*, p.138 and footnote no. 5.
21. The *Hua-Yen* (Jap. *Kegon*; Sanskrit, *Avatamsaka*) school was based on the *Hua-Yen* sutra, and stands in relationship to Zen as the Kabbalah would be to Hasidism. The only English treatment on this school is by Garma Chang, *The Buddhist Teaching of Totality*.
22. This is a key concept from master *Lin-chi* (in Japanese Rinzai).
23. Paul Ricoeur, *The Symbolism of Evil*.
24. As cited by Scholem, *op. cit.*, p. 190.
25. *Op. cit.*, p. 191.
26. J. G. Weiss, "The Kavvanoth of Prayer in Early Hasidism," *JJS*, vol. 9/1 & 2 (1958), p. 163.
27. Historically, the northern Zen school and the Hua-Yen school were both patronized by Empress Wu around 700 A.D. and active around the capital in the north.
28. Scholem, *op. cit.*, p. 195f.
29. This is one area of contention between the Chinese and the Tibetans. *See* Paul Demieville, *Le Concile de Lhasa* for this historic confrontation. Tibetan Tantra in this sense is more Kabbalah and more communal.
30. Weiss, *op. cit.*, above, p. 167. *See also* Scholem, *Major Trends in Jewish Mysticism*, lecture no. 8, on the transition involved here.
31. Weiss, *op. cit.*, p. 188.
32. *Op. cit.*, p. 177.
33. Weiss, "Kavvanoth of Prayer in Early Hasidism," *JJS*, vol. 9/1 & 2 (1958), p. 168 and footnote 11 on p. 169. Baal Shem drew from an anthology of haggadic passages of the Talmud collected by an Italian Talmudist, a standard work for the untutored with good intentions.
34. *See* his life story in *The Platform Sutra*.

35. Section 20 of *The Platform Sutra*, a discourse on the Trikaya (Three Bodies) theory, was based clearly not on the original Sanskrit terms but the Chinese words used for translating them.
36. Both the Zen and the Hasidic genre here are formidable; for the latter, *see* the random selection in Louis I. Newman, *The Hasidic Anthology*.
37. Yampolsky trans. *The Platform Sutra*, p. 67.
38. *See* opening section of *The Platform Sutra*; a comparable scene can be found in *Lin-chi lu* (Jap. *Rinzai roku*, collected sayings of master Rinzai).
39. Enough to cause him to be exiled for fear of his plotting against crown. Shen-hui won imperial favor later due also to his popularity.
40. Scholem, *Major Trends*, p. 337.
41. *The Platform Sutra*, sections 1, 32, 38, 47, 55, 56, 57 all supported this idea.
42. *Hu Shih* ed., *Shen-hui yu-lu* (Collected Sayings of Shen-hui), p. 176.
43. This prayer-vow is to be repeated three times, *see* section 21 of the *Platform Sutra*.
44. *The Platform Sutra*, section 6, my translation.
45. *The Platform Sutra*, section 15.
46. There is a range of possibilities here, spanning the contemplative mysticism of the Great Maggid to the more community-conscious faith of Rabbi Nachman, *see* Weiss, "Contemplative Mysticism and 'Faith' in Hasidic Piety," in *JJS* vol. 4 (1953), pp. 19-29.
47. Scholem citing S. J. Agnon in Scholem, *Major Trends*, but Dan Ben-Amos and Jerome R. Mintz' trans., *In Praise of the Baal Shem Tov* gives a more objective picture of the traditions.
49. A representative Zem poem. For more, *see Zen Poems of China and Japan: The Crane's Bill*, trans. by Lucien Stryk and Takashi Ikemoto.
50. Scholem, *The Messianic Idea*, p. 249. *See also* p. 198.

A Psychiatrist's Experiential View of Hasidism and Zen

Benjamin Weininger

I am a clinician in full-time practice of psychoanalytic psychotherapy. I am also the co-founder, with the late Hans Hoffman, of the Southern California Counseling Center, a pioneering learning community composed of lay persons learning to do counseling on those who have life problems with which they cannot cope. We later included preventative counseling, such as for mothers with their first child, parents with pre-teenagers who anticipate teenage problems, "empty nest" syndrome, pre-retirement counseling several years before retirement, and persons first discovering chronic or organic diseases.

Having been declared a heart patient at the age of twelve, I learned to live with it, restricting some activities, and have now reached the age of seventy, feeling well and healthy. It was early in medical school that I developed a duodenal ulcer from the stress of meeting deadlines. In addition, I was unhappy at that time, suffering from vague conflicts about doing poorly in my relationships with women. My other friends seemed more at ease in this area. Also I felt increasing stress about competition in school, and about my poor health.

I began to stay often in bed, sleeping on a screened porch, drinking milk and cream and taking alkaline powders. During this anxious and unhappy state, a friend of mine talked to me about Leo Tolstoy and Krishnamurti. He talked to me about love. When he left I was astounded at the feelings within me. I felt a great sense of relief as if a burden had been lifted from me. I felt a sense of wholeness, a sense of love. Everything in the universe seemed brighter. I felt we had one God, the Father, and that we were all brothers, although quarrelsome. I soon realized that men live by love.

My ulcer symptoms disappeared. I quit my milk and cream diet and became a vegetarian. I began to take long walks, arose at sunrise, went to bed at sundown, woke at midnight, read religious literature, especially Tolstoy, the Sermon on the Mount, and Krishnamurti by kerosene lamp. The experience was so powerful that my life now took a new direction. In the last fifty years since that time, I have never found it necessary to look for another meaning in my life. I did not understand then what had happened to me. It was that event that eventually led me to choose psychiatry as a profession. Years later I received some clue as to what had happened.

I had been in conflict in many ways; unconsciously in conflict with my mother, competitively in medical school, competitively with the boys in relationship with girls in which I was unsuccessful, and troubled by my recurring ulcers. This had developed in me a low sense of my worth. I felt that my friend had accepted me unconditionally; just as I was. This effected a complete subsidence of any anxiety. As the anxiety dropped, my sense of wholeness was there. I perceived the world as brighter. It was just as bright before, but I had not seen it because I was looking inward. I was withdrawn into myself. This sense of isolation seemed to be caused by external factors actually. I have since learned that the sense of isolation and alienation is not due to a lack of persons or friends, especially in an overcrowded world. I learned it was caused by withdrawing into myself. I was hiding, but it appeared that others were isolating me. I have had this happen to me on a number of occasions, but not in recent years.

Because of my sustained feelings of anxiety, frustration and depression, I withdrew to protect myself from further hurt, and as the anxiety dropped away, I was able to take my eyes off myself long enough to look around and see the brightness of the universe. There was not a division at this time between inner and outer. There was a sense of joy. The inner experience of joy and outer experience of light were one. I realized why some mystics called it "seeing the light." It was like walking out of a dark movie and into the sunshine.

Since I remained in the country my life was simple. My diet, for the time being, was vegetarian. I felt good, walked a great deal. I probably was having a Vitamin B deficiency, and stopping the milk and cream, and eating some nourishing food, was also a factor in feeling good. It is not unusual for a mystical person to follow a vitamin deficient diet. This is especially noticeable for those persons fasting for spiritual purposes.

However, when I returned to medical school after that summer, the old conflicts reappeared. But the message that men lived by love remained, and to a certain extent, I was able to put this into practice from time to time. That men live by love was for me like a compass pointing to the North Pole, and as a compass wavers when it is disturbed, I lost my way many times. When things quieted down it was confirmed again and again to me that people live by love.

William James, in "The Varieties of Religious Experience" beautifully described the religious experience of seeing the light and also the sequence of events that led up to it: extreme conflict, depression, a sense of hopelessness, a giving up the fight, and *then* the mystical experience. In his entire book I observed that he did not make any connection between this type of experience, and another human being acting as a trigger. He described it as if it occurred out of the blue when the person gave up the struggle.

In my experience, the person gives up the struggle to solve his conflicts when another person becomes involved with him deeply and in a non-condemning way. Persons have reported the experience when they were alone, but they did not report their contacts with significant people in the preceding days before this happened. I would not say that it never happens without a personal influence, but in most autobiographically reported cases such a personal influence can be found.

The consciousness that appears is within oneself. It is not from the other person. "The Kingdom of Heaven is within you," and it makes itself manifest when anxiety is absent. The deep contact with the other person is often essential for the anxiety to subside. The "I-Thou" relationship in which a new dimension, a new awareness, a new relationship happens, was not felt in either person before. The experience is so overpowering that one forgets that it was a person who had triggered it. The effect seems to be so much greater than anything personal, that it appears to flow from the creative forces of the universe. It does, in my opinion.

I am aware of the uniqueness of each person, not only psychologically but genetically. The differences between individuals and religious experiences are important. There are varieties of religious experience. Usually the differences are stressed. I prefer to stress the similarities. I had this view from my first peak experience of awareness. It was strengthened by my psychoanalytic training. "We are all more simply human than otherwise." The sanest man has more in common with the most irrational person than he has a difference.

I became aware of a peak experience when I was twenty-one. In reflecting on my past, I realized that I had had many mini-peak experiences of short duration, but was not fully aware of them as such.

For example, during my teens (and all of us have this at times but do not recognize it as peak experiences), under an intensely star-studded sky conducive to a meditative mood, I felt an aura, a sense of mystery about life and the universe; or a sense of silence in the morning light in the mountains, or at the sound of pounding waves, or at twilight. They occur more frequently when there is an inner sense of aloneness.

During the first twenty-seven years of my life I lived in a completely orthodox Jewish environment in the west side of Chicago. Most of my friends were Jewish. When I left for psychiatric training in Baltimore and Washington, most of the people around me were non-Jewish, with a few exceptions. While there I became interested in Martin Buber's writings. I had met Martin Buber in Washington, but did not have enough time with him to get to know him. But his writings stimulated such an overpowering sense of delight and joy, I could hardly contain my feelings. I talked about these teachings with such friends as Rabbi Henry Rabin who brought back to me much of the Hasidism I had been applying unconsciously, though it was always a part of me. It was from him that I learned how the Hasidic fire demonstrates what a genuine community is really like, with the Rebbé and the Hasidim engaged in a dialectical unity, dedicated to a common cause which could bring the kingdom of heaven right here on earth, where one can experience it.

Though Jews were living in a society of alienation, Hasidism was a community movement, reaching tremendous proportions of communal intensity. They had found a way to break through to the great joy in life, endowing the simplest acts with enormous intensity and feeling. The Jews, living in an atmosphere of alienation, developed Hasidism as a defense operation to prevent being overcome by a feeling of not belonging. Buber's recital of Hasidic lore was a universal teaching that spoke from an ancestral dark. But before I was able to awaken my inner essence, I realized I could not find that essence until I knew what it really was. Hasidism helped, making it easier for God to enter, to avoid our escapes, or continual hiding out. These were some of the thoughts that my friend, Henry Rabin, brought up to my consciousness, and I realized I had somehow retained the warmth and enthusiasm and joy of my Hasidic inheritance.

I had become interested in Buddhism and Zen, because of Krishnamurti, and saw many similarities between Hasidism, my mystical experiences and the teachings of Buddha and Zen. More specifically, though there were differences in the outer-forms, there was not much difference in the basics in Hasidism and Zen.

To be in touch with the eternal Oneness (a new word) is the implied objective of both Hasidism and Zen. All religions agree, the Kingdom of Heaven is within us. We are the sparks of the Divine, coated by layers of learned and conditioned responses. Hasidism calls these layers shells. Zen designates them as ego—the conditioned self, of "dependent origin." The real Self is what we are born with, called essence by Gurdieff and Sufis. Our real self, or essence, is a spark of the divine. Man has often fallen away from his essence, and is covered with many shells. He seeks. His quest is to find his real Self underneath the conditioning. The search involves being aware of the shells or ego defenses.

One cannot seek the divine directly or through concepts. The sense of the Eternal comes when we are not looking, not searching. It comes through grace, unexpectedly and by surprise. The paradox is that we search through curiosity, and only when all our inquiries and thinking comes to an end. There is a letting go as we see there are no answers, a dropping of the incessant effort to find a meaning to life. The mind is permitted to fall silent. At that moment, the inner conflict ceases and the sense of wholeness, awareness of the eternal, happens. The divine—hidden when the mind is noisy, groping—finally appears. Thus the paradox: the search is necessary, but it is also in the way. The miscarriage of the revealed often happens because the person perceived the event as an end in itself, rather than as a part of the life process. The sense of the eternal is transient. The unresolved conflicts within the person are there, probably for the entire lifetime, but from time to time they decrease in intensity.

In both Hasidism and Zen a rededication in daily life is essential. In the one through prayer, singing and dancing with joy in spite of one's personal suffering. The way is pointing. The way cannot be given by another. Curiosity itself shows the way. The overt activity and the quiet meditation of Zen may have been influenced by climate and diet. Vitamin deficiency makes one more easily vulnerable to the mystical. However Hasidism does not stress the mystical, but the everyday life. Zen emphasizes the mystical, but not as an end in itself. The spiritual is not maintained in isolation, but by fully attending to our involvements in everyday life with others, in work, our relationships to things, and gathering together in communal meetings from time to time. The religious is a private awareness given expression within the communal. It is not an individual matter lived in isolation.

In Zen there is meditation sitting quietly doing nothing, both alone and in groups. Involvement in work and especially use of the hands is part of the process. Meetings and discussion with the Master have their Hasidic correspondences in discussions with the Rebbe. In my view, these are surface matters. The Buddha isolated himself for a while, and then taught what he had learned: compassion and harmlessness for all living things. The Westerner often sees the detachment of the Buddha as isolationism. It only appears so. Compassion is not isolation. The meaning of the word 'detachment' is beautifully described by Spinoza. We need to view things from the aspect of eternity. I call it seeing things with a perspective. This happens more frequently as one's defenses decrease in intensity. One gains altitude with another perspective.

The basic similarity between Hasidism and Zen occurs to me when I visit an orthodox synagogue on the day of Yom Kippur. The people are praying and chanting, each one at his own pace, as if in direct communion with the Unknown. Yet there is a feeling of sharing with the group. The surprising silent reverence that I feel, between the expressed words, is of the utmost significance to me. Although there is movement and chanting, there is the silence. In Zen, while meditating, seemingly doing nothing, thoughts and words wander in and out of the mind. In between the thoughts, words, there is the severest silence. At this point they meet, and in the stillness, when the mind is empty of content, a sense of wholeness and being, in contact with the life-force of the universe, happens. Even though it may be transient, it points the way.

The Jews had gone through innumerable massacres and pogroms. For escape they had tried everything—immersion in the sea of Talmud, Kabbalah, the messianic movements and more. But nothing had helped. The greatest teachers of the Hasidic movement went into solitude, were touched by the spiritual fire, and then came back into the human community, bringing with them great ecstasy, freedom and community spirit. They were a turned-on people in tune with nature, getting their inspiration essentially from nature.

The Hasidic tales are full of legendary realities. The teachings of the Besht took the Great Maggid out of his asceticism and into the community of man. The warm relationship between Baal Shem Tov and Dov Baer had the value of sound psychotherapy. A warm, loving relationship is the only basis for effective therapy. The Maggid never had to talk much. Somehow (as a hint at the psychotherapy of the future), it was his way of living that mattered. One can feel the power of a community that has a dedicated core. It is a genuine community with genuine leadership. The Hasidim needed a Rabbi, their leader, for them to turn on in their community, and vice versa. It was a tremendously important interrelationship.

There is a story told of the Besht (Baal Shem Tov). It was the day after the Day of Atonement. He wanted to make the prayer over the new moon. The clouds would not dissipate to reveal the moon, no matter how hard he prayed. It was important that he see the new moon with clarity. The Hasidim began dancing and singing toward the end of the service which he was conducting. They asked the Baal Shem Tov to join the circle. He took up the dance with them, and all of a sudden, the clouds disappeared. He was able to see the new moon with great clarity, and so was able to make the blessing. The joining in the circle and taking up the dance with them was a dialectic relationship; there is the one who quickens and those who are the quickeners. The two have to work together in concert. Then something takes place and they are dedicated to bringing the Kingdom here on earth.

Common reverence and common joy of soul are the foundations of genuine human community. You cannot know about love of God unless you love a human being. You go from the love of a mother to the love of a sweetheart to the love of the world. In the Hasidic community, the love for the Rebbe gave the Hasids a taste of the greater love for humanity. It gave focus to that love. Hasidism took the social form of a great popular community. It was not an order of the secluded, nor a brotherhood of the select, but a popular community in all its medley, in all its spiritual and social multiplicities. Never yet, in all the history of Europe, has such a community established the whole of life on the basis of the perception of unity. This Hasidism addresses itself to the central malaise of our society; the alienated individual. It offers a way out, a way of life.

In our groups I told Hasidic stories and we elicited reactions from the group about each story. We responded in return. We listened to Hasidic music and danced, and at noon had a simple communal lunch and prayer over the food. In the afternoon we began with Zen philosophy and told Zen stories, and again we received responses, and added ours in return. It left all of us with a great sense of community. Another form of our encounter group thus evolved with an effect similar to others.

My participation in the workshop began with Buddhist philosophy. How can one be involved and detached at the same time? I felt I had a certain detachment and yet I was involved. Though Buddhism is often associated with a sense of detachment, it is a misinterpretation to consider it a removal from involvement. It is incorrect to consider it a withdrawal from life. Actually, it only appears to be so. It is involvement with a sense of perspective, viewing things, as Spinoza said, from the aspect of eternity. We gain altitude when we are less anxious. Our view, therefore, of the world is larger. We lost altitude as we become more anxious, and our view becomes narrower. The degree of involvement is actually greater if we have a larger view. We are then less afraid of the consequences of involvement, because we have gained a clear perspective. Under these circumstances, we see that there is less to fear than we thought, and therefore we take more risks of commitment. This is associated with a sense of detachment, not a sense of withdrawal or indifference.

My interest for many years was in the mystical. Through two of my teachers, one a psychotherapist, Harry Stack Sullivan, and the other, a mystic-psychologist-philosopher, T. Krishnamurti, and then the teachings of Sigmund Freud, my interests shifted to the psychology of the defensive ego. It is through diminishing the effect of the defensive ego that a sense of wholeness or involvement is possible on a more enduring basis.

A mystical experience bypasses the defensive ego and we get a glimpse of what is possible. But the ego is still there. In this instance I am not using the term ego as referring to the strong part of the person. The analysts use "ego strength" to refer to the healthy part of the person. But I am using it in the sense of our defenses and fears against involvement in life, in which there is a fear of possible and even probable unpleasant consequences.

Surprisingly, Sullivan's and Krishnamurti's views of personality are similar, not only in theory but also in language. It is surprising to me because Sullivan is a pioneer in interpersonal psychiatry, and Krishnamurti is a self-educated mystic-philosopher-psychologist. There is one difference that I observed; Sullivan was more aware of the interpersonal, especially of the other person first, then also of himself. Krishnamurti was also aware of the interpersonal, but was more aware of himself first. Krishnamurti, in my experience, has a clearer awareness of the operational processes of the defensive ego than anyone I have personally met, having spent two summers sharing talkings with him several times a week.

My basic interest is in awareness of the habitual responses that inhibit involvement with life. I find these to be maintained by what Freud called the super-ego, meaning our acquired conscience. I make this distinction from the existential conscience with which we are genetically endowed.

The relevance that the mystical experiences have had in the course of my life have been considerable. They have been sometimes a hazard, but on the overall, favorable. From my psychiatric experience, mystical experiences do not always lead to a favorable outcome. Leo Tolstoy had his religious experience late in middle life following a severe depression in which he contemplated suicide. They often occur when a person has reached an impasse in his life, where his former approaches to life are not working very well in the new and present circumstances. In Tolstoy's situation; being saturated with having lived a life of indulgence, he was searching for a meaning in life, a reason why he should continue to live. Then a religious conversion happened to him. A few years ago I learned from Tolstoy's youngest daughter, then eighty years old, the immediate circumstances of her father's conversion. In his search, he often visited the peasants. The circumstances of their lives were harsh. They were poor, often sick. There were frequent deaths. The peasants usually responded: "It is God's will." It was the peasants who triggered Tolstoy's conversion.

In my situation, I was an overprotected, only child. My interests were mostly academic and chess. I was mainly concerned with myself. This approach to life was not working well for me at age twenty-one. My conversion was an *intuitive outbreak* from our inherited common consciousness, to show me another way. A clergyman once said, "When all seems lost, God throws one a lifeline." I became more socially conscious, an essential survival need for my age and circumstances.

I see mystical experience as an intuitive happening from our genetic inheritance to help us continue our development, especially when there has been too much of a block in a given area of our personality. In the Western culture, these peaks appear to take the form of a breakout in the areas of the social sense, a necessity for survival in persons who are too much self-centered and lack a social sense. Hasidism emphasizes the aspects of the communal nature of man. In the Orient the opposite is true. In everyday life, the importance of the family rather than the individual self has priority. So, in Zen Buddhism, the mystical serves as a breakthrough in the need for privacy, a perception of the uniqueness of the person in his sense of unity. In this way, a person who is over-balanced in one area moves towards more of a balance, becoming a unified instead of a divided person.

Religious conversion is less likely to occur in the "healthy minded," as William James pointed out. It occurs more often in troubled souls.

Whether the outcome is hazardous or favorable depends on the age and the degree of underlying strength the person has developed before his conversion. A young person with not much life experience and a troubled anxious childhood, encountering repeated setbacks and failures in life, often has a break-out (what is usually referred to as a psychotic or a schizophrenic episode). He, too, has a revelation of being a messiah. He has a mission to save the world, but in these circumstances there is a rapid alternation between being a savior and being among the damned, where everyone is dead and he is the cause of it. He is in a state of panic and terror because the world he knows has suddenly disintegrated, and another level of consciousness appeared which was too overpowering to deal with. Even in this situation, if the person meets a therapist or an understanding and non-condemning friend who sees in this break-out an attempt to a new integration into a healthier reality than the person was living before, then the outlook for a more favorable outcome is good.

I spent many years trying to regain the mystical experience until I later had enough good life experience to realize that I no longer needed it. In most areas of my daily life I was functioning and responding to the needs of the day as best I could, often bungling, but more often appropriately responding. The error in my perception was: I did not realize that my unsolved problems from the past would take a life-time of increasing awareness and working through, and that they would never be completely finished.

The beauty of life is that even though one perceives that one always dies, leaving things uncompleted, life in the everyday is complete in itself. It is a taste of the Eternal Now. I feel that the Hasidic and Zen mystics have areas of consciousness open to them that are, in essence, similar. Their discussion of these events differ, depending on their cultural differences and the circumstances under which these events happened. Aimee Palliere wrote in "The Unknown Sanctuary" that he was studying for the priesthood and walked into a synagogue on Yom Kippur. He saw the men chanting and praying, wearing their prayer shawls, and suddenly he had an illumination in which he felt he knew what Jesus meant when he spoke of the Father. He became converted to Judaism and later became a rabbi. Palliere used almost the same words in which I understood the Father.

Freud stated: "To be completely honest with oneself is the best effort a human being can make." Here again is a direction, not a goal to be realized. At moments we are capable of being completely honest with ourselves. What interferes is the degree to which we seek psychological security guarantees. We need to have our basic security needs met Looking for guarantees in any area of life is a carry-over in most of us from childhood, when the guarantee of having mothering was essential for survival.

The religious in all religions gives us a glimpse of the unity of all things. There is in each of us an impulse towards the sense of unity. This sense of unity is more accessible to us during a peak or mystical experience, or religious experience. It then becomes essential to have the sense of unity integrated into the everyday life so that the peak experience itself ceases to be important.

The barriers to this happening are the difficulties in the way of being self-honest. We see things selectively in order to avoid feeling threatened or humiliated. In being aware of myself, I paid most attention to two areas that were in the way of my being self-honest more often than not. Always being self-honest is not now my goal.

One area is the attempt to maintain my pride. The images of myself from being threatened and my being hurt; the images of being a good father, a good therapist, a good husband, a good friend, a good lover and so on. I discovered that only by risking humiliation, acknowledging the gaps in my image without condemning myself for the setbacks, but being aware of them and living through the hurts, not rationalizing, was a way of a loosening of the images so that there are spaces in the daily life struggle where these images play no part. Under extreme stressful situations, the images are restimulated and of shorter duration.

The second area of discovery, an awareness of the insatiable dependency needs and the inevitable frustration that follows, persisted in me long into middle life. As my psychological craving diminished, so did the sense of frustration. As the awareness of the pride related to images and their consequences became clearer, living in the everyday was more real. This kind of awareness is more possible in relationship with many other persons.

It is understandable that a child needs his pride bolstered and his basic needs met, and that humiliation is intolerable for him. For the adult, the reverse is true. He needs to risk humiliation rather than avoid it, and to acknowledge that one cannot have one's way and live with others too.

For me, the sense of the eternal is in the NOW. The rapid changes that have occurred in the objective world in the last fifty years appear to me to be surface changes only. The process of life, in essence, has always been the same, forever changing, with peaks of balances and harmony.

Many years ago I proposed the development of a Universal Religion with symbols that most of us could agree upon. Such as, five minutes set aside each week in silent meditation and prayer to remind ourselves that we are all brothers, even while belligerence continues. Five minutes of silence each week, throughout the world, when one could retain one's loyalty to one's own religion or to no religion at all. Apparently, the awareness of one's suffering leads to self-pity; the awareness of one's own suffering and the suffering of others *leads* to a sense of compassion and love.

Hasidism teaches loving kindness and that God is One. Buddhism .teaches compassion and harmlessness to all living things. These disciplines, and psychiatry, should help us express our love, understand our own shortcomings, and forgive the shortcomings of others.

The Inner Passage

Steve Sanfield

I

Finding myself alone on the Greek island of Hydra, a little despairing
over a broken love affair, I took to drugs and traveling around the
Mediterranean and North Africa. By the time I returned to the island
almost a year later my prime concerns were mysticism and the
pursuit of it through the use of LSD. That was in 1962 when neither
were the popular basis of an underground culture. My only guides
were the few books on mysticism I could acquire (Huxley's 'The
Perennial Philosophy' and James' 'The Varieties of Religious Experience').

Once I offered LSD to a Greek friend who lived on the island. I
promised to guide him through the experience and encouraged him
to speak out if he ever found himself lost or bewildered; but he and I
sat in silence in my small house for eight hours. Finally he got up and
left, saying only, "Thank you."

He returned the next morning, a leather-bound book under his arm,
and said: "There's something I want to read to you." He then proceeded to read the entire text of the Bardo Thodol. I was totally
astounded; for here it seemed was an accurate guide to my LSD
experiences. (Later, Timothy Leary published a book called *The
Psychedelic Experience* based on *The Book of the Dead*.) Hearing it
struck me so deeply I could not speak and my friend left again. This
time it was I who said, "Thank you."

That same evening I went to visit him. I was filled with questions,
and he was able to answer most of them. We spoke until dawn about
Tibetan Buddhism and its seeming similarity to the LSD experience.
Soon he got for me a set of the Oxford University editions of Evans-
Wentz's work on Tibetan Buddhism. Here at last was a system of

thought and practice that fitted in with my own inclinations and experiences. I continued using LSD, studying the texts, and living somewhat like a hermit. (The house was built into the side of a huge boulder—giving the main room the appearance of a cave and satisfying all my romantic cravings.)

At one point against all of Evans-Wentz's advice about trying these exercises without the personal guidance of a teacher—I began to practice the Yoga of Psychic Heat. The Tibetans call it Tumo, and it refers to a method of extracting prana from the inexhaustible supply of prana in the universe and storing it in the body. The yoga involves meditation, visualizations, and physical and breathing exercises. After performing these correctly the yogin will begin to feel the psychic-physical heat begin to rise from the base of his spinal column (Kundalini). I gave myself over to this practice for six days until I began to feel a physical warmth rising up my spine. It became stronger and stronger until I could do nothing but sit quietly and feel it. I've done it!, I thought. But within moments the heat began to pass and was replaced by an intense cold. Soon my entire body became numb with cold. It wouldn't go away. I searched the text for an answer, a way out but could find none. I repeated the exercises over and over again. There was no relief. No matter how many clothes I wore, no matter how many goat skins I lay under, no matter how hot the brazier got I was cold to my bones. I was sure I was going to die. Now that it was too late I remembered the warnings about not practicing such yogas without proper guidance. I promised myself that if I survived I would set out to find a proper teacher. Three days and nights of fear and shaking, and suddenly the cold in my body vanished as quickly as it had appeared.

Days of questioning, of trying to understand, left me without an answer but only the resolve to find someone who did. A few days later I was having morning coffee in a cafe along the agora when an old friend joined me. The last time I'd seen him was over a year ago when he left Greece for a journey to India. Here he was back: the same long, black beard, the same mad gleam—maybe a little madder—in his eyes, and about thirty pounds lighter. He began to tell me of his adventures, but soon all we were speaking of was his experiences among the Tibetan refugees in Nepal and Northern India. He told me how welcome earnest Westerners were among the Tibetan lamas. He also told me how the refugee camp at Dalhouse was looking for people to teach young incarnate lamas the English language. This seemed like the perfect opportunity for me. The Baal-Shem has taught that "there is no accident." All so-called coincidences are only hints at hidden relationships whose significance we must fathom.

Here then was my way. I would go to Dalhouse, work with the Tibetan refugees, and find a teacher among the lamas.

The logistics were more complicated. What route? With what money? And most important I felt I would be setting off on a journey without return and that I had to put a final end to my life and obligations in America. I decided to first return to America, settle my personal life, sell my library, and use the money to go on to Dalhouse via the Pacific Ocean.

II

My journey took me to London for a meeting with Christmas Humphreys at the Buddhist Society. He had little to tell me, (perhaps I looked too ragged to take seriously) but he did fill my arms with Buddhist sutras and texts. He also put me in touch with a representative of the Tibetan refugees who promised me a place with the Tibetans in Dalhouse. I told him I'd be there within three months.

Upon returning to America I met an old friend who told me of a Tibetan lama who'd started a small monastery in New Jersey. I went to visit him, but sitting before him, sharing tea and tangerines, I found myself unable to speak. All the questions I'd planned to ask now sounded foolish to me. It was enough to be in his presence. Geshe Wangyul seemed ageless, wise, and infinitely kind. He began asking me questions about myself. "Why had I given up writing? Why was there still tension between me and my family?" One after the other until it became clear he knew everything about me. I had read of such powers, thought I believed them to exist, but until that moment I never really believed them. Now there was no doubt. Geshe Wangyul told me I could "stay and study with the boys" if I wanted to. He also said he thought I should keep moving; and, no, it wouldn't be necessary for me to learn Tibetan.

I went outside, feeling very peaceful. Without much thought I found myself back at the gas station that also served as the bus station. I left without saying good-bye.

A month later I was living in a small house in Hollywood, working parttime in a bookstore. My library had been sold, my personal life seemingly taken care of, and my arrival was expected at the Dalhouse Tibetan Refugee Center. All that remained was to book passage to the Far East. I had lived and worked in Hollywood before and soon began to run into old friends. One who came to visit was Peter Goodrich. Peter was a man of many talents. He had always been a good friend and a teacher of sorts to me. He began to tell me of a man he'd met recently: "a Japanese cat, a Zen master who really had his head together." I'd never heard Peter speak with such admiration for another man before. A girl friend of his had taken him to meet this Zen master and do zazen. I asked Peter if he was going back, and he said: "It's not my bag, man, but he's great, really great. You should meet him."

I wasn't particularly interested in Zen Buddhism. I was sure of my path, but my friend's enthusiasm won me over. A few nights later his girl friend took me to a nondescript house on a deadend street in Gardena. We arrived late and tiptoed in. We found two places on the tan and sat down. I looked around and saw half a dozen people sitting in the za-zen posture. I tried to assume the same position but found it impossible. A Japanese man with a shaved head and black robes came and stood in front of me. He began to manipulate my body with incredibly strong hands. My body gave up all resistance, and soon I was sitting like the others.

After a few moments it became excruciating. My back and legs began to ache, but the mood of the place made it impossible for me to move. Finally a bell rang, and everyone stretched their legs. The relief was enormous. Then more za-zen. Then another series of bells, and it was time for san-zen. In those early years Joshu Sasaki Roshi would see anyone in san-zen. As the number of people who came to him—many out of curiosity, as I did—stricter regulations were set up. Now a student must sit at least ten sessions of za-zen before he is admitted to san-zen.

I was instructed in the bowing procedure and entered the san-zen room. There was Sasaki Roshi, sitting even quieter and stronger than the statue of Buddha outside the room.

"Your name?"

"Steve Sanfield."

"Do you believe in God?"

"Of course!" Why else would I be here? All the mystics from all the traditions made it clear they were speaking of the same thing. God was immanent and transcendent. All things were God. "In all ways shall you know him

"Show me the voice of God."

"Hello."

"You're a fool." And then his bell. The interview was over.

I returned to my seat on the tan, sure that I had manifested the voice of God merely by speaking. I was right. After all, I was close to being a holy man. Hadn't my friends in Greece told me so, treated me as such? This man can't call me a fool.

Driving back to Hollywood, Dianne told me Sasaki Roshi had come to the United States in 1962 to teach Zen to Americans. He had been a monk since he was 14, and the abbot of Sho-jun Temple. He was now 57 years old and was meagerly supported by a few students and patrons.

I arranged for freighter passage to Japan, began to make final preparations for the next step in my journey. But in the next few days I began to think more and more about this man who would not accept my answer. I returned, determined to convince him I was right.

This time there were birds singing outside the window.

"The birds are singing."

"Good answer but not enough. That is one sound. Dog sound is another sound. That, too, is God voice, Buddha voice. All sounds are the sound of God. How can you create that sound?"

Another time: "Each sound alone is the sound. But what is that sound alone? The sound of God is the sound of one hand clapping. The sound is the truth. You hear it without hearing. It is silent and yet it speaks. How do you realize it?"

And so it went for a few weeks. No matter what answer I gave, Sasaki Roshi would not accept it. I was resolved to answer the question before I left for the Tibetans. Finally, there was only a week left before my boat left. Should I go or should I move to Gardena? There was no choice. I was trapped. So one day I packed my pack and walked (my own pilgrimage) through the streets of Hollywood, Los Angeles, and Watts, the 14 miles to Gardena. I would stay until I heard or could manifest the voice of God.

The problem obsessed me; yet it was more than that which brought me to a tiny, rented room behind a poker club in this outgrowth of Los Angeles. After each session of za-zen tea was served, and the students would sit around and socialize. I held myself aloof from it all, feeling that this small talk had nothing to do with holiness or the quest for truth. Yet, as I sat there I couldn't take my eyes off of Sasaki. The way he drank his tea, sat at the table, the way he moved, the sparkle in his eye when he spoke. I'd never seen anyone move like that. The sureness, the absolute rightness of every gesture.

"What was most important to your rebbe?"

"Always just what he was engaged in at the moment."

And did not a Hasid travel hundreds of miles only to watch the Zaddik tie his shoelaces? Having seen that, he was able to return home. It was enough.

Within a few weeks I was living in the garage attached to Roshi's small house. We built a zendo in it, and he began to hold za-zen every morning and evening. More and more students came—some staying only long enough to find out how uncomfortable to a Westerner za-zen could be. Others stayed longer. I stayed for three years: cooking, cleaning, doing za-zen, san-zen, craving to become a monk. The empty holiness and pride I had brought with me were stripped away bit by bit.

"You don't drink, Steve? Have a glass of scotch. Have some more saki. In the monasteries we call it prajana hot water."

"You don't like meat? Try some of this whale meat."

I was still trying to answer the original question Sasaki Roshi put to me, but more and more I wanted to understand it. My unquestioning belief in God was slipping away.

"When you hear the God voice you do not need God because you have become God. A child does not need his mother if he is happy. But that does not negate his mother."

My understanding grew, but it was far from enough.

"All is God. All is Buddha. You are Buddha. You are God. Understanding is not sufficient. You cannot understand truth. You must experience it. You must realize it. We can realize our Buddha nature in everything we do, at every moment."

That was the most difficult part for me. I was still working at the bookstore. I couldn't concentrate on what I was doing. Finally I was fired and glad of it. Now I would be able to spend all my time at the zendo. But Sasaki wouldn't allow it. He insisted, as he did with all those who would be his students, that I get a job. One of his patrons was the head gardener at Marineland, and I was hired on as a gardener. Each day I would rise at 5 a.m., make tea, prepare the zendo, do za-zen and san-zen, cook breakfast, clean, go to work, return to the zendo, do my tasks, za-zen again, serve tea, and finally fall onto my mat exhausted.

And so it became my daily life, and it was there that lay the secret of "nothing special."

III

Someone asked: "What is Zen?"

Roshi answered: "When your feet itch, don't you scratch them?"

Another time: "Zen is really very simple. When I face east, my back points west. Just like that."

Once, while having tea with his students, Roshi said: "Everything in the universe is supposed to be perfect. You are perfect, but as soon as you think something is lacking or that you have something else to do, then you become imperfect. If you think there is something you must do outside this group or away from the activity of the now, then you chase away your perfection. If you're living in thoughts of the past or the future, then perfection is blemished. So now let us drink our tea in completion and perfection!"

"You live twenty-four hours a day, and at certain moments you may exclaim, 'Oh my God!'. Is that God or something you have added? Does God only live for you at that moment?"

Roshi addressed his students: "All of you are earth-bound, tied up by time and space. If any of you here are not earth-bound. If any of you are not time-bound, come up and shake hands with death." No one went forward. Roshi laughed and returned to his quarters.

After working all day in the rock garden in front of the zendo, the final three stones in one corner of the garden had been set. Sasaki Roshi stepped back and looked at the rocks for a long time. Finally he said: "Top rock, down a half inch." At that he retired to his quarters. The rock weighed over 200 pounds, and most of it was buried. His student, Yo-hsin, wishing to test his teacher, moved the dirt around the stone, and after an hour called Roshi. Roshi looked quickly at the rocks and said: "Still one half inch."

Another time while working in the garden with his students a rainbow appeared. "Roshi, a rainbow!" exclaimed one. "Very beautiful", said Roshi and returned to his work. The students, however, continued to look at the rainbow. Roshi looked up and shouted: "Very beautiful but one time is enough."

A visitor asked: "Does an enlightened man have thoughts in za-zen? Is his mind still?"

Roshi said: "I will answer you when you are enlightened."

'In Buddhism we speak of the Great Death. But this death is not death of the body. It is the death of the ego-self. You must die the Great Death to be born into the religious world."

"What does *Prajna-paramita* mean?"

"Eat, eat, eat until you are no longer hungry."

On the Buddha's birthday, Roshi addressed the assembly: "Today is the day of the birth of the Buddha. It is the time that blossoms on the tree begin to fall and in their places seed pods begin to appear. It is thus with all plants. So we celebrate both. There is no need to eat fine food, drink, or dance. Just put a flower in your lapel, drink a glass of fresh water, and say hello to yourself in the mirror. If you want to do more, run in the street and shout freedom and equality.

"Equalities that do away with differences are not the truth. Differences that do away with equalities are not the truth. Mountains are high; the sea is low. What a difference. What an equality. As long as we see things dualistically, we shall never see the truth. When one is awakened one sees the world non-dualistically; and to see things non-dualistically is to see things all on an equal level. They are equal, but this does not do away with differences. Man is man; woman is woman. They are equal, but to do away with differences would be the end of humanity. Men, women, tall, short—let us partake of tea together. Different though we are we can share in this equality. What could be more joyous!"

Speaking to a group of students in Laguna Beach, Roshi said: "Many roshis say different things. They teach in different ways. Some say you must become good men. Others say discipline yourselves. All that is fine, but my teaching is different than that." Roshi began to laugh, and after a few moments everyone in the room was laughing with him. Suddenly he clapped his hands and let out a scream. Everyone was silent. Roshi continued: "When you laugh, how are you? There is no thought of self; no thought of laughter. There is only laughter. Laughter is the perfect za-zen posture. I think that only men can laugh. I do not think monkeys can laugh. We speak of heaven, but what is heaven but laughter. Maybe because man can laugh he thought up heaven and hell. In Zen one goes through stages. First, he is concerned with rules and position. Next he is concerned with developing his character. But ultimately he must become a man of laughter. Others have come from Japan and told you you must become good, you must become kind. But I come to tell you you must become men of laughter."

A professor came from U.C.L.A. and explained to Roshi the experiments that had been done among Zen monks in order to measure their Alpha waves and E.E.G.'s while they did za-zen. When he asked Roshi if he would be willing to participate in the experiment, Roshi replied: "My head is not a machine. If you wish to study my head, you must study it with your head."

In honor of his sixtieth birthday, Sasaki Roshi's students and patrons gave a great feast in his honor. Roshi rose and addressed them: "I would like to shake hands with all of you without any gloves, but gloves are still necessary. The gloves are my translator. What is your opinion of that glove. If you think it's favorable, clap your hands. All of you were born, in a sense, beautiful into this world. And I'm very happy of the fact that when you were born, you were born whole and perfect. So now I will celebrate all of your birthdays. All of you have a chance to be born anew all the time with your true nature. No matter how much I think and try to form words I just cannot find the proper words to convey my appreciation for this celebration on my behalf. It seems my nature has become harmonious with the universe itself. I feel I have no need of words to explain that to you. So while I'm in this mood I will sing a haiku.

I have nowhere to go.
I have no need to go anywhere
Since I am one with the universe.

Everybody, Happy Birthday. Yes! On this happy occasion, the question is do you people have a past and a present and a future? However, you clapped your hands in tune with the universe. While you were celebrating my birthday, you were celebrating your own. So with that understanding I want all of you to be born anew today. Thank you."

After za-zen one evening Roshi said: "The question for tonight is: How am I insufficient? And where you are insufficient you resolve how to become sufficient. If a child cannot play a game today because he was too busy, he is not disappointed. He is happy and resolves to play it tomorrow. So should a Zen man resolve to become sufficient in what he was insufficient in today."

Someone asked: "Is there ever a time when you are sufficient?"

"Perhaps only when we die. My teacher's teacher, Banryo, used to say that Buddha—wherever he might be now—is still practicing discipline. You grow rice, harvest it, and have enough for this year, but it's not sufficient for next year; so you plant again.

"In monasteries za-zen is only a small part of each day. Each monk must work six hours every day. Rinzai said: 'Sitting is Zen. Walking is Zen.' Calm is Zen. Trouble is Zen."

A student asked: "Is there anything which is not Zen?"

"No, not even your foolish question."

A professor of theology came and was served tea. He asked Sasaki Roshi if he was familiar with Hasidism. Roshi was not but had heard of Martin Buber. The visitor then related that Nyogen Sensaki had once been in Jerusalem and was brought to see Buber. He entered Buber's study and finding him seated behind a writing table seated himself opposite. Without preliminaries, Sensaki asked: "What is truth?" Buber withdrew a plain white envelope from his desk, sealed it, and handed it to him. Sensaki accepted it, rose from his seat, bowed, and left the room. That was their first meeting.

Everyone at the table laughed, including Sasaki Roshi. When the laughter died down, Sasaki was still chuckling and said: "Both children."

Later when asked why he called them both children he replied: "Children's game. They both read too many books."

Often when Roshi would work, or gather rocks for the rock garden, or go mountain climbing, he would wear Western-styled clothes that his students had given him. Because of his build, they were ill-fitting and he always looked a little ragged. When someone suggested he get better fitting clothes, Roshi replied: "It is good. When clothes do not fit good, people think the man is poor. In America no one notices a poor man.

"If Zen is to grow in America, it must wear American clothes. When Zen came to Japan from China, it put on Japanese clothes. Now it must put on American clothes."

Four students were laying a stone path. Roshi had injured his arm and was directing the work. When tea was served, Roshi refused, saying: "No work. No tea."

Picking fruit one day, Roshi said: "Always leave the lower branches for the children."

Someone asked Roshi if he was homesick for Japan. He replied: "I do not understand such questions. I have no home. I have no country. But I am human and must have a place to sleep, so now I live in Gardena. People have homes, families, jobs. They are very attached to them. What heavy burdens. A Zen man has no attachments. Very free."

Another time: "When you sit in a chair, that is your home. If I ask you where you live and you tell me Los Angeles, that is dualistic thinking. It is only a convenience. Your home is where you are."

"In Zen it is said that the answer is in the question. If you must ask a question looking for an answer, you will never find it. It is like smoking a pipe. You must put it to your mouth to smoke it. You can't smoke it by holding it in your hand."

Without a translator Roshi gave the following lecture to a gathering of psychologists and professors in Hollywood: "It is now spring, and the weather is getting warmer. It is very easy to catch a cold. Please try not to catch cold."

A group of women visited the Zendo and asked Roshi about miracles. He turned to a student and said: "Ron, drink that glass of water." When he had done so, Roshi said: "There is a great miracle. Many people come to me looking for miracles. I turn my head to the left. I turn it to the right. Is there a greater miracle than that? When we wake, we open our eyes. When we sleep, we close them. A bird flies and we can watch it. When it is hot we can eat ice cream. These are all miracles. My aim, my work is not to show you how to perform miracles. It is not to make outstanding people of you. It is not to help you make money. It is only to try and lead you to discover true freedom—the freedom that comes when you awaken to your true self."

Another time Roshi said: "If you want to be truly free, you must realize through yourself your true freedom. At that time you have become truth itself. This truth—since it is free—is neither good nor bad, right or left, fair weather or foul. It has nothing to do with birth or death. Zen is your daily activity. It is not apart from it. If it is true Zen, then you are not bound up by daily activity. You are free in whatever you do. There is still ego, still desire. There is no man without it. But once you awaken, you see things differently. You know through yourself that you are that flower, that beautiful woman. There is no desire to possess, because you are everything from the start. Then you are able to partake of the beauty of flowers. You are able to accept people's kindness. You are able to cry when a child cries. Is there anything more wonderful than this?"

A student asked: "What is the ideal of Zen?"

"Zen has no fixed ideal. If you must have some idea as a goal, it must be nothing. Simply do your work as best you can."

At a conference of religious leaders Sasaki Roshi said: "The world has a great need for a free, naked religion so that man can walk in true freedom. Only when he discovers his true nature is he completely free."

"I will not die until Zen is born in America."

IV

At the beginning of those years I really had no idea of what was going on. I didn't know anything about Zen training or Zen metaphysics. My background was Western mysticism and the rarified heights of Tibetan Buddhism. I was totally baffled. Only the day to day presence of my teacher gave me the faith to continue.

I began to read about Zen, starting with Suzuki's books. I felt a little guilty about my reading. When people would ask Sasaki Roshi to recommend books on Zen, he would tell them books were for scholars, that books on Zen were "no more than a mirror for your face. If you look at picture postcards of the Grand Canyon, you might think you have seen it. But you must go to the Grand Canyon yourself to truly see it."

Once while visiting friends in Santa Barbara, both of whom were students of Roshi's, Joel began reading to me from a book: "Unless we believe that God renews the work of creation every day, our prayers and obeying the commandments grow old and accustomed and tedious. As it is written in the psalm: 'Cast me not off in the time of old age'—that is to say, do not let my world grow old. And in Lamentations it is written: 'They are new to us every morning: great is thy faithfulness.' That world is new to us every morning—that is your great faithfulness." Immediately I remembered a lecture Sasaki Roshi had given about Rinzai where he quoted this Tang Dynasty master as saying: "Unless you yourself create the universe and everything in it each day, you are no better than dead."

My friend continued to read: "Infinity shall be contained in every deed of man, in his speaking and seeing, listening and walking, standing still and lying down."

In those days many people came to Roshi with their own idea of what Zen should be like. They had images of rock gardens and tea ceremonies—doing everything in a special Zen way. Maybe they were more interested in things Japanese than in Zen. Roshi soon became aware of this and tried to direct his students to their daily tasks—no matter what they were. A favorite question of his was: "Where is your Buddha-nature when you're driving on the freeway?" He said many times: "Zen is sitting, walking, laying down. Zen is praying, shitting, working."

The book was Martin Buber's collection of Hasidic sayings, *Ten Rungs*. I bought a copy and used to read it along with my books about Zen. I read by candlelight when the day's tasks were done, and I felt guilty about it. It was almost like a sacrilege, like heretical literature. As a matter of fact, I still felt a little guilty about reading anything at all. Didn't Bodhidharma say that the teachings were apart from the scriptures? I once asked Roshi about the sutras, and he said, "Sutras were a dream of the Buddha's for weak-minded students. Throw away the sutras." Still he suggested I study the Diamond Sutra. I read it and told him I had. "Read it one hundred times. Then you can begin to study it." It was the only text I never felt any conflict about reading.

Buber's book was my first contact with Hasidism in those years. I had seen Hasids in the town where I grew up in Massachusetts, but whenever I asked about them I was told they were a little crazy, that I shouldn't pay them any attention. I didn't make any connection between what I was reading and what was in my blood, the feeling of being a Jew. I simply found within that book from another tradition a verification of what I was learning by following my Zen life.

Dov Baer said: "I will teach you the best way to say Torah. You must cease to be aware of yourselves." Each session of za-zen ended with the chanting of the four Bodhisattva vows. When students would ask Roshi to translate them into English, he would tell them: "No need translation. Just chant. Forget yourself."

V

By the fall of 1967 the small zendo in the garage had become inadequate for the number of daily visitors. Clearly a larger place was needed, and a concentrated effort was made to raise funds for expansion. I went to New York to try and gather support and money for the project. I stayed with a friend on the Lower East Side, then the center of the "counter-culture" on the east coast. Trying to find his apartment on my first day in the city, I stopped on Second Avenue, and there, boldly displayed on a theater marquee, was "Timothy Leary in The Enlightenment of Buddha". How far it's all come, I thought.

Largely through Leary's proselytizing, the use of LSD had spread to all levels of society. It was not just the young and more adventuresome who were using it. Praise for its power could be heard from doctors, teachers, and theologians. Many equated it with a religious experience and approached it as such. Churches were started with LSD as the sacrament. And there were many people who were drawn to formal disciplines because their experiments with psychedelics left them with too many unanswered questions. Sasaki Roshi recognized the importance of such drugs in the lives of some of his students, but he asked them not to use them any longer. He said that drugs clouded the mind and that a clear mind was needed to practice Zen. LSD was fine if it made you start questioning the nature of the universe and yourself, but further use would not bring you any closer to the answers. "LSD is like medicine. When you are cured, you have no need for the medicine anymore."

Convincing people to donate money for a zendo 3,000 miles away was difficult, but with the help of the American yogi, Richard Hittleman, and his partner, Morton Levitt (both early supporters of Sasaki Roshi), I did manage to raise some. While at Brandeis University I met a young rabbi who asked me why I, a Jew, had chosen to follow the path of Buddhism and not, like so many Jews of my generation, the way of Hasidism. He spoke of the similarities between the two ways and suggested that if I had the chance I should visit the Hasidic Rebbe in Montreal. That was the second time in less than a month he was mentioned to me.

In New York I met the Canadian poet, Leonard Cohen, whom I had known in the Greek Islands. We exchanged tales of our wanderings and adventures, but what interested him most were my experiences with my teacher. I talked and talked until finally there were no more questions. (Five years later, Cohen became a serious student of Sasaki's.)

One Sunday another friend was to take us to meet a group of young Hasids. These were men who had come to Hasidism only recently, after years of searching in other directions. As we crossed Washington Square Park we saw a large circle of people had gathered. Sitting in the center was Swami Bhaktivedanta leading those around him in chanting a mantra. This was his first visit to America, and the Hare Krishna movement was just beginning. Soon Alan Ginsberg joined them and the circle grew larger. They chanted and danced, played drums and finger cymbals, and many of those participating seemed to be in a trance. There was no talking, no explaining—only the singing of the mantra.

Leonard wanted to stay, so Morton and I continued to our meeting. We entered an old brownstone where, seated around a large kitchen table, were five bearded and black-hatted men, all about my age. Introductions over, we fell into easy conversation. I had come to share what little I had learned and to listen to what they had learned. Perhaps we could help each other by sharing our individual journeys. But soon they were asking me why I didn't lay tefilin. Didn't I know how important all the mitzvahs were? How could I call myself a Jew? And so it went until we left. I had come to share and, hopefully, to learn, but I went away feeling I had been attacked.

Back at the park the Hare Krishna circle was just breaking up. "Nice song," was Leonard's comment; and he told me he had been doing some singing and dancing with the Hasids in Montreal. He found it a great nourishment. He also mentioned the Montreal Rebbe, and I thought to myself that someday I would have to meet him.

Later that night Leonard told me the story of Sabbatti Zevi in great detail. I had never heard the tale of the false messiah before, and I sat spellbound. When he finished, I asked him why he had told it to me. "I don't know," he responded. "I just thought you ought to know about it."

Soon after that I returned to the zendo in Gardena and resumed my studies, but somehow the story of Sabbati Zevi consumed me. For weeks and weeks it invaded my thoughts. My za-zen was filled with it. Had my friend brought it into my life because he thought there was a connection between Zevi and my own teacher? No, that didn't seem right. Actually, I did not spend much time speculating on it's meaning. It was the story itself that gripped me. To this day I still don't understand why it obsessed me as it did.

VI

More money had been raised for a new zendo, and plans were being made for the purchase of an old Catholic School in Los Angeles. But I was not to be a part of it. I, who had lived a close to abstinent life for three years, fell in love. It happened suddenly and with great force, and there was no denying it. I wanted to live with this woman and she with me. When I told my teacher he seemed pleased. He had always discouraged me a little from following a monk's life—perhaps because I sought it so avidly. But when he found the woman was the wife of a friend and fellow Zen student, he told me I must leave the zendo and not return for six months. He never tried to talk me out of it, never made a moral judgement. He only said it would be best for the Sangha if I was not there.

We moved to the Santa Ynez mountains, south of Santa Barbara, and began to live a poor but idylic life. Weeks later Roshi sent word that he wanted to see me. I went to Los Angeles, a little afraid of what my teacher might say to me. He told me my actions had caused some trouble among the other students. Some were quite concerned with the right and wrong of it, but that was not his problem. He said that if I loved this woman, I must stay with her and marry her and raise a family. And so a little over a year later, Jacquie (who was three months pregnant) and I were married by Roshi at the Los Angeles zendo.

Little by little, living the life of a householder, I found myself with a need to turn back to my roots. I began to read Buber's tale of the Hasidic Masters, fascinated by the similarities between them and so many Zen tales: the central importance of the relationship between master and disciple, the humble occupations of so many masters from both traditions, the same vital spirit, and, of course, the emphasis on experience rather than learning. The Baal Shem Tov taught that every Jew, no matter where, no matter when, could offer prayers acceptable to God. and in the Zenrin Kushu it says, "Every man needs only a square of ground beneath his feet to do za-zen on." What drew me deeper and deeper were the living truths that emerged from these tales. It was not theory, not metaphysics, but the daily lives of these great zaddiks that carried the lessons. I t was for me to understand the principles behind them and incorporate them into my own life.

We began to celebrate some of the Jewish holidays, light the Shabbas candles, observe the Sabbath in our own fashion: resting from work, reading selections from the Pirke Abbot, simply being aware that it was a special day. Once, just before Yom Kippur, I had the urge to hear the shofar blown. I had memories from my childhood of the power of that moment and wanted to experience it again. I called a nearby synagogue and asked if I could come to pray on the High Holidays. The woman on the phone asked if I belonged to the congregation and then said I would have to buy tickets. I told her I was a Jew who simply wanted to pray and was too poor to pay any money. Her response was, "Well, I don't know how I can help you then." I hung up in a rage. Jews. Prayer. They were not to be found in the temples.

And when my son was born the following spring, it was I who conducted the ceremony at his circumcision. At first I was told it would be out of the question for me to be there. After all, it was just a simple operation that's given no more than a passing thought in hospitals today. No, I insisted it was much more than that. It was a covenant that had been kept alive through the centuries—even in the face of death—and it was my son. Thanks to an understanding doctor, I was allowed to be there and say the prayers.

Soon after his birth we moved to the foothills of the Sierra Nevadas, where we built our own house and began to make our dreams a reality. It was here that my Jewish roots became more and more important to me. I began reading Jewish history and lore, asking questions I had never considered important: What did it mean to be a Jew in today's world? What joys? What sorrows? What had been given? What must be continued?

Yom Kippur was observed by going alone to the woods or the river all day, fasting and remaining silent. Passover became an important time for us, a time of renewal. We celebrated it with a seder that grew larger each year, using a Haggadah we put together ourselves. We took what was meaningful to us and left behind anything that didn't speak to us directly. We incorporated material from the American Indian, Chinese Buddhist, and Hasidic traditions and we included the songs and poems of our friends and contemporaries. It became our great spring festival: celebrating the fertility of the earth and continuing the oldest moon festival in the world. We retold the tales of the day, remembering the past and our link to it.

Such times were deeply satisfying. "To observe this ritual in the absence of priests, of an ark, of a listening sky is a rich discipline," writes a Canadian poet. But I began to feel I was in exile. Though there were other Jewish men around, men who, like myself, were beginning to look towards their own traditions, I felt the need to speak with others. With my family I planned a trip to the east coast to visit some of the men who had been important in my life. Perhaps they could help me. Perhaps there was another way to follow.

I went to see Cantor Morton Shanok, the man who had prepared me for my Bar Mitzvah. He had been my teacher more than twenty years before, and I'd always had a great respect for him. He was one of the few Jewish leaders I knew whose concern with the spirit and goodness of man never got lost behind the secular concerns of bigger and richer temples. He encouraged me when I told him of seeking new prayers, new songs, new ways of worship. He showed me how the prayer books and liturgy were continually changing. Now, more than ever, he felt a need for such change, but he cautioned me about change merely for its own sake. Certain traditions had survived through the years only because they touched the spirit of man; as long as they do so they must be maintained. And he warned me about discarding anything too soon. I must always be patient enough and open enough to allow the meaning of any ritual to make itself clear to me.

It was good to speak with my old teacher, but I also saw there was no place for me in the established forms of Judaism. Other men I visited were only interested in their Jewishness as a cultural identity. Their deepest commitment seemed to be to the delights of Jewish food. Still others had turned so far to other faiths, like science, they weren't even interested in dialogue.

I went to Canada to visit Leonard, and he said he would try to arrange a meeting with the Montreal Rebbe. He called a friend of his, Robert Hershon, who was a disciple and supporter of the Rebbe. It was the Canadian Thanksgiving, and the rebbe happened to be celebrating the day with Hershon and his family at their country home; but it was not to be that simple. First Hershon would speak to me, and then, perhaps, a meeting could be set up.

He appeared late that night, a huge man dressed in a black hat and a cape. As he stood swaying in the doorway, a little drunk from the day, I saw him as a figure from another time and place. Was it Paris? Casablanca? We drank wine and smoked cigarettes. He asked me why I wanted to meet the Rebbe. Why? Wasn't it enough that he was a rebbe and I was Jew? What did I want to ask him? I would know when we met. Did I believe in him? He was capable of miracles, but one had to believe. Hershon had seen the rebbe do incredible things. He could read men's thoughts, heal the sick, keep the world in balance with his prayers. Yet, I believed everything he said, but how could I believe in a man I'd never even seen? We talked almost until dawn, and finally Hershon said he would try to arrange a meeting.

Early the next morning the Rebbe called. Why did I want to see him? I was a Jew trying to find some understanding of my roots, a way to feel at home in the world. O.K., he would see me, but first I was to meet with some of his assistants. I went to the Yeshiva to meet the man he suggested. He was busy with a class of children but would be available soon. An hour later I was sitting at a long table in the library with three young Hasids. The same questions: Why had I come? What was I looking for?—and the same answers. Then more questions: Did I speak Hebrew? Did I lay tefilin, do the daily ablutions? Why didn't I wear a yarmulke? It was destined to be a replay of my meeting with the Hasids in New York. Finally my anger mounted. I smashed the table with my fist and screamed, "Did the Baal Shem attack those who came to him? Didn't Dov Baer welcome everyone, drunkards and thieves included? I've come almost 4,000 miles seeking help or advice or something, and all you can do is put me down for not following rules. Enough. I don't need it." And with that I stormed out.

Two days later, just as we were leaving for the bus station, the phone rang. It was Hershon. The Rebbe had been told of the meeting and would see me. Too late. I was leaving. It was not to be.

VII

Hasidism is a way of life, a spirit, and the teachings are only a commentary on it. For me it was impossible to enter the formal world of ear locks, tefilin, the 614 mitzvahs. It was also impossible for me to remain in the formal world of Zen. I think either path followed completely and directly would have been simpler. When I lived with Sasaki Roshi, I craved the daily rules and regulations practiced in Zen monasteries; just as I later craved the fellowship and rituals of the Hasids. My teacher told me again and again that monastery life was easy; it was living in the world that was difficult. He also told me, "A Zen man has no regrets."

Last winter when no rain had fallen on the land and spirit for so long, I set out on a journey in search of a rainmaker. I took it upon myself that clouds passed without dropping any life-giving rain, that the springs were going dry. I visited Sasaki Roshi on Mt. Baldy in Southern California, but my search ended in the Hopi Indian village of Hotevilla,

Arizona. It was there that David Monongye, the grandfather of his village and a traditional religious elder, told me, "Return to your home. Purify your heart. Ask nothing for yourself."

I have tried to that, and it seems a worthy if not impossible task. Following no formal way but pursuing what speaks clearly to me, I finally come to this poem:

Religion

Only a method a tool
    like hunting
the end is the kill:
    how men prepare
    stalk the game
    take part in death
determines everything.
The secret is the daily life.
All else is commentary.

BIOGRAPHICAL DATA ON THE CONTRIBUTING AUTHORS

Harold Heifetz: Editor/Compiler of ZEN AND HASIDISM; Novelist and playwright with a long history of interest in Jewish and Japanese culture, and in the sociology of prejudice. He has been a guest lecturer at the University of California at Los Angeles. He is the author of two novels, *The Hard Charger,* and *Jeremiah Thunder*, which will be made into motion pictures.

Three of his plays have been produced on the West Coast, one of which—*Harry Kelly*—dealing with the Japanese War Relocation Camps, toured 28 cities in 1977. He has just completed a new novel dealing with ethnic stratification and prejudice in Hawaii.

He is a member of the Writers Guild of America, West, and the Dramatists Guild of New York.

Christmas Humphreys: Former Senior Prosecuting Counsel to the British Crown, and Commissioner to the Central Criminal Court in England. Founding President of the Buddhist Lodge, London, now known as the Buddhist Society. Well-known author and leading British Buddhist.

R. Schatz: Professor in Jewish Mysticism, Hebrew University, Israel. Born in Argentina, author of two volumes of Jewish mysticism. She is a graduate of the Hebrew University.

Chaim T. Hollander: Rabbi, ordained in Cleveland, Ohio. Master's degree from St. Louis University. Torah educator for 25 years; author of numerous articles on orthodox Judaism.

Jacob Yuroh Teshima: First Japanese to graduate from the Hebrew University in Jerusalem. He received a doctorate from the Jewish Theological Seminary in New York. He has been an instructor at the University of Judaism in Los Angeles, California. A close associate and translator into the Japanese language of Abraham Joshua Heschel's numerous works. Fluent in Hebrew, Teshima now resides in Tokyo and is based at the Tokyo Bible Seminary.

William Kramer: Rabbi; Professor of Religious Studies at California State University, Northridge. Author of many books and articles in religion and art. Kramer formerly taught at the Hebrew Union College. He is senior contributing editor of Heritage Publications. He is a graduate of Case-Western Reserve University and of the Hebrew Union College-Jewish Institute of Religion. He has conducted a seminar on mysticism at the Essalen Institute in Big Sur, California and is currently engaged in further post-doctoral studies in law.

Paul Wienpahl: Born in Wyoming in 1916, Wienpahl read existentialism at the Sorbonne in 1954-55, having moved on from the positivism and pragmatism of the early years. He practiced Zen Buddhism in 1959 at Daitoku-ji in Kyoto, Japan. Out of this experience he wrote *The Matter of Zen* and *Zen Diary*. Wienpahl has been a professor of philosophy at the University of California, Santa Barbara, for 31 years.

Louis Ginzberg: Late Professor of Talmud and Rabbinics, Jewish Theological Seminary; Rabbi and author of many works on the Talmud and Jewish law; author of *The Legends of the Jews*, 7 volumes; *The Geonim and Their Halachic Writings*; and *A Commentary on the Talmud of Jerusalem*, 3 volumes.

Jiyu Kennett: Roshi Kennett is a Zen Master, trained in the Soto Zen tradition. She is the Abbess and Spiritual Director of Shasta Abbey, a Zen seminary and training monastery at Mt. Shasta, California. She was formally ordained in the Chinese Rinzai tradition in Malaysia and went on to study Soto in Japan. She is also an instructor at the University of California Extension and a member of the faculty of the California Institute of Transpersonal Psychology. She is the author of *Zen is Eternal Life; How to Grow a Lotus Blossom;* and *The Wild, White Goose, the Diary of a Zen Trainee.*

Steve Sanfield: A graduate of the University of Massachusetts, he lived and travelled in the Mediterranean area and North Africa for two years. He lived and studied for three years with Joshu Sasaki Roshi and has settled in the Sierra Nevada foothills of Northern California. He published two volumes of poetry in 1974 and 1975, and three more in 1976, 1977.

Whalen Lai: Graduate of the International Christian University, Tokyo;

received his Ph.D. in Comparative Religion from Harvard University, specializing in Chinese Traditions. He is presently Assistant Professor at the University of California, Davis and is editing with Prof. Lewis Lancaster a book on Early Ch'an in China and Tibet for the Berkeley Buddhist Studies series. Lai has worked primarily in the history of Chinese Buddhism, and has published in many journals, including *Philosophy East and West*. His doctoral thesis was on the Awakening of Faith in Mahayana.

Hidenori Tashiro: Professor of Philosophy at Tokai University in Tokyo, Japan. He is a graduate of Tokyo University, with a major in Philosophy. He studied Zen Buddhism under Unkan-kusshaku Daibiroshi and Seiryu-kutsu Nakagawa Kando.

Martin Buber: Late philosopher and theologian, one of the spiritual leaders of his generation, a prolific author and a giant amongst thinkers. He was Professor of Philosophy at the Hebrew University, Jerusalem, Israel.

John Blofeld: English Buddhist and author of many books such as *The Way of Power* (Allen & Unwin, 1970) on meditational methods of Tibetan Buddhists; *The Wheel of Life; People of the Sun; City of Lingering Splendour,* and others; and translator of *The Zen Teaching of Huang Po; The Zen Teaching of Hui Hai* and most notably *I Ching (Book of Change).* Blofeld has studied under Tibetan Lamas of both the "Yellow Hat" and "Red Hat" sects. He now resides in Bangkok, Thailand.

Zalman Schachter: A Hasidic Rabbi who received his training in Europe and at the Lubavitcher Yeshiva in Brooklyn, N.Y. He is a graduate of the Hebrew Union College. His interest in the common search for spirituality has led to the exploration of Zen, Sufi, gestalt and other growth centers. He is currently Professor of Religion in Jewish Mysticism and Psychology of Religion at Temple University, Philadelphia, Pa.

Gary Snyder: Pulitzer Prize poet, 1977. Mystic, New Age spokesman on man and his environment in such publications as East/West Journal, now resides in Nevada City, California.

Benjamin Weininger: A graduate of the University of Illinois College of medicine, now in private practice as a psychiatrist and psychoanalyst in Santa Barbara, California. He is co-founder and co-director of the Southern California Counselling Center in Los Angeles. He has written extensively on factors involved in the religious experience. He has participated with Erich Fromm and D. T. Suzuki in workshops in Zen Buddhism.

Abraham Kaplan: Professor of Philosophy, University of Haifa, Israel; currently Andrew W. Mellon Visiting Professor of Philosophy at the California Institute of Technology, Pasadena. He is President of the Israel Philosophical Association, and the author of *Power and Society; The New World of Philosophy; American Ethics and Public Policy; The Conduct of Inquiry; Individuality and the New Society; and Love and Death: In Pursuit of Death.*

Jiri Langer: late Czech poet and author, who lived in Belz for many years, leading a strictly Hasidic life. Noted for his religious inflexibility. Taught Hebrew to Franz Kafka. He wrote "Songs of the Rejected," a collection of poems, and Erotik der Kabbala in which he applied Freudian theories to the material. He spent the last years of his life in Israel.

CONTRIBUTORS

Harold Heifetz

Christmas Humphreys

Meister Echart

Jiri Langer

John Blofeld

Louis Ginzberg

Nagarajuna

Jiyu Kennett

William Kramer

R. Schatz

Chen-Chi Chang

Hyman Enelow

Hidenori Tashiro

Jacob Yuroh Teshima

Akihisa Kondo

Paul Wienpahl

Zalman Schachter

Chaim T. Hollander

Gary Snyder

C. G. Jung

Martin Buber

Abraham Kaplan

Whalen Lai

Benjamin Weininger

Steve Sanfield

QUEST BOOKS

are published by
The Theosophical Society in America,
a branch of a world organization
dedicated to the promotion of brotherhood and
the encouragement of the study of religion,
philosophy, and science, to the end that man may
better understand himself and his place in
the universe. The Society stands for complete
freedom of individual search and belief.
In the Theosophical Classics Series
well-known occult works are made
available in popular editions.

Another important Quest book is called

by **Charles Poncé**

About this book, The Library Journal writes:

"Here at last, is a ... readable study of the ancient Jewish mystical system, the Kabbalah ... an unusually clear and inspiring explication ... a valuable work for both public and academic libraries."

Available from:
The Theosophical Publishing House,
306 West Geneva Road, Wheaton, Illinois 60187